How to Invest in Real Estate and Pay Little or No Taxes

How to Invest in Real Estate and Pay Little or No Taxes

Use Tax Smart Loopholes to Boost Your Profits by 40 Percent

Hubert Bromma

McGraw-Hill
New York Chicago San Francisco Lisbon
London Madrid Mexico City Milan New Delhi
San Juan Seoul Singapore Sydney Toronto

The **McGraw-Hill** *Companies*

1 2 3 4 5 6 7 8 9 0 FGR/FGR 0 9 8 7 6 5 4

ISBN 0-07-144378-9

This publication is designed to provide accurate and authoritative information in regard to the subject matter covered. It is sold with the understanding that neither the author nor the publisher is engaged in rendering legal, accounting, or other professional service. If legal advice or other expert assistance is required, the services of a competent professional person should be sought.

—From a Declaration of Principles jointly adopted by Committee of the American Bar Association and a Committee of Publishers

McGraw-Hill books are available at special quantity discounts to use as premiums and sales promotions, or for use in corporate training programs. For more information, please write to the Director of Special Sales, McGraw-Hill Professional, Two Penn Plaza, New York, NY 10121-2298. Or contact your local bookstore.

This book is printed on recycled, acid-free paper containing a minimum of 50% recycled, de-inked fiber.

Contents

Introduction

For more than a quarter of a century, savvy investors have been buying real estate and related investments on either a tax-free or tax-deferred basis. By avoiding or minimizing the taxes due in a real estate transaction, investors can enjoy a huge increase in yields from compounding in a tax-free environment. In addition, if a real estate asset is held for a significant period of time, investors also enjoy the advantage of having more available cash as a result of not being required to pay taxes. There are numerous tax shelters available for real estate transactions, but most people are unaware of how easy it really is to take advantage of such shelters.

This book explains how you can buy and sell real estate on a tax-free or tax-deferred basis using 1031 exchange rules, IRAs, 401(k)s, special exemptions provided by the Internal Revenue Service and the Department of Labor, and various combinations of these mechanisms. This book will show you legitimate, accepted methods for avoiding tax on investment real estate transactions, and how to avoid pitfalls and errors made by others. Once you understand the world of choices available for making tax-deferred and tax-free real estate investments, you will be able to diversify your investment portfolio and protect your assets at the same time. When you finish this book, you will have a clear understanding of your tax shelter options for basic real estate transactions, real estate options, notes, income streams, leveraging property, purchasing tax lien certificates, and more. Simply by learning a few rules and doing proper planning, you can easily and legally defer or even avoid paying taxes on your real estate investments.

This book is written from two points of view: the person who wants to make tax-deferred and tax-free investments; and the trustee and administrator, qualified intermediary, and other third parties making the transactions work. This provides a unique insight on the decisions you make and how they are discharged.

The book is divided into three parts, with chapters describing the legal nature of tax-free and tax-deferred capabilities, examples of actual transactions, and the mechanics of how transactions actually are made.

PART 1

REAL ESTATE IN IRAs AND 401(k)s

This part provides the reader all the necessary understanding, examples, and mechanics to self-direct investments in real estate using Individual Retirement Accounts and qualified plans as the source of capital. Self-directed plans have been around since 1975, when the Employee Retirement Income Security Act of 1974 (ERISA) became effective. At that time mostly qualified plans, such as Defined Benefit, Profit Sharing, and Money Purchase Pension Plans, were self-directed. From that time on, real estate and notes were one of the investments of choice among small companies. Mostly attorneys, accountants, and real estate brokers were involved. In 1981, Individual Retirement Accounts became deductible for many citizens. Banks, insurance companies, and stock brokers captured the IRA marketplace. Even today, these institutions provide almost all the investment product to the consumer and to qualified plans as well. Most of the population is not aware that IRAs and qualified plans can be self-directed.

The popularity of IRAs and qualified plans as tax-deferred investment vehicles has increased since the difficulties in the stock market, decrease of interest rates, and concerns regarding corporate citizenship among large, previously highly regarded corporations, and even large accounting firms. The self-directed plan industry in general might comprise less than 1 percent of the total investments of all types. The IRS has yet to report self-directed IRAs and plans separately. Of that total, real estate is still less than private placements in IRAs and qualified plans.

Part 1 provides you with insight into the details of real estate in tax-deferred plans from not only you the investor, but also from inside institutions that perform the activities required to make your real estate transaction be and stay free of tax. Tax-deferred investing is a partnership of you the client, the trustee and administrator, the Internal Revenue Service, and the Department of Labor. Without any one of these, the self-directed Real Estate IRA would not exist. This part is oriented to you, the investor.

How to Use This Part

This part provides you with important information about the many investment options available through various tax-deferred retirement savings mechanisms. Much of the information is drawn from the Internal Revenue Code and various Treasury Regulations. Some of the numbers are cross-referenced in the first and second parts.

The first chapter, "How to Get Started," provides an overview of IRAs, Roth IRAs, SEP IRAs, SIMPLE Plans, Coverdell Education Savings Accounts, or ESA's, (formerly education IRAs), and Qualified Plans (formerly known as Keogh or HR-10 plans) and discusses how to do real estate transactions in a tax-free or tax-deferred environment.

The second chapter, "Transactions," gives you examples of actual transactions using retirement plan funds to buy and/or sell various assets in and out of your plan while retaining their qualified status as tax-deferred or tax-free.

The third chapter, "Mechanics: Opening Accounts," provides the details of how you open an account, who you see, and what you need. The time it takes to open an account is small, but the other mechanics might take longer than you think. The opening of an Individual 401(k) which you self-trustee is also covered. This chapter also includes rules regarding plans, what types of investments are or are not permitted, and information on unrelated business tax (UBIT) and debt-financed property.

The fourth chapter, "What to Do and Not Do to Get the Best Tax Results," includes important aspects of IRA investments, such as what is statutorily prohibited, how assets are distributed to you personally, how real property improvements are made when owned by an IRA or qualified plan, how rental income is treated, what happens when property is debt financed, and other relevant information to defer tax and get the best benefit from self-direction.

CHAPTER 1

How to Get Started

Generating Income with Your Tax-Deferred Plan

For many people, the purpose of a retirement plan is to set aside funds to provide an income for the future. While saving money for the future is an important first step, you can also put your self-directed retirement plan to work and use it as a vehicle to generate tax-free and tax-deferred income.

This chapter outlines the various retirement plan options and their requirements. It also provides examples of a variety of real estate transactions so that you can become familiar with what to look for and what methods to use to ensure that your transactions are handled correctly.

Tax deferral in retirement plans became available to the general public and employers as a result of the Federal Employee Retirement Income Security Act, which was passed by Congress in 1974 and became effective in 1975. Tax deferrals prior to that time were only available through customized vehicles developed for specific employers or individuals, often using insurance products.

Since 1975, numerous legislative changes have impacted the appeal of different types of retirement plans, making some plans more popular and others less so. The portability of IRAs, Roth IRAs, and qualified plans has made tax deferral using such plans very popular. The reason for the popularity of the traditional IRAs and 401(k)s, for example, is the ability to defer paying taxes on deposits until funds are withdrawn from the account. The appeal of the Roth IRAs is that you pay taxes now so that you can withdraw the money tax free in the future.

How Difficult Is It?

Admittedly, handling real estate-related assets ("nonstandard" assets) in an IRA or 401(k) is more complex than handling "standard" assets, such as stocks, mutual funds, or certificates of deposit. A real estate transaction can involve legal descriptions, price negotiations, title insurance, closing instructions, filings, note preparation, payment terms, and more. At first, this can seem overwhelming—like any area involving financial and legal matters, the language and the paperwork required can be daunting. The first time you fill out a note or review an escrow instruction form, it probably seemed hard to understand. The second time, it gets easier. If you invest a relatively short amount of time looking at the examples in this chapter, you'll quickly gain an understanding of the basic processes involved. The examples go through the typical issues and documents involved in a variety of real estate transactions. These examples will help you familiarize yourself with what to do and expect so that when you do your own deals, you will be comfortable with the process.

The tax-deferred and tax-free vehicles described in this chapter are:

- Individual Retirement Arrangements
- Simplified Employee Plans
- Keoghs and other qualified plans

What Are the Steps?

There are four basic steps to follow in making self-directed investments with your retirement accounts:

- Find an administrator, custodian, or trustee who provides self-directed plan services.
- Determine which type of retirement plan meets your needs or situation.

- Fund the account.
- Buy assets with the funds in your self-directed account.

Tax-Deferred and Tax-Free Retirement Investment Vehicles

Traditional and Roth IRAs

An IRA is a depository account from which you buy or sell assets. An account is created by a written document. Only an individual can establish an IRA. IRAs may not be established by trusts, joint tenants, or tenants-in-common. All of the assets in the account are placed or "vested" in the name of the trustee, custodian, or administrator for your benefit and/or for the benefit of your account.

There are two types of non-employer-originated IRAs: traditional and Roth. With a traditional IRA, contributions may be tax deductible—earnings grow tax free but all withdrawals are taxed as income. You can contribute to a traditional IRA in addition to another retirement plan; however, you might not be able to deduct all of your contributions. Contributions to a Roth IRA are not tax deductible, but you can withdraw the funds tax free after age 59-1/2. You can have a Roth IRA in addition to another retirement plan as long as you meet certain earnings requirements.

Both traditional and Roth IRAs have the following basic requirements:

- The trustee or custodian must be a bank, a federally insured credit union, a savings and loan association, or an entity approved by the IRS to act as a trustee or custodian.
- The trustee or custodian cannot accept contributions of more than the maximum allowable contribution for the current tax year. However, rollover contributions can be more.
- Your contributions must be in cash, unless it is a rollover contribution.
- The amount in your account must be fully vested at all times.
- Money in your account cannot be used to buy a life insurance policy.
- Assets in your account cannot be combined with other property, except in a common trust fund or common investment fund.
- You must start receiving distributions from your account at the required age, as determined by the type of IRA you have.

Your return in the traditional IRA is almost immediately more than it would be if you made the same investment outside the IRA, assuming you have a tax rate of 30 percent after deductions. The worst case in a traditional IRA or qualified plan is that you will have to pay tax when you withdraw the funds. The following example shows the benefits of saving money in an IRA:

If you open an IRA with $13,000, it will take 25 years to double your money at a 10-percent annual return; $140,851 in the IRA and $70,557 for non-IRA investments at a 30-percent tax rate on income. Then you decide to withdraw the money all at once. You now get $98,596. That is still $28,000 more than the non-IRA investments and is due solely to the differences in compounding in a pretax versus after-tax environment.

If your returns are less than 10 percent, say 5 percent, your return would be equal after 25 years after you pay tax, versus after 10 years at a 10-percent return.

IRAs and qualified plans are powerful tax deferral tools that everyone interested in real estate investments can use. The returns are your responsibility, along with when you want to take the money or property out. Real estate, notes, and other nonstandard investment assets provide opportunities for those who have experience in working with them, or for those who are willing to take the time researching the potential benefits.

IRA Contribution and Compensation Limits

To contribute to a traditional or a Roth IRA, you or your spouse must have received taxable compensation during the year. Compensation includes wages, salaries, tips, professional fees, bonuses, commissions, and other amounts you receive for providing personal services. All taxable alimony and separate maintenance payments you receive under a decree of divorce or separate maintenance are treated as compensation.

If you are self-employed (a sole proprietor or a partner), compensation is your net earnings from your trade or business (provided that your personal services are a material income-producing factor), reduced by your deduction for contributions on your behalf to other retirement plans and the deduction allowed for one-half of your self-employment tax. Compensation also includes earnings from self-employment that are not subject to self-employment tax because of your religious beliefs.

When you have both self-employment income and salaries and wages, your compensation is the sum of both amounts. If you have a net loss from self-employment, do not subtract the loss from salaries or wages you receive when figuring your total compensation.

Compensation does not include any of the following items:

- Earnings and profits from property, such as rental income, interest income, or dividend income
- Pension or annuity income
- Deferred compensation received (compensation payments postponed from a past year)
- Foreign earned income and housing cost amounts that are properly excluded from income
- Any other amounts that you are entitled to exclude from income
- Income from an investment in a partnership if you do not provide services that are a material income-producing factor

Simplified Employee Pensions

An SEP allows an individual to make contributions towards his or her own retirement (if self-employed) in a traditional IRA established for his or her own benefit. It may also be used by an employer to make contributions towards his or her employees' retirement, in a traditional IRA established for the individual employee. In either case, an SEP allows for retirement savings without the need to establish a complex retirement plan.

> ***Tip:*** *An SEP cannot make contributions to a Roth IRA. However, a traditional IRA established to receive SEP contributions may be converted to a Roth IRA if the recipient qualifies for a Roth conversion.*

You can set up and contribute to an SEP-IRA up to the due date (plus extensions) of your income tax return for that year. Contributions must be in the form of money (cash, check, or money order). However, in some cases you may be able to transfer or roll over property from another retirement plan to your SEP-IRA.

For purposes of an SEP, a self-employed individual is considered to be both an employee as well as an employer. You are considered an employee if you meet all of the following requirements:

- Are at least 21 years old
- Have worked for the employer for at least three of the five years immediately preceding the tax year
- Have received from the employer at least $400 in compensation in the tax year

An employer can establish less restrictive participation requirements for its employees than these, but not more restrictive ones.

An employer can exclude the following individuals from coverage under an SEP:

- Employees covered by a union agreement and whose retirement benefits were bargained for in good faith by their union and their employer
- Nonresident alien employees who have no U.S.-source earned income from their employer

Leased employees might be entitled to participate in an SEP plan. To be considered a leased employee the following conditions must be met:

- Your services are provided under an agreement between the recipient and the leasing organization.
- Your services are performed for the recipient, or for the recipient and related persons, on a substantially full-time basis for a period of at least one year.
- Your services are performed under the primary direction and control of the recipient.

Savings Incentive Match Plans for Employees

A SIMPLE allows an employer with 100 or fewer employees to make elective contributions on behalf of each eligible employee. SIMPLEs must be maintained on a calendar-year basis. You can set up a SIMPLE using IRAs or as part of a 401(k) plan.

With a SIMPLE, the employer is required to either match the employee's elective deferral or make a nonelective contribution on behalf of each eligible employee.

A SIMPLE must be the only retirement plan to which the employer contributes. However, an employer who maintains a qualified plan for union employees can have a SIMPLE IRA for any nonunion employees.

An eligible employer who establishes and maintains a SIMPLE for at least one year is considered an eligible employer for two years following the last year actually eligible.

An employee who received at least $5000 in compensation during any two years preceding the calendar year and is reasonably expected to earn at least $5000 during the current calendar year can elect to have the employer make contributions to a SIMPLE retirement account. You can establish less restrictive eligibility requirements for employees, but not more restrictive ones. An employee's right to the contributions cannot be forfeited.

The following employees do not need to be covered under a SIMPLE:

- Employees who are covered by a union agreement and whose retirement benefits were bargained for in good faith by their union
- Nonresident alien employees who have no U.S.-source earned income from the employer

During the 60-day period before the beginning of any year, an eligible employee can elect to have the employer make contributions (called elective deferrals) to the SIMPLE retirement account on his or her behalf. The employee's contributions are excluded from the employee's adjusted gross income. An employee can also choose to stop making elective deferrals at any time during the year. The employer must either match the employee's contributions or make nonelective contributions. No other types of contributions are allowed with a SIMPLE.

Coverdell Education Savings Accounts (ESA) (Formerly Education IRAs)

Education IRAs, now called Coverdell Education Savings Accounts (ESA), are a way to set aside funds for education expenses. Contributions are not tax deductible, but earnings accumulate tax free and withdrawals are not taxed when used for qualified education expenses. Here are the basic rules governing ESAs:

- You can contribute up to $2000 annually for each child under 18.
- You are eligible to contribute if your gross income is between $190,000 and $220,000 if married and filing jointly, or $95,000 to $110,000 for single filers.
- You can use the funds for tuition for elementary and secondary schools as well as for college and university expenses.

Qualified Plans

Qualified plans are retirement plans that are approved by the Treasury Department. Although it is not mandatory that a retirement plan be approved, it is advisable to have the IRS determine whether the plan qualifies under Internal Revenue Code.

Only employers can open qualified plans, but all employees, including the employer, can participate in the plan. The employer is responsible for maintaining the plan. If you own your own business but do not have employees, you are still considered an employer. Qualified plans set up by a self-employed person are interchangeably referred to as Keogh or HR-10 plans.

There are two basic types of qualified plans: defined benefit plans and defined contribution plans. Defined benefit plans require actuarial assumptions and computations to figure out contributions. Because you need continuing professional help to have a defined benefit plan, they are not addressed in this chapter. With a defined contribution plan, contributions are based on a percentage of compensation or profits.

A profit-sharing plan is a defined contribution plan. Contributions to profit-sharing plans are discretionary and may vary from year to year. Unless the plan is designed to take advantage of permitted disparity rules, each employee receives the same contribution. Contributions are usually based on business profits, but according to the IRS rules, they can also be based on compensation. The maximum deductible contribution to a profit-sharing plan is 25 percent of eligible compensation, up to $41,000 for 2004. The employer takes the deduction for this contribution. The employer's contribution to each employee's account is not considered taxable income to the employees for the contribution year.

A profit-sharing plan can include a cash or deferred arrangement (401(k) plan) under which the employer and eligible employees can elect to contribute part of their before-tax earnings to the plan rather than receive the pay in cash. This contribution, called an elective deferral, together with any earnings resulting from the elective deferral, remain tax free until distributed by the plan. If the plan permits, the employer can make additional matching contributions to the 401(k) on behalf of the employee.

Selecting a Custodian or Trustee for an IRA or SEP IRA

All IRAs must have a custodian or trustee. Under the current income tax regulations, the terms "custodian" and "trustee" are synonymous for IRAs. Administrative or record-keeping firms, often referred to as Third Party Administrators (TPAs), also offer self-directed accounts. These administrators contract with one or more banks to provide self-directed services, and the bank acts as the custodian or trustee.

All banks are subject to regulation and examination by various state and federal agencies. Those regulatory agencies require that banks ensure that the TPAs comply with the same controls, policies, and procedures as the bank itself. As part of any examination, the regulatory agencies will verify that the TPAs are in compliance with applicable state or federal banking law. Some banks contract with TPAs in several different states to serve local and regional self-directed needs.

All banks provide insurance for deposits through the Federal Deposit Insurance Corporation (FDIC), which protects uninvested cash in your account up to a maximum of $100,000. However, you should always check whether your uninvested cash is FDIC insured, because some custodians place uninvested cash in other than FDIC insured accounts. If your uninvested cash is not FDIC insured, you will need to evaluate the risk you wish to take, if any. Also, under the Internal Revenue Code, nonbank trustees may offer IRAs, in which case your uninvested assets will not be FDIC insured. Note that FDIC insurance only covers uninvested assets; invested assets are not insured by any government plan.

> ***Tip:*** *Companies that offer to take a fee to find a self-directed custodian often look for new investors for their product, which they place with trustees or custodians whom they choose. It is best to do your own due diligence and ask your own questions.*

Selecting a Self-Directed Retirement Plan

To fully maximize your investment options, you need to have a retirement plan that allows you to select the types of investments you want to make. A fully self-directed retirement plan allows you to invest in any assets that are not prohibited by Treasury Department regulations and the Internal Revenue Code.

You can use an individual retirement arrangement, such as an IRA, or an employer-sponsored tax deferred plan (also referred to as a Qualified Plan), including 401(k)s, to make the investments you want. This section provides an overview of the types of retirement plans you can set up either as an individual or as a self-employed person. If you already have a retirement plan that is not self-directed, "Investment Provisions" below tells you how to transfer or roll over the funds to your self-directed account.

Determining Whether the Account Is Self-Directed

The administrator, custodian, or trustee must provide you with an IRA custodial or trustee account disclosure and agreement. One article must outline the self-direction features of the plan. The following sample language, written originally by the author, is typical of completely self-directed plans.

Investment Provisions

All contributions shall be invested and reinvested by the Administrator or Custodian as directed by the Depositor. It is understood and acknowledged by Depositor that the Custodian and its Administrator shall assume no responsibility, expressed or implied, for any loss or diminution of account, and Depositor indemnifies and holds harmless Entrust Bank & Trust and Affiliates, without limitation, against any and all losses, costs, expenses, or liabilities of any nature whatsoever incurred as a result of Custodian's and/or Administrator's execution of Depositor's investment instructions. Depositor agrees that all uninvested cash shall remain on deposit in an interest-bearing account offered through Custodian. The Depositor shall receive interest based on the then-published terms of such account that may, from time to time, change. The Custodian may, but need not, establish programs under which cash deposits in excess of a minimum set by it will be periodically and automatically invested in interest-bearing FDIC insured deposits.

Investment of Contributions

At the direction of the Depositor, the Administrator shall invest all contributions to the account and earnings thereon in investments acceptable to the Custodian, which may include but are not limited to marketable securities traded on a recognized exchange or "over the counter" (excluding any securities issued by the Custodian or Administrator), real estate, trust deeds, real estate limited partnerships, private placement offerings, certificates of deposit, and other investments to which the Custodian consents, in such amounts as are specifically selected and specified by Depositor in orders to the Administrator in such form as may be acceptable to the Custodian, without any duty to diversify and without regard to whether such property is authorized by the laws of any jurisdiction as a trust investment. The Custodian shall be responsible for the execution of such orders and for maintaining adequate records thereof. However, if any such orders are not received as required, or, if received, are unclear in the opinion of the Custodian, all or a portion of the contribution may be held uninvested without liability for loss of income or appreciation, and without liability for interest pending receipt of such orders or clarification, or the contribution may be returned. The Custodian may, but need not, establish programs under which cash deposits in excess of a minimum set by it will be periodically and automatically invested in interest-bearing investment funds. The Custodian shall have no duty other than to follow the written investment directions of the Depositor, and shall be under no duty to question said instructions and shall not be liable for any investment losses sustained by the Depositor.

Registration

All assets of the account shall be registered in the name of the Custodian or Administrator or of a suitable nominee. The same nominee may be used with respect to assets to other investors whether or not held under agreements similar to this one or in any capacity whatsoever. However, each Depositor's account shall be separate and distinct; a separate account therefore shall be maintained by the Administrator, and the assets thereof shall be held by the Administrator in individual or bulk segregation either in the Custodian's or Administrator's vaults or in depositories approved by the Securities and Exchange Commission under the Securities Exchange Act of 1934.

Investment Advisor

The Depositor may appoint an Investment Advisor, qualified under Section 3(38) of the Employee Retirement Income Security Act of 1974, to direct the investment of his IRA. The Depositor shall notify the Custodian in writing of any such appointment by providing the Custodian a copy of the instruments appointing the Investment Advisor and evidencing the Investment Advisor's acceptance of such appointment, an acknowledgment by the Investment Advisor that it is a fiduciary of the account, and a certificate evidencing the Investment Advisor's current registration under the Investment Advisor's Act of 1940. The Custodian shall comply with any investment directions furnished to it by the Investment Advisor, unless and until it receives written notification from the Depositor that the Investment Advisor's appointment has been terminated. The Custodian shall have no duty other than to follow the written investment directions of such Investment Advisor and shall be under no duty to question said instructions, and the Custodian shall not be liable for any investment losses sustained by the Depositor.

No Investment Advice

The Administrator and Custodian does not assume any responsibility for rendering advice with respect to the investment and reinvestment of Depositor's account and shall not be liable for any loss that results from Depositor's exercise of control over his account. The Custodian and Depositor may specifically agree in writing that the Custodian shall render such advice, but the Depositor shall still have and exercise exclusive responsibility for control over the investment of the assets of his account, and the Custodian shall not have any duty to question his investment directives.

Disclosures and Voting

The Custodian shall deliver, or cause to be executed and delivered, to Depositor all notices, prospectuses, financial statements, proxies, and proxy soliciting materials relating to assets credited to the account. The Custodian shall not vote any shares of stock or take any other action, pursuant to such documents, with respect to such assets except upon receipt by the Custodian of adequate written instructions from Depositor.

The above information must be disclosed to you in this or a similar form. The provisions establish the authority of the administrator to purchase the investment you selected on your behalf, and that title to that investment can be perfected in the name of your trustee, custodian, or administrator for your benefit.

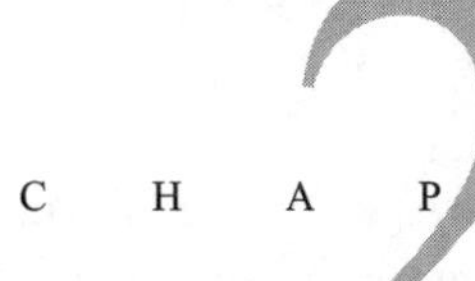

CHAPTER 2

Transactions

Buying and Selling Real Estate-Related Assets with Your Retirement Account

Case History of Linda's IRA Investment in Real Estate and Notes

For several years, Linda has been using her self-directed IRA to purchase real property and notes, and has had leveraged property in her IRA for rehab projects in Florida.

Linda started out using her retirement plan funds for real estate when she began her career as an agent for a residential broker. She started a Keogh plan in 1975 and contributed to her plan account when she could. She did this by being her own trustee and custodian, and having a professional Third Party Administrator (TPA) perform the plan administration functions. At the time Linda created her plan, some TPAs also did asset record keeping. Being in charge of her Keogh, she was able to do the transactions she wanted. That meant simply that her pension trust purchased notes for her account, and all earnings were tax deferred.

In 1981, she opened her first self-directed IRA. In the case of an IRA, she had a TPA that provided self-directed IRA services through a trustee bank.

Linda's Retirement assets have grown to more than $1,500,000 over three decades. Here is an overview of how it works:

- Put money away in an IRA. A Roth IRA is generally preferable if you qualify, as the gains are never taxed. The amount you put away is taxed in the year you make the contribution. Pay the tax with money outside your Roth IRA. If you do not qualify for a Roth, the old traditional IRA works, and gains are taxed when you start taking money out later.
- If you already have an IRA and wish to convert it to a self-directed IRA, all you have to do is complete a self-directed IRA application with the trustee or custodian of your IRA, and transfer the assets in the old IRA to your new self-directed IRA. If you previously had a 401(k), TSA, 403(b) or government-sponsored 457 plan from a previous employer, you may roll these over to any traditional IRA. The paperwork is easy and it takes only two to four weeks to complete the rollover process. This time frame permits the transfer or rollover of assets from IRAs and qualified plans (if applicable).

The First Purchase of Real Estate: Linda's first real estate transaction involving her plan was the purchase of a duplex. She made an all-cash offer of $40,000 for a property she had been familiar with, knowing that the tenants had been there for more than five years and were not going to move. The current owner needed cash, and the timing was ideal. The cash flow on the property was $9600 per year gross, and $6000 net. This fit into her goals for her plan.

Linda's transaction was accomplished as follows:

Linda completed a buy direction letter for Real Estate for the purchase of the property, and sent it to the trustee for her IRA. Linda made a good-faith deposit of $2000 with personal funds, which would be returned to her out of escrow at closing, being replaced by the cash from her IRA. Title was to be vested in the name of her IRA as follows: Entrust Administration, Inc. FBO Linda's IRA.

In Linda's case, Entrust Administration, Inc. is the third-party administrator, or TPA.

Linda obtained a preliminary title report, which showed no prior liens or other conditions that would preclude the purchase.

All documents were read and approved by Linda and signed on behalf of her IRA by the agent for the Trustee bank, Entrust Bank and Trust.

The agent for the trustee, having sent the funds to escrow, along with the completed documents, closed escrow.

After Closing: The purchase was recorded, with the recorded deed being sent to Entrust Administration, Inc. as agent for the trustee, Entrust Bank and Trust. The trustee's agent maintained the deed in safekeeping.

The tenants were instructed to make payments to Entrust Administration, Inc. FBO Linda's IRA. The income was deposited to the FDIC insured cash account at the trustee bank for the benefit of Linda's IRA.

All bills for expenses, such as taxes, hazard insurance, maintenance, gas, electric, and disposal services were sent directly to the IRA administrator to be paid from IRA funds at the trustee bank.

As you can see, the purchase of a property in an IRA is as straightforward as making that purchase personally, except that there is an intermediary, such as a trustee or TPA performing the transaction on behalf of your IRA.

Buying a Property and Rehabbing: Linda knew the real estate market, and she decided that she could achieve very high yields in rehabilitating properties, or rehabbing. One of her first transactions was the purchase of a single-family fixer using her IRA.

Knowing that the yields in her IRA were far better than regular transactions in a year that she would pay taxes, she located a property that would make the most money after rehabilitation.

The purchase price for the rehab property was $30,000 and the work on the house was estimated to be $5000. Linda had budgeted $15,000 from her IRA to start with, so she needed an additional $20,000 to complete the transaction. Because she liked the idea of using other people's money, she decided to try borrowing from a bank rather than partnering with others.

Real Estate Option Purchased by Debra's IRA: Debra found a property in Tucson, Arizona, which had been partially developed. The contractor had run out of money and out of town. The owner of the property, Jack, wanted to recover his investment and was anxious to find an investor or buyer. This had been going on for about a year, and he was delighted that anyone would talk to him about the property as it was only partially developed.

Debra knew that there were builders in Las Vegas who were looking at an opportunity to buy a property in the fast-growing Arizona real estate market. She had done business with the Las Vegas developers before, and decided that the best way to buy Jack's property was not with cash but with a real estate option.

The real estate option gave her control of the real estate without buying it. Debra would have the exclusive right to either purchase the property or not. She decided that the opportunity was an excellent possibility for her traditional IRA

She made an offer on behalf of her IRA in the form of an option agreement for the right to purchase the property for $2,000,000 in 90 days or less. The option consideration was $30,000.

Jack, who had been paying the ongoing costs of a property that was not cash flowing, was happy to see any cash at all, and $10,000 per month for 90 days seemed like a better deal than no deal at all. His taxes were due on the property on the assessed valuation in another month, and this would make Jack happy.

During the option period, if Jack sells the property to someone else, while Debra's IRA holds this option, the IRA is entitled to receive cash paid more than the $2,000,000 which Debra, through her IRA, agreed to pay. If Jack sells the property for less than what Debra's IRA (through the option agreement owned by her IRA), the IRA can collect the difference from Jack.

Debra's IRA, at the direction of Debra, has the exclusive right to purchase the property or not to buy it. If she elects not to buy it, she loses the $30,000—worst case. Because she does not wish to have any issues with simultaneous closing, she lines up a nonrecourse line of credit from a hard money lender for her IRA for $2,000,000, based on the commitment from the Las Vegas investor.

The Option Agreement is signed by her IRA administrator, after Debra has read and approved the final version. Jack will receive his copy signed in original along with a check for $30,000 as consideration. The option agreement stipulates that the $30,000 is not returnable if the option is not exercised by the IRA or assignee.

The Las Vegas buyers look at the property in question with Debra and like the possibilities of building the rest of the project out. They have the property appraised separately and find that it has a value of $2,200,000.

Because this is commercial real estate, no comparable values were available, so a commercial valuation was performed. Debra knew it was time to sell her option based on the valuation and directed her IRA to sell her option to the Las Vegas investors for $70,000, a major boost in Debra's IRA balance. The sellers gladly accepted the offer, as Debra had found the property for them at her expense, and they would save $130,000 on the purchase of the property. Jack would receive the $2,000,000 he wanted, as well.

Buying Notes Secured by Real Estate to Maximize Earnings to Your IRA or Qualified Plan

Herman Buys a Note and Income Stream

Herman is a note investor in San Diego. He is always looking for a great deal from people who wish to sell their notes because they want cash in advance. He always purchases notes secured by real estate, and in fact he is really buying the income stream. In all cases the debt obligation must be transferable to Herman, and he has been buying these notes for almost 20 years using IRA funds.

Herman has his IRA buy performing debt instruments with a long history of no delinquencies. In every case he likes to make sure that there is a prepayment penalty on years' payments, whenever possible. He also prefers high rates of interests, short amortization terms, and low loan-to-value ratios.

As notes produce a gain in value from interest, the owner of a note can sell some of the payments, which transfers some of that gain (for cash), and yet collect the full value of the loan from the remaining payments.

Herman found that Walter wants to sell the second mortgage he carried back when he sold his house. The original principal was $18,000. The mortgage is for five years at 8-percent interest. The payer, Joe, made 14 payments on Walter's note, and still owes $14,417.69.

Walter is looking to have a return for the remaining 44 months of 20 percent. To determine the purchase price he is willing to offer Walter, he determines the cash flow over the remaining term of his desired return. This works out to be $11,253. He offers $11,000 for the note to Walter. Walter finds that this works for him.

Herman directs his IRA administrator to purchase the note secured by deed of trust for $11,000.Title is perfected by the Trustee and Administrator for the Benefit of Herman's IRA. Joe is instructed by Walter to make future payments to Herman's IRA. Herman follows up to make sure, as in past experience he has had problems with checks going to the last note owner. Herman has his new note serviced as part of his IRA by the administrator.

IRAs Borrowing Money

IRAs may not be used as collateral for loans for personal use. However, obtaining debt financing for property in an IRA is considered to be for the benefit of the IRA and therefore is not prohibited. The biggest issue is finding lenders. Most institutional lenders do not lend to plans generally because such loans are not salable in the secondary market. Community Banks and other portfolio lenders, such as mortgage companies and hard-money lenders, in general will lend to plans.

Here is what you need to know about obtaining a loan for your plan:

- The loan-to-value ratio is important for any lender.
- The loan to your plan must not permit recourse to you as an individual.
- You may not guarantee a loan, but a third party who is not related to you may guarantee the loan.
- You can use other or additional collateral for the loan.

Many banks like an 80-percent loan-to-value (LTV) ratio on single-family dwellings. It is unusual for a lender to loan your IRA on this high a ratio. On the other hand, some banks, and hard-money lenders in particular, will lend on a 50-percent LTV.

Commercial properties are treated differently. Such properties are often evaluated on the basis of cash flow, occupancy, return on capital, and other factors. Your personal ability to repay becomes less of a factor when commercial property, such as four-unit residential dwellings, strip centers, multiunit apartment buildings, and commercial buildings are concerned.

In Linda's case, she had a good banking relationship at her local independent bank, which agreed to make the loan to her plan. Because plans are trusts and the IRS Code disallows Linda's guaranteeing the loan, a nonrecourse loan was needed. The community banker was sophisticated enough to understand that this loan would be a portfolio loan, and the analysis of suitability of the loan in the bank's portfolio was not dissimilar to the analysis required for a commercial real estate loan. As a backup, Linda had a private mortgage company who would lend to her plan as well, but at a higher interest rate and points.

As stated above, the cost of the house was $30,000, so the funding went as follows:

She directed the IRA trustee to purchase the house using $10,000 from her IRA, and a loan from the Bank to the IRA for $20,000. Closing costs were included.

The trustee noted that the Buy Direction Letter and the property in question conflicted with each other, based on the preliminary title report. There had been a lot line adjustment during the life of the property, which had been recorded, but the seller had not been aware that this was important to complete the purchase from the trustee's point of view.

The comparison of the Buy Direction requirements to the documents provided by title and escrow are a major aspect of the administration of the plan by the trustee, custodian, or TPA as agent for the trustee.

On receiving a corrected Buy Direction Letter, the escrow was funded by the custodian for the benefit of Linda's IRA, and the lender. On receipt of the HUD-1, the final settlement was made, with the transaction adjustments being properly accounted for by the IRA TPA.

Repayment of the Loan

Normally the loan, which the IRS calls "debt-financed property," will be paid by the trustee or administrator, as rental income comes in and generates cash flow from which the payments can be made. If rental or other cash is not available to make loan payments, the loan payment cannot be made. In Linda's case, the property is going to be rehabbed, and no rental income is available to make any loan payments.

Linda negotiated with the lender for an interest-only loan for 90 days, renewable for an additional 90 days. The $5000 remaining in the IRA was to fund the rehab costs and allow for the interest carry on the loan. Linda had presold the property to a willing buyer for $56,000, under contract, and her risk was minimized as a result (see Table 2.1).

The transaction unfolded as shown in Table 2.1.

TABLE 2.1. Linda's Rehab Property

Total Purchase Price	$30,000		
IRA Portion	Original Investment	Rehab Costs	Total Costs
	$10,000	$5,000	$15,000
Loan Portion	Original Amount	Interest Expense	Total Loan Expense
	$20,000	$1,000	$21,000
Total Cost of Acquisition and Rehab	$36,000		

Linda also used the services of a third-party administrator to make payments to subcontractors. This made the project easier to handle and avoided concerns about violating any provisions of the Internal Revenue Code.

What Happens if There Is Shortage of Money in the IRA

The rehab went according to plan. If an unexpected problem arose that cost more money than the plan had available, Linda's options would include the following:

Make a Contribution to Her IRA

This would be the easiest option if she had not already made a contribution exceeding her contribution limit. If excess contributions result, penalties of 6 percent on the amount overcontributed may be assessed for each year the excess contribution remains in the IRA.

Transfer or Roll Over Funds from Another IRA or Qualified Plan

This would be another relatively easy solution, provided that those funds were available.

Increase Her "Debt Finance"

This option is more complicated, as it would require the completion of additional paperwork with her banker, with additional points and some more interest.

Sell Another Asset in Her Plan to Raise Cash

This would be an easy way to raise money. Linda could sell all or part of a note in her IRA or Profit Sharing Plan and use the proceeds to complete the rehab project. She could also sell part of a stream of income from a note for a short period, if the amount she needed to raise was small. In any case, this option would result in a discount of a note she owned in her IRA or plan.

Bring In Partners

This option is fairly complicated, as it would involve having to go through a sale process involving both her bank and her IRA and would require that Linda give up an undivided interest in the property and some of her profit along with it. She could also do this using a Limited Partnership or Limited Liability Company, although this would add more expense. She could not, after the original purchase, partner with herself or "disqualified persons" such as ascendants or descendants and spouses thereof.

Sell the Property As Is

This is the least preferable option, and the IRA would probably lose out on the profit interest.

The Sale

The property rehabbing was completed 110 days from the purchase date, and the sale went forward into escrow. Linda completed the sell direction letter for $56,000, and the escrow company handling the closing contacted Entrust. The loan of $20,000, plus accrued interest of $1000, was repaid out of escrow, which left $20,000 as gross profit to Linda's IRA. Of this $8333.33 was attributable to the IRA (see Table 2.2).

Unrelated Business Income Tax on Debt-Financed Property in an IRA

Because Linda's IRA made a gross profit of more than $1000 on borrowed funds, which had not been taxed previously, the IRS code requires payment

TABLE 2.2 The Sale

Proportions:	
IRA + Loan	
41.67 percent	Percentage Not Subject to UBIT or IRA portion
58.33 percent	Percentage Subject to UBIT or loan portion
Sales Price	$56,000
Gross Profit	$20,000
IRA Profit	$8,333

of tax on the 58.33 percent of the property that was debt financed. Along with payment of the tax, Linda must file an Unrelated Business Income Tax return, IRS form 990 T, for the IRA.

Linda hired her accountant to prepare the tax return for execution by the agent for the custodian. The unrelated business tax was $3419. This amount takes into account the expenses involved in the rehabbing that did not contribute to the value or appreciably prolong the life of the property, such as repairs needed to meet code requirements; incidental plumbing, electrical, and miscellaneous repairs; depreciation; interest and other related expenses. With her IRA now increased by $16,509, which included the $5000 in rehab expense, Linda is satisfied that her rehabbing experience was a positive one. The final breakdown was as shown in Table 2.3.

TABLE 2.3 Final Breakdown

IRA Profit from non-UBIT portion	$8,333
Profit Allocation: to Loan Subject to UBIT Expenses	$11,667
Allocated to UBIT	$2,917
Amount subject to UBIT	$8,750
UBIT paid by IRA	$3,491
Profit on Loan Portion After IRA paying UBIT	$8,175
Total Net Profit to IRA	$16,509
Percentage net profit to IRA	82.54 percent

The Same Transaction Involving a 401(k) Plan

Here is an overview of how the process works if Linda makes the same transaction in a 401(k) Profit Sharing Plan (the "Plan").

- Open a qualified Plan with a 401(k) option, or an Individual (k) for your business (the "Plan").
- If you already participate in a profit-sharing or other defined contribution plan, amend and restate your plan to one that permits complete self-direction.
- Start looking for transactions on which you would like to earn tax-free or tax-deferred income.

Purchase of Real Estate

Linda completed a buy direction letter for Real Estate for the purchase of the property that she processed for herself as trustee and custodian. She made a good faith deposit of $2000 with a trust check from her Plan. Title was to be vested in the name of her Plan as follows: Best Properties 401(k) plan, FBO Linda's 401(k) account, Linda trustee.

A preliminary title reported no prior liens or other conditions that would preclude the purchase. All documents were read and approved by Linda and she signed on behalf of her Plan as the Trustee for Best Properties 401(k) plan. She compared these documents back to her Buy Direction Letter, for good measure to make sure that all terms were as she had agreed initially. Although it seems redundant, a double-check is always helpful.

Escrow was closed with Linda as trustee of her Plan sending the funds to escrow as well as the completed documents signed by Linda on behalf of her Plan. The purchase was recorded, with the recorded deed being sent to Best Properties 401(k) plan. The trustee, Linda, maintained the deed in safekeeping.

The tenants were instructed to make payments to: Best Properties 401(k) plan, FBO Linda's 401(k) account, Linda trustee.

The income was deposited to the Plan's cash account at Linda's bank for the benefit of her Plan account. All bills for expenses, such as taxes, hazard insurance, maintenance, gas, electric, and disposal services were sent directly to the Plan to be paid by Linda from funds maintained at her bank exclusively for the Plan.

As you can see, the purchase of a property in a Plan is as straightforward as making that purchase personally, except that there is an intermediary, such as a trustee [or a Third Party Administrator ("TPA")] performing the transaction on behalf of the Profit-Sharing 401(k) Plan.

401(k) Plans Borrowing Money

401(k) and other Qualified Plan accounts may borrow money, on a nonrecourse basis. Borrowing from a 401(k) for personal use is permitted but is not usually recommended for investment purposes, as the account may make investments directly. Loans for personal use made to an account holder may have the loan amount secured by assets in the plan, although other collateral may be used. One may not borrow in excess of $50,000 over a five-year period for personal purposes.

Linda, as the Plan Trustee, Is Instructed by Herself as the Plan Account Holder

She directed herself as the Plan trustee to purchase the house using $10,000 from her Plan account, and a loan from the Bank for $20,000. Closing costs were included.

Repayment of the Loan: Normally the loan, which the IRS calls "debt-financed property," will be paid by the custodian of the Plan as rental income is received and generates cash flow from which the payments can be made. In this case, Linda is both the custodian and the account holder. If rental or other cash is not available to make loan payments, the loan payment cannot be made. In Linda's case, the property is going to be rehabbed, and no rental income is available to make any loan payments.

Linda negotiated with the lender for an interest-only loan for 90 days, renewable for an additional 90 days. The $5000 remaining in her plan account was to fund the rehab costs and allow for the interest carry on the loan. Linda had presold the property to a willing buyer for $56,000, under contract, and her risk was minimized as a result.

The transaction unfolded as shown in Table 2.4.

TABLE 2.4 Linda's Rehab Property

Total Purchase Price	$30,000		
401(k) Portion	Original Investment $10,000	Rehab Costs $5,000	Total Costs $15,000
Loan Portion	Original Amount $20,000	Interest Expense $1,000	Total Loan Expense $21,000
Total Cost of Acquisition and Rehab		$36,000	

What Happens if There Is Shortage of Money in the Plan Account

The rehab went according to plan. However, if an unexpected problem arises that costs more money than the plan has, some of Linda's options would include the following:

- Make a contribution to her plan. This would be the easiest option if Linda had not made a contribution already exceeding her contribution limit. Although excess contributions could result, excess contributions are treated differently in qualified plans than in IRAs.
- Transfer or roll over funds from another IRA or from another qualified plan left over from a previous employer. This would be another relatively easy solution, provided that those funds were available.
- Increase her "debt finance." This option is more complicated, as it requires the completion of additional paperwork with Linda's banker, with additional points and some more interest.
- Sell another asset in her plan to raise cash. This is an easy way to raise money. Linda could sell all or part of a note in her Plan and use the proceeds. She could also sell part of a stream of income from a note for a short period because the amount she needed to raise was small. In any case, this option would result in a discount of a note she had as a Plan asset.
- Bring in partners. This option is more complicated, as it would involve having to go through a sale process including her bank and her Plan account and would require that Linda give up an undivided interest in the property and some of her profits along with it. She could also do this using a Limited Partnership or Limited Liability Company, although

doing so would add more expense. She could not, after the original purchase, partner with herself or "disqualified persons" such as ascendants or descendants and spouses thereof.

- Sell the property as is. This is the least preferable option, and her Plan account would probably lose out on the profit interest.

The Sale: The loan of $20,000, plus accrued interest of $1000, was repaid out of escrow, which left $20,000 as gross profit to Linda's 401(k) (see Table 2.5).

TABLE 2.5 The Sale

Proportions:	
401(k) + Loan	41.67 percent
Percentage 401(k) portion	58.33 percent
Percentage loan portion	
Sales Price	$56,000
Gross Profit	$20,000
401(k) Profit	$20,000

Unrelated Business Income Tax on Debt-Financed Property Involving a 401(k)

Unrelated Business Income tax does not apply to acquisition of debt-financed property, but does apply to operating income received in a 401(k) or other qualified plan. (Internal Revenue Code § 512, Unrelated business taxable income; § 514 Unrelated debt-financed income.)

Gary's Purchase of Paper within an IRA

Gary Black decided that notes were going to be an important part of his plan portfolio. Cash flowing notes were an essential part of his long-term strategy of diversification with a major emphasis on real estate. He decided to purchase packages of paper, which had some significant problems. He found notes supported by mobile homes and real property, which he could purchase at 10 cents on the dollar. He felt that with aggressive collection as well as restructuring due dates, and moving current payments to the end of the loan term, or by extensions, he could make a decent tax-deferred and tax-free profit.

He directed Entrust to purchase $250,000 of the notes for $25,000. He purchased them from an attorney in New York, and the notes and deeds of trust were assigned and the mobile homes were rerecorded as"Entrust Bank and Trust, FBO Gary Black IRA" as lien holder. (The vesting is analogous to real property, note, stock, bond, or any other asset.) See Table 2.6.

TABLE 2.6 Purchase of Paper within an IRA

Discounted Note Purchase		Earnings Percentage	Earnings Dollars	Earnings Percentage in IRA after investment	IRA Due IRA	Tax due if non IRAs 30%	Percentage return after tax
Total funding needed:	$25,000						
Face Value of Notes	$250,000	0.500%	$1,250				
Note restructure	$50,000.00	4%	$2,000	8.00%	$0.00	$600.00	5.60%
Foreclosure and Carryback	$100,000.00	6%	$6,000	24.00%	$0.00	$1,800.00	16.80%
Uncollectible	$50,000.00	0%	$0	0.00%	$0.00	$0.00	
Totals			$8,000	32.00%	$0.00	$2,400.00	3.73%

The only difference between this transaction being performed with non-IRA funds rather than by the IRA is the taxable event that may result from non-IRA profits. By turning a $25,000 purchase into $150,000 of earning assets, the yields increased dramatically, without any current taxable income. The tax is deferred until withdrawal takes place. The tax is also deferred in any traditional, SEP, or SIMPLE IRA until withdrawal takes place. This transaction done by a Roth IRA would have no taxable consequence even at withdrawal.

Cashing Out Partners and Receiving Notes for Payment

Gary and his partners sold property for $100,000 for a total profit of $40,000. His plan owned 50 percent and his partners owned the other 50 percent with his spouse, his personal funds, and three other unrelated persons. As part of the sale, he elected to take his profit interest for his Plan in the form of notes, effectively cashing out his other partners. In this way he had earning assets in first position while his partners received the cash they wanted for other investments (see Table 2.7).

By using funds found in IRAs and other people's 401(k) plan accounts, as well as using partners and personal funds, the participants were able to plan easily, creatively, and effectively for the growth of their assets in a tax-free and tax-deferred environment. The tax law changes in 2002 and 2003 and other creative tools made the process straightforward and easy to understand.

Gary's Purchase of Paper within a Qualified Plan with Gary as Trustee

Gary would act as trustee for his plan for the plan participant, Gary Black. He would direct the trustee, Gary Black, to purchase the asset for his benefit. The vesting would be Black Commercial Properties, Inc. 401(k) Plan, FBO Gary Black as lien holder. (The vesting is analogous to real property, note, stock, bond, or any other asset.) Qualified Plans [including those with a 401(k) option] permit the employer or his or her designee to act as trustee for their company's plan.

The only difference between performing this transaction outside of the 401(k) as opposed to within his Plan account is the taxable event. By turning a $25,000 purchase into $150,000 of earning assets, the yields increased dramatically, without any current taxable income. The tax is deferred in his Plan until withdrawal takes place. Gary could also partner with other IRAs such as his Roth IRA and other entities that he owns or is a partner in.

Commercial Property IRA

Bill Heller is a Broker and is interested in purchasing additional real property for investment purposes.

TABLE 2.7 Cashing Our Partners

Sale of Property Owned by Gary and His Partners	Original Investment	Sales Proceeds	Profit	Cash Proceeds	Carry-Back Note	Net Cash Result from Profit	Notes Bought by Gary's IRA from partners
Gary's IRA portion	$30,000	$50,000	$20,000	$12,000	$8,000	$4,000	
Norbert's SEP-IRA portion	$6,000	$10,000	$4,000	$2,400	$1,600	$4,000	$1,600
Larry's SIMPLE-IRA portion	$2,400	$4,000	$1,600	$960	$640	$1,600	$640
Linda's Personal Portion	$8,400	$14,000	$5,600	$3,360	$2,240	$5,600	$2,240
Norbert's Personal Portion	$13,200	$22,000	$8,800	$5,280	$3,520	$8,800	$3,520
Totals	$60,000	$100,000	$40,000	$24,000	$16,000	$24,000	$8,000
Total after Gary's Note	$30,000	$50,000	$20,000	$12,000	$8,000	$4,000	$8,000
Purchase							
Reconcilement of Gary's IRA at end of transactions							
Original Investment	$30,000						
Notes	$16,000						
Cash	$4,000						
Total	$50,000						
Net Profit to IRA	$20,000						

Locating the Property

Bill locates the property in January. He has done so by checking through the MLS and through personal contacts for potential rehabs in an area with which he is familiar. The property he found is a 36-unit apartment building and has land adjacent to it available for expansion.

Funding the Purchase

As part of the funding, he is going to use his own cash and funds in his traditional IRA. Bill will fund half of the purchase personally.

Bill completes a Buy Direction Letter supplied by the agent for custodian. The letter contains the details of the transaction. At this point, the agent completes the rest of the transaction for the custodian or trustee. Entrust is informed through the Buy Direction Letter that Brentwood Escrow is handling the title and escrow matters, and that Brentwood Escrow will contact Entrust to complete the transaction.

Escrow is opened at Brentwood Escrow for the property, and the deposit is taken. Although it is sometimes customary for escrow to just hold on to the check, in this case the deposit is made to the escrow account. Escrow is to close in 60 days.

Bill also engages American Title (ATCO), and he asks for a preliminary title report. Entrust asks ATCO for the copy of the deed, which will be recorded in the purchasers' names. The vesting will show 50 percent undivided interest in subject property in the name of Bill Heller as a married person as his separate property, and the "Entrust Administration, Inc. for the Benefit of Bill Heller IRA" for the remaining 50 percent.

Closing

At closing, the Settlement Statement (such as a HUD-1) provides a breakdown of the costs and charges allocated among the buyers and sellers. The earnest money deposit is split: $3600 remains in escrow, and $3600 is refunded to Bill Heller. The refund to Bill Heller is for the portion in which his Plan has an interest; otherwise, it would be considered a contribution. Bill will make out a check to the escrow company for the amount needed to fund 50 percent of the purchase price, including $3600 that was refunded to him personally.

The sale closes and the seller is happy with the deal, and Bill now owns the property, 50 percent each in his name and his Plan's name (see Table 2.8).

TABLE 2.8 Bill Heller Buys a 36-Unit Apartment Building with 50-percent IRA and 50-percent Personal

Purchase Price		$720,000
Earnest Money	$7,200	
IRA	$3,600	$360,000
Personal	$3,600	$360,000

Income

Assignment of Rental Agreements and Income Allocation: The rental agreements for the apartments are assigned to Bill and his plan equally. Bill advises the renters that checks need to be made out to his plan. The IRA custodian or agent receives the payments and keeps accurate records of them. The Custodian or agent will divide the income in exact proportion between Bill and his plan. In the case of co-ownership by an IRA or other persons or entities, it is advisable to employ the services of a property manager or outside bookkeeper.

Expenses

Expenses for the apartment building, such as hazard insurance, taxes, and repairs will be divided pro rata between the Plan and Bill. The Trustee, Entrust Bank and Trust, or a third-party servicer will pay for any repairs or other expenses from the cash account established for this property. Bill will pay for the other 50 percent of the expenses. Keep in mind that a third-party servicer may not be a disqualified person such as the account holder or owner, ascendants or descendants, or be part of any relationship in which the owner (in this case, Bill) would receive a current benefit.

The transaction and first–month's rental income and expenses appear in Table 2.9.

TABLE 2.9 Bill Heller Buys a 36-Unit Apartment Building with 50-percent IRA and 50-percent Personal Funds

	Total		IRA	Personal	
Purchase Price	$720,000		$360,000	$360,000	
Earnest Money	$7,200		$3,600	$3,600	
Income on 36 Units					
Apartments at 3412 Etiwanda	Beginning Balance In Bank	Credits	Ending Balance In Bank	IRA	Personal
Income Deposits Balance	$15,000		$15,000	$7,500	$7,500
Forward					
Rental Payments 01-Jan	$40,000		$55,000	$20,000	$20,000
Total Income			$55,000	$27,500	$27,500
Trust Fund Deposits	$72,000		$36,000	$36,000	
Trust Fund Deposits 01-Jan	$2,000		$74,000	$1,000	$1,000
Total Trust Funds	$74,000		$37,000	$37,000	
Debits					
Expense	$74,000				
Utilities	$3,500		$1,750	$1,750	
Water Heater	$4,000		$2,000	$2,000	
Tax Impound Account	$700		$350	$350	
Insurance	$9,500		$4,750	$4,750	
	$17,700		$56,300	$8,850	$8,850
Reserve Account for Expenses	$5,500		$50,800	$2,750	$2,750
Net Monthly Cash Flow	$50,800		$25,400	$25,400	

Additional Investments

Because his pro rata Plan income is $40,000 per year and pro rata expenses are only $7000, he has his Plan purchase discounted mobile-home paper with $25,000, as the cash flow permits.

Commercial Property Purchase in a 401(k)

Funding the Purchase

If Bill decided to use a 401(k) Plan, the scenario would look like this. As part of the funding, he is going to use his own cash and funds in his 401(k) plan account for the real estate brokerage firm, a "C" corporation of which he is the majority shareholder. Bill has found out that because his traditional IRA is made up of pretax dollars, he can roll the cash he needs from the IRA over to the profit-sharing plan. (He will leave the private placements and notes in the IRA, as his IRA custodian is providing the servicing for those assets.) Bill can do this because the tax laws changed in 2002 and 2003 to permit this. Bill feels that it is more convenient to do this transaction through the qualified plan for the following reasons:

- He is the trustee of his own plan and can do the closing personally using funds from a single source, his Plan account.
- Because this is an apartment building, Bill recognizes that there may be a liability issue concerning tenants. Although he has sufficient insurance based on his personal risk profile, the qualified plan has an antialienation provision, which will protect his qualified plan assets from creditors. (The antialienation provision only functions when there is at least one common-law employee in the qualified plan.)
- Because Bill does his own record keeping, he will be able to collect all the rents and divide them between his personal account and the profit-sharing plan without having to hire a property manager. (He actually will have his bookkeeper do this for the plan.)
- Bill wants to move quickly. The purchase contract shows him as the buyer. Because he knows that until the actual close of escrow, the sales contract is assignable, until closing there is no issue of self-dealing or

prohibited transactions involving the Plan account. The terms of the deal are that Bill provides all cash for $720,000 and earnest money of $7,200 to the Seller, Lori, through escrow.
- Bill will fund half of the purchase personally.

Bill completes a Buy Direction Letter for his account with the details of the transaction. Bill will also act as the trustee for the Plan.

At this point, Bill, as trustee and custodian for his plan account completes the rest of the transaction. As trustee, he acts on his Buy Direction Letter, which states that he will contact the title and escrow companies to complete the transaction.

Escrow is opened at Brentwood Escrow for the property, and the deposit is taken. Although it is sometimes customary for escrow to merely hold on to the check without depositing it, in this case the deposit is made to the escrow account. Escrow is to close in 60 days.

Bill also engages American Title (ATCO), and he asks for a preliminary title report. Bill asks ATCO for the copy of the deed, which will be recorded in the purchasers' names. The vesting will show 50-percent undivided interest in subject property in the name of Bill Heller as a married person as his separate property, and the "Bill Heller Profit Sharing 401(k) Plan, for the Benefit of Bill Heller 401(k) Account, Bill Heller, Trustee" for the remaining 50 percent. Closing will occur in the same manner as with the IRA, with Bill closing the transaction on behalf of his plan.

Assignment of Rental Agreements and Income

The rental agreements for the apartments are assigned to Bill and his plan equally. Bill advises the renters that checks need to be made out to his plan and him personally. Bill's bookkeeper receives the payments and keeps accurate records of them. The bookkeeper will divide the income equally between Bill and his plan and will write two checks: one to the Plan and one to Bill personally. In the case of co-ownership by an IRA or other persons or entities, it is advisable to employ the services of a property manager or outside bookkeeper. In that case, the checks would be made payable to the property manager, who would receive the rent checks and split them proportionally between the Plan and Bill personally. That company may not be owned by Bill or any other disqualified person.

Expenses

Expenses for the apartment building, such as hazard insurance, taxes, and repairs, will be divided pro rata between the Plan and Bill. Bill has the ability to write a check on the spot for any repairs or other expenses from the trust money market account he established at his brokerage.

The transaction and first–month's rental income and expenses appear as shown in Table 2.10.

Additional Investments

Because his pro-rata Plan income is $40,000 per year and pro-rata expenses are only $7000, he has his Plan purchase notes and other assets as cash flow permits.

Using an IRA to Buy Discounted Notes

Recently a realtor, Lee, discovered problem loans on a property that she had sold. The loans were brought to her attention by a collection agency.

Property at 18 Main Street

The original financing on this property was for $100,000. When the borrowers were about to go into foreclosure, a third party was able to arrange private financing and purchase the obligation from the bank prior to foreclosure. A group of three investors provided the private financing. Two of the investors, Martha and Eddie, each had a 25-percent interest in the two notes that resulted from the refinancing, and a third investor owned a 50-percent interest. Both notes were for a term of 30 years at 15 percent interest per year.

Two years later the borrowers had problems again, and the investors decided to engage a local collection agency. The loans were being collected, and the 50-percent investor in the $100,000 note decided that he wanted to sell out.

Lee knew the principals in the transactions, was aware that there was a fair amount of equity value in the property, and knew about the events preceding the potential foreclosure. Although payments were slow, they were being made.

TABLE 2.10 Bill Heller Buys a 36-Unit Apartment Building with 50-percent IRA and 50-percent Personal Funds

	Total				401(k)	Personal
Purchase Price	$720,000				$360,000	$360,000
Earnest Money	$7,200				$3,600	$3,600
Income on 36 Units						
Apartments at 3412 Etiwanda		Beginning Balance In Bank	Credits	Ending Balance In Bank	401(k)	Personal
Income Deposits Balance	$15,000	$15,000		$7,500	$7,500	
Forward						
Rental Payments	01-Jan	$40,000		$55,000	$20,000	$20,000
Total Income				$55,000	$27,500	$27,500
Trust Fund Deposits		$72,000			$36,000	$36,000
Trust Fund Deposits	01-Jan	$2,000		$74,000	$1,000	$1,000
Total Trust Funds				$74,000	$37,000	$37,000
Debits						
Expenses	$74,000					
Utilities		$3,500		$1,750	$1,750	
Water Heater		$4,000		$2,000	$2,000	
Tax Impound Account		$700		$350	$350	
Insurance		$9,500		$4,750	$4,750	
		$17,700		$56,300	$8,850	$8,850
Reserve Account for Expenses		$5,500		$50,800	$2,750	$2,750
Net Monthly Cash Flow				$50,800	$25,400	$25,400

Lee has a plan with $180,000 in uninvested funds and other assets. Recognizing the opportunity, she decided to make an offer to all of the investors. The offer consisted of $50,000 for the $100,000 note. The 50-percent investor negotiated a purchase price equal to 75 percent of the value of his interest. Recognizing that the 50-percent investor wanted out and had negotiated what appeared to be a reasonable deal, Martha and Eddie sold as well. The plan bought the note for $75,000. The principal balance outstanding at the time the Plan purchased the note was $98,900.

The plan owner would direct the trustee of the IRA to purchase the note on behalf of the IRA (see Table 2.11).

TABLE 2.11 Purchase of Notes at Discount

18 Main Street		Original Face	Current Balance	Discount	Plan Purchase
		$100,000	$98,900		
Lee	50%		$49,450	0.75	$37,088
Martha	30%		$29,670	0.75	$22,253
Eddie	20%		$19,780	0.75	$14,835
	100%		$98,900		$74,175

The note payments are relatively regular, albeit slow. Again, the income received on that note is tax deferred. The note is being serviced externally at a 1-percent fee from the mortgage servicer. This fee may be tax deductible as an accounting fee that the trust pays. (The amount of these fees and plan administration fees, as well as other accounting fees, must meet conditional tests as a percentage of income to be deducted from taxable income.) The deductible amounts should be reviewed with a tax professional. As this plan is intended to be for buy and holds, the owner not only has income in the plan, but also a first position note. If foreclosure would be necessary, the plan would then own the property, and be able to sell, with or without a carryback note, lease option the property, or just rent it out. In any event, the profits net after expenses are tax deferred.

The other part of the uninvested fund was invested in a managed account in which the client gave specific direction to a securities broker as to her goals and objectives for income and growth. One of the objectives was that the remaining balance was to be liquid enough so that within a 60-day period, the managed account portion could be liquidated to be placed into another real estate opportunity. Good managers of assets are able to balance the needs of clients' short- and long-term financial objectives and still achieve reasonable results. A securities broker who understands clients' needs and the real estate market can be a valuable asset in handling self-directed accounts.

Using a 401(k) to Buy Discounted Notes

The plan owner as trustee would direct herself to make the purchase on behalf of her 401(k), and then follow the same process as above for IRAs. The only difference would be that all income would be credited to the 401(k) for the benefit of Lee. Lee is either a participant, or could also be the trustee, custodian, and administrator (see Table 2.12).

TABLE 2.12 Purchase of Notes at Discount

18 Main Street		Original Face	Current Balance	Discount	Plan Purchase
		$100,000	$98,900		
Lee 401(k)	50 percent		$49,450	0.75	$37,088
Martha	30 percent		$29,670	0.75	$22,253
Eddie	20 percent		$19,780	0.75	$14,835
	100 percent		$98,900		$74,175

Tax Lien Certificates

Purchasing Tax Obligations

A tax lien certificate documents the purchase of a tax obligation from a taxing authority. This obligation is unpaid by the property owner of record. The taxing authority (in this example, a county) sells the obligation to private individuals, usually at a public sale, to receive immediate income.

Sometimes these obligations are auctioned. The taxing authority receives the tax money it is owed, and the purchaser of the debt receives interest on the amount paid. The owner of record may redeem the tax lien certificate at any time, but must also pay interest on the obligation. The obligation may bear interest at relatively high rates—18 percent annually or more. In this example, the intervening time prior to redemption is three months, and the return is 8 percent over four months.

You may purchase such obligations from a taxing authority that offers tax lien certificates directly or by mail. This labor-intensive asset requires your attention. The purchase amounts can be small, so sometimes plans purchase a large number, which means more administration and more costs.

In the case of auctions, the administrator can accommodate your purchase up to the amount of available cash in your account through special drafts for that purpose.

When you purchase a tax lien certificate, the administrator receives the actual certificate for your benefit (Certificate of Purchase at Tax Sale). It includes the purchase amount, which is remitted on your behalf to the county. The terms of the sale are also included in the certificate.

Sarah Buys a Tax Lien Certificate

Sarah purchases Tax Lien certificates (TLC) regularly at auction. She has an arrangement where she receives a number of cashier's checks to take to auction to purchase the TLCs in her IRA. A Purchase direction letter is used for obtaining the cashier's checks, and the title becomes vested in the name of the IRA.

A Certificate with Sale Book Number is often a registry of such certificates. The references to Certificates include the Sale Book number. Make sure that the certificate number conforms to what you purchased. In her case, she purchased a certificate from Polk County, Iowa. The original asset was purchased for $181 three months prior, bearing an annual interest rate of 8 percent for four months (equaling 24 percent in a year).

The original Buy Direction Letter is sent to the administrator or trustee of the IRA to purchase the TLC from the jurisdiction, Polk County, Iowa to be vested in the name of the administrator or trustee For the Benefit of Sarah's IRA.

This direction letter provides the information needed for the administrator to send certificates for redemption. In this case, the account owner follows up on each tax lien certificate bought and redeemed. Through this cooperative process, the cost of administration is reduced, resulting in a higher return for the plan.

AVCO Financial Services redeemed the Certificate for $205 and is the beneficial owner on title for the asset. The total amount is usually included in a letter regarding Surrendering Certificates. When a tax lien certificate is redeemed, the county sends the plan a check for the amount due. The receipt of the funds is subject to surrendering the certificate to the county treasurer.

Tax Lien Certificates Purchased in a Qualified Plan

Sarah Buys a Tax Lien Certificate Using Her 401(k) Plan: Sarah, as the trustee of her plan, purchases a number of cashier's checks to take to auction to purchase the TLCs with her 401(k).

The original Buy Direction Letter is completed by Sarah as the Trustee of her 401(k) plan account to purchase the TLC from the jurisdiction, Polk County, Iowa, to be vested in the name of the "Sarah 401(k), for the Benefit of Sarah 401(k) Account, by Sarah, Trustee."

Sarah completes a Buy Direction Letter to document the activities in her plan. This direction letter provides the information needed for Sarah, as the custodian of her 401(k), to send certificates for redemption. In this case, Sarah, as the 401(k) account owner, follows up on each tax lien certificate bought and redeemed.

Using LLC and other Company Forms for Purchases in IRAs

IRAs have been used to invest in stock of publicly traded and private or closely held corporations since retirement plans and similar accounts were first created. However, federal tax laws limit investments in companies if the IRA account holder has a personal interest in the company in question. The issues regarding such ownership by IRAs center mostly on the percentages of ownership that are permitted under applicable tax laws and regulations. In many cases, ownership of a corporation in which an IRA invests will result in disqualification of an individual relative to an IRA. Disqualification in and of itself does not mean that a taxable event occurs. For example, if the beneficial interest owner of a Limited Liability Corporation that an IRA owns is disqualified, it means that the entire benefit of the LLC must inure to the IRA. Once the disqualified person (the beneficial interest owner of the IRA) receives any personal benefit, the IRA ceases to be an IRA as of the end of the previous year in which the violation occurred. This is a short version of a prohibited transaction violation involving an IRA. Most individuals who seek proper legal counsel and understand the issues involved in owning LLCs do not have any problems. A carefully crafted document is necessary.

If the company in which the IRA invests is an operating company, pursuant to the Plan Assets Regulation, ERISA Reg. Section 2510.3-101, the IRA assets generally include the equity interest in the operating company but do not include the underlying assets of the operating company. ERISA Reg. Section 2510.3-101(a)(2). However, if the IRA owns all of the outstanding equity interests (other than director's qualifying shares) in an entity, the IRA's assets include those equity interests and all of the underlying assets of the entity. ERISA Reg. Section 2510.3-101(h)(3). In other words, if the IRA owns all of the outstanding stock of an operating company (other than the director's qualifying shares), there is a "look-through" to the underlying assets of the operating company, and such underlying assets (as well as the shares of stock) are IRA assets.

The non-IRA stockholder of the operating company should have veto power because of ERISA Reg. Section 2509.75-2 ("IB 75-2"). IB 75-2 is an Interpretive Bulletin issued by the Department of Labor relating to prohibited transactions. IB 75-2 generally provides that if a transaction between a disqualified person and an IRA would be a prohibited transaction, then such transaction between a disqualified person and a corporation or partnership will be a prohibited transaction if the IRA may, on its own, require the corporation or partnership to engage in the transaction. For example, the sale of any property between the IRA depositor and his IRA is a prohibited transaction. Code Section 4975(c)(1)(A). The sale of any property between the IRA depositor and a corporation would also be a prohibited transaction under IB 75-2 if the IRA could compel the corporation to sell the property to the IRA depositor. If the non-IRA stockholder has veto power, the IRA cannot, by itself (even if it owns 99 percent of the stock) compel the corporation to engage in a transaction.

Even assuming that the IRA owns less than 100 percent of an operating company and that the non-IRA stockholder has veto power, prohibited transaction issues can still arise. The stock of the operating company that is held by the IRA is an IRA asset, and a transaction involving such stock could be a prohibited transaction. In this regard, particular attention should be paid to the fact that Code Section 4975 prohibits indirect transactions that involve plan assets.

Most individuals who purchase closely held stock have no issues regarding ownership among themselves and disqualified persons, as these purchases have a broad enough ownership base to not come close to violation of percentage of ownership matters.

Checkbook control is an often-used idea that people have regarding doing transactions using an LLC, for example, to effect the purchases of real estate and notes. If the beneficial owners are self-directing their plans or IRAs to purchase controlling interest in a new LLC (not previously owned by a disqualified person), the IRA is directed to have the beneficial owners be responsible for the purchases and sales within the LLC by assuming an official position, such as managing member or president. The custodial function of the IRA is only that of the LLC. The LLC must adhere to all rules and regulations promulgated by the regulatory authorities. The IRA custodian or trustee should have no part in the formation or operation of the LLC unless the custodian wishes to be potentially considered a fiduciary or active trustee/custodian.

The LLC is then responsible to ensure:

- No personal benefit is provided to the beneficial owner or other disqualified person, such as family members, including siblings;
- No prohibited transactions occur within or in connection with the operation of the LLC;
- Profits are distributed in accordance with the LLC, which may or may not be taxable;
- Unrelated Business Income Tax, if due, is paid.

When used properly, this form of ownership can facilitate transactions effectively and easily. An example of case law involving similar transactions is also shown in the Appendix: *Swanson v. Commissioner*.

Using LLC and Other Company Forms for Purchases in Qualified Plans

Qualified Plans have invested in stock of publicly traded and private or closely held stock since retirement plans and accounts began in 1975.

Example of an LLC Using Retirement Funds as Investors: Diversification and Tax-Free Investing

A group of commercial brokers has discovered a wonderful investment opportunity—a putting green. The brokers established a Limited Liability Corporation (LLC) for the purpose of a real estate acquisition. The main real estate purchases were to be investment properties. Because tax-deferred vehicles should not be used for the purpose of running a business, it was essential that the acquisition purpose of the partnership be so limited. The partners, all members of the same firm, were otherwise unrelated parties. They funded the original issue stock acquisition as follows:

Two transferred all of their assets to the self-directed plans. One opened an SEP IRA with $41,000, the maximum amount permissible in 1994. They had sufficient income to fund the 25-percent maximum of their adjusted gross income. Another opened an Individual (k) and funded $21,000 under the assumption that that amount would cover 25 percent of her gross income, including her $14,000 401(k) contribution. (She was 50, so she could also use the catch-up provision for $1000.) All of the members of the partnership share the same tax accountant. This made the overall transaction fully advised from a tax point of view. (It is advisable that one seek tax advice when making contributions to any tax-deferred plan if one is self-employed and has the intent of sheltering a good portion of one's income. The tax advisor can help establish the amounts needed to fund self directed plans.) The LLC made the acquisition with both tax-deferred and non-tax-deferred funds. Some partners elected to use non-tax-deferred funds. The managing director in this case was not an investor.

The partnership had "preleased" a putting green to a professional operator. The lessor paid a fixed amount, as determined by the lease terms, to the partnership. The general partner, after paying minimal costs, distributed income to the limited partners. This is a fairly straightforward use of a self-directed plan. It is important to recognize that this type of partnership investment had different characteristics than many publicly offered limited partnerships. This is true because the partners all knew each other and they all had a commonality of interests and received their information and administration from the same source. Coordination of the entire transaction was, as a result, very straightforward and expeditious. From beginning to end, the transactions took one week. The transactions would have occurred in an even shorter period of time if an express mail package with one of the partners' funds had not been misrouted.

The return on the partnership net to the self-directed accounts is 12 percent. The individuals who transferred all of their existing investments may liquidate them when they decide to make purchases that are not handled or managed by regular broker dealers. In this case they have the advantages of both options, and they won't be charged administration fees for stock, bonds, and mutual funds.

Using Your 401(k) Rolled Over to an IRA to Make Your Real Estate Business Work

A husband and wife want not only to invest Roth IRA funds to rehab properties but also to use the same funds to run their business.

At the time we originally spoke, they had two deals working, which meant using about $100,000 to buy two single-family houses. They sold these houses, netting $150,000. They also had a couple of other deals in the works during the next few weeks with similar results anticipated.

Both husband and wife had 401(k) funds from previous employers. A couple of years ago they had asked about Roth IRAs. We had told them that if they qualified, they could roll over the 401(k) funds from their old employers to traditional IRAs, and then, if they qualified, by having Modified Adjusted Gross Income or W-2 wages of less than $100,000, they could convert the traditional IRAs to Roth IRAs. Because they also thought about making additional contributions for their business, the traditional IRAs remained under their newly established Simplified Employee Pension IRA. The regular or traditional IRA would then be available to make their SEP-IRA contributions every year, without administrative difficulties. (This also works for SIMPLE IRAs and in-service withdrawal rollovers from Qualified Plans to IRAs.) Having paid the taxes, the clients have a basis in excess of $500,000 in their Roth IRAs. (The basis is the amount they have in the Roth after tax. The clients paid the taxes using money not in their plan. They could have used IRA funds to pay the tax also, but that would diminish the amount available for tax-deferred and tax-free gains.)

In the meantime, they needed to run their business. With all the money in the Roth, they could take out the basis up to the amount they have, or in this case $500,000, and live on it, put some into their business, whatever they want, as they would have no tax implication on those funds. We suggested that one approach they should consider is to take the amount they currently need to run their business and personal expenses from their basis, and then roll that amount back in within 60 days, thus protecting that amount of their Roth. At the same time, they can also use part of their basis to make deals and get current income. For example:

They need $50,000 for the next two months to live on. They withdraw $50,000 from their Roth Basis money and use it for that purpose. At the same time, they want to make some deals to show income outside their Roth. They take an additional $50,000 of their basis and make a net $10,000 in the next few weeks. That shows on their income statement. As they only needed $10,000 to live on, they can roll back that $50,000 profit they do not need.

From then on, it is a matter of budgeting. If they make more deals like the ones they have a record of accomplishment with, they could make enough to live on and repatriate more of the basis they withdrew from their Roth (as long as they do it within 60 days of the withdrawal date). They could always just keep the income-producing money outside their Roth. Because it is basis money, there is no tax on the money they keep.

At the same time, they are going to make deals with the Roth money. There the profit stays in the Roth, remembering all the while that the basis remains forever. In this case, the basis is still at $400,000, which can be withdrawn at any time. Of course, when these clients reach 59-1/2 years old, in 20 years, they can withdraw any amount of money, from both the basis and the profit, at any time.

Table 2.13 shows how this worked for them.

In addition, they can continue to make contributions based on earned income. These clients are well informed enough to make sure that at various times their earned income and contribution levels need to drop to remain consistent with Roth conversion rules.

TABLE 2.13 Funding a Business Using 60-Day Rollover Rules—Two Roth IRAs, Each with $250,000

IRA #	Martha and Eddie	Take a Distribution	On Date	Use Funds Personally and clear (This is taxable)	Amount of Original Distribution Remaining	Roll Back Distribution to Roth	Make Investment with Roth (See note A)	Principal Amount Left in Roth
1	$50,000	$50,000	01-Jan	$10,000	$50,000	28-Feb	$50,000	$500,000
2	$50,000	$50,000	28-Feb	$8,000	$50,000	30-Apr	$50,000	$500,000
3	$50,000	$50,000	30-Apr	$0	–$50,000	Not Returned	$0	$450,000
4	$50,000	$50,000	01-May	$7,000	$50,000	30-Jun	$50,000	$450,000
5	$50,000	$50,000	01-Jul	$9,000	$50,000	30-Sep	$50,000	$450,000
6	$50,000	$50,000	30-Sep	$10,000	$40,000	15-Oct	$40,000	$440,000
7	$50,000	$50,000	20-Oct	$20,000	$60,000	28-Nov	$60,000	$450,000
8	$50,000	$0		$0	$0		$50,000	$450,000
9	$50,000	$0		$0	$0		$50,000	$450,000
10	$50,000	$0		$0	$0		$50,000	$450,000
Totals	$500,000			$64,000	$250,000		$450,000	$450,000

Notes

A This amount is investable in the IRA once returned as a rollover amount. All rollovers need to be the same property (in this case Cash).

(1) The distribution taken on April 30 was not returned within 60 days. This amount was Roth basis money, which reduced the amount in the Roth basis, but was not taxable. If this had been a Traditional IRA, the amount would have been taxable as a distribution, with possible 10-percent penalties if one or both owners were under age 59-1/2.

(2) The distribution rolled over on 10/15 was short by $10,000. The following month, on 10/28, rolled back the additional $10,000 as well as the $50,000 withdrawn on 10/20.

Note that all distributions are shown as taxable events. The rollover with 60 days is reported on one income tax return.

Another way they can accomplish some of their longer-term business and tax-free goals is to leverage some of the deals they are making in their Roth with nonrecourse loans. Remembering that leveraged deals in any type of IRA are subject to Unrelated Business Income Tax, they will be out of a leveraged situation for a year prior to sale, if the profit is more than $1000. They will repay the debt from other cash funds in their IRAs.

The assets that you direct your plan's administrator, trustee, or custodian to purchase are placed in your plan's account. (References made to trustees, custodians, and administrators are interchangeable and refer to both IRA and qualified plan trustees or custodians.)

The trustee of a self-directed plan does not usually find or recommend investments, so the first step is finding an asset you wish to purchase. The trustee signs the final documents on behalf of your plan, but the initial work is up to you.

For some transactions, you might encounter a "black ink" requirement. Black ink signatures are not as common as they once were, but some states and jurisdictions still require special pens to sign real property plat maps and the like. If you do not have a black pen, it is worth acquiring one to avoid having paperwork returned to be redone.

It is crucial that you understand the type of investments that you are making, and what is involved. This chapter gives an overview of some of the more general documents involved in purchasing real estate-related assets. For examples of various actual transactions and deals, see the subsequent chapters.

For examples of various actual transactions and deals, such as purchasing real estate and notes, see the subsequent chapters. They provide you with the framework in which typical transactions in plans are made, although there are many ways to do any of the deals presented.

You can make any deal you want, provided that it does not violate prohibited transaction or self-dealing rules.

The information provided in this chapter is not to be considered legal, accounting, tax, securities, or investment advice. We recommend that advice be sought from professionals in those fields. All reviews of any documents by administrators, custodians, or trustees in no way indicates, states, or implies that investment advice is being given, or that property or investments made in self-directed plans or accounts are suitable investments for any purpose. The beneficial owner assumes all risks for all transactions.

Questions Regarding Purchase and Sale of Real Estate and Other Assets

I have a self-directed profit-sharing plan and several IRAs. In my prototype plan, I am only allowed to invest 10 percent of plan assets (I am the plan trustee/administrator) in real estate investments such as buying homes, land, etc.

The plan originator says the reason I cannot invest more in real estate is that real estate is illiquid at certain times. However, I recently read that you can buy real estate through self-directed IRAs. I do not want to invest in real estate trusts or the like. I want to control the plan and make my own investments and my own decisions and act as the trustee or administrator myself.

To respond to your question, my first question is: Do you have employees in the plan other than yourself, a spouse, or partners? If you do, you can have a Profit Sharing, and/or Money Purchase Pension plan that permits complete self-direction for each employee. You may then make any investments you want, as may the employees. You may also cover employees additionally under 404(c) of the Internal Revenue Code and offer them a group of diversified funds. There are also certain audit and bonding requirements for Plans that are comprised of 5 percent of nonstandard assets and that include participants and common law employees.

I have a 401(k). Can I use it to invest in real estate?

Anytime that you wish, provided that your plan allows investments in real estate. If your current plan does not currently permit such investments, it can be amended and restated to permit self-direction in earmarked accounts. Ask your plan administrator about self-direction, and if it is not currently permitted, ask your employer about making the change you would like.

I currently have investments in various mutual fund accounts all registered either in the name of my trust or for the benefit of my profit-sharing plan. Can all of these accounts be made self-directed? Converted to profit sharing, or to an IRA or Roth IRA?

All retirement accounts, be they IRAs or Qualified Plans, as well as Coverdell Education Savings Accounts can be made to be completely self-directed. You can transfer to a self-directed IRA from any other IRA, and you may amend and restate your Qualified Plan to be self-directed. For Qualified Plans, you may also apply for an amendment of the investment provision to make investments self-directed in earmarked accounts.

Can I use my 401(k) money to invest in mobile homes?

You may do so provided that your plan document permits investments in such assets and does not limit investments to specific investment types. Generally, such investments are made through "earmarked" plan accounts. You should ask your plan administrator, or consult the plan investment provisions.

If IRA rollover funds are used to purchase rental real estate, how are the monthly proceeds and expenses distributed/disbursed? Can I keep any of the monthly proceeds (without tax penalties) and how would maintenance expenses be paid?

If any IRA funds are used to purchase real estate, the real estate becomes an asset in the plan, as the IRA actually purchases the property. The rent payments are s ent to the custodian of the IRA to be credited to your account and are available for investing. Expenses are also paid from your IRA, although they are subject to your review to ensure they relate to the property in the plan. The IRA cannot pay for expenses that are not related to the property. You may also have your IRA contract with an independent property manager for these services.

You may also choose to collect the rents personally, but the checks must then be sent intact to the custodian. You may not keep rent payments. However, you may take distributions from your IRA, without penalty, if you are age 59-1/2 or older, or in the case of a Roth IRA, if you are 59-1/2 or older and have had the Roth IRA for five years or more. If you do keep the rent payments, they will be considered distributions to you, and such retention by you may be considered a prohibited transaction, which may disqualify your IRA or plan from being a tax-deferred or tax-free plan. The penalties may range from 15 percent to 155 percent of the amount of the distribution, if not corrected.

The above restrictions also apply to qualified plans, such as profit sharing and 401(k) plans.

Can my IRA and I buy a property together using the IRA as a down payment? Specifically, can I buy real estate as follows: My IRA makes the down payment, and I finance the balance of the purchase price with a mortgage in my name. Then the IRA and I each own a percentage of the property based on the relative amounts of the purchase price paid. The point being, this gets around the problem of lenders not wanting to lend to an IRA. Would that be illegally loaning money from the IRA to myself?

What you propose is one of the methods we suggest individuals adopt in order to use their IRAs (or Qualified Plan) for purchasing real estate on a leveraged basis. Your suggestion not only gets around the lender issue, but also any unrelated business income tax that may apply with IRAs owning debt-financed property. Because you are partnering with yourself on an undivided interest basis, you would not be lending money to yourself. You would be an investor along with your IRA. The lender would be lending 100 percent on the portion of the investment you own. For example:

A $100,000 property with a $20,000 interest vested in your IRA and $80,000 vested in another person (say you) would result in an $80,000 loan to you from the bank. If the bank values the property at more than $100,000, the proportionate percentage ownership would still be the same, as the purchase price doesn't change. You would personally make the payments on the $80,000.

I have an SEP IRA through my employer. Can I set up a self-directed IRA and do a "trustee to trustee" transfer from my SEP IRA in order to make an investment in a family-owned project? This is going to be rental property that should provide a nice return.

You may hold the IRA connected to your employer's SEP anywhere you wish, unless the SEP Plan states that it must be opened initially at a particular institution. You may always transfer it after the deposits are made, as you are always 100-percent vested in the benefits of that IRA.

The Internal Revenue Code specifically prohibits your IRA (and therefore, your SEP IRA) from purchasing an interest in a property in which you, or family members who are ascendants or descendants, currently own an interest.

You may, of course, purchase completely new investment property with which you do not have a prior connection. You may also partner with yourself, your plan, and others and their plans, if you buy a new investment property.

Can you pledge your IRA as security for a loan to buy real estate?

You may not pledge your IRA for a loan. Pledging your IRA is a disqualifying event, and the tax-deferred or tax-free treatment would be lost as a result. Your IRA may purchase investment real estate, and that property may be used, on a nonrecourse basis, as pledged collateral for the loan. The IRA [also 401(k)] is responsible for the payment of the debt from funds in the IRA (or 401(k).

My husband and I own an office building now. The current value is approximately $350,000. We own several notes equaling $175,000 and we each have $60,000 in our respective IRAs. We currently lease one-half of the space to our company and lease the balance to an unrelated tenant. We are considering moving out and leasing our space to some other unrelated tenant. Is there any approved way to put our IRA funds into the building notes or ownership via a trustee? Are there any other options you might suggest?

Because you own the office building now, there is no way in which it can be placed in your own IRAs. Other persons' IRAs (and qualified plans) who are not owners of the building could own the interest in the property, and also one who does not lease space in the building. All investments made using your IRAs must be in assets that you do not currently own.

Any benefit from the purchase, such as rental income or income from a sale would be shared pro rata between you and the IRA, as would expenses.

Can I use my IRA or Qualified Plan (including 401(k) funds) to purchase land on which I plan to build a home when I retire? If so, can the tax be averaged over a period of years?

Your IRA may purchase investment property.

You may build on that land using IRA and/or qualified Plan funds. You may also:

Leverage the asset and build on the land using the borrowed funds; or

You may partner with yourself and others in acquiring the land and building on the land on a pro-rata basis.

Be aware that there are unrelated business income tax issues for debt-financed property.

During the time that the home is in your IRA, you may not receive a current benefit from it. This means that you may not use it, even if you pay rent, nor may other disqualified persons. Of course, you may take distributions from your IRA, or in-service withdrawals from your plan, once every 12-month period. During this time, the assets become your personal property to use for whatever purpose you wish, including renting a property out and receiving current taxable income thereon. You must roll that property to an IRA or plan within 60 days for this distribution not to become a taxable event.

That property may be distributed to you after age 59-1/2, at which time you will be taxed on the fair market value of the property, if this is part of a traditional IRA or Qualified Plan. The tax is paid on your tax basis in the year the land is distributed to you. You may not average the resulting tax over a number of years.

However, you may take the property in a series of undivided interests over a number of years. You may not live in or use the property, other than as an income property, until it has been completely distributed to you. You will only be taxed on the fair market value of the undivided interest distributed to you. Remember that the asset will remain income property for your IRA and/or your qualified plan until you take the final distribution of the asset. Good planning will provide you with the tax answer you are seeking.

If you were to make the purchase with Roth IRA funds, for example, by rolling your qualified plan funds to a traditional IRA and then converting to a Roth IRA, any distribution will be tax free to you. If you do this transaction entirely with a Roth IRA, you will need the Roth in place for five years prior to taking distributions without penalties, unless the property is equal to the amount of cash or property originally contributed or converted to the Roth (the basis). If the property is the asset that is converted to a Roth IRA, then that property is the basis of the Roth. That property, having had taxes paid on it, may be removed at any time without taxes or penalties. If you wish to hold the asset as an income-producing property without tax consequences, then you must roll it back to a Roth IRA within 60 days of removal.

You may also, on obtaining a Prohibited Transaction Exemption (PTE) from the Department of Labor, purchase that property with cash. (That cash replaces the property in your IRA or Plan.) No tax would be due in this event.

Providing that I qualify, can I take out a mortgage personally and use IRA funds for the down payment? I would essentially be partnering with myself, but would only pay capital gains on the profits from the debt-financed portion when I sell (or maybe do a 1031 exchange and start over). I know there is a 1031 exchange provision to defer capital gains. Does any similar mechanism exist to "roll over" value without exposure to tax?

If you do a 1031 exchange, the IRA will hold the proportionate interest it held before. Your IRA will not be exposed to tax, as the amount in the exchange will not change the percentage of ownership by the IRA, and the IRA will have no debt-financed position as a result of the exchange.

If property in your IRA or Plan is part of a 1031 exchange, the 1031 exchange rules apply. You are a disqualified person, as are others as identified under Internal Revenue Code Section 4975. Because your IRA or Plan does not file the schedules normally associated with exchanges, the exchanges are reported by one side only. In addition, any property exchanged to the IRA or plan is subsequently treated as tax deferred (tax free for Roth). Unrelated Business Income Tax (UBIT) does apply for any debt-financed portion of the transaction. To the extent that the debt-financed portion of the exchange can be minimized, the UBIT result is also proportionately affected.

My current 401(k) plan allows me to take out a loan to buy a home and pay it back to the plan. It is not considered an early distribution. If I roll over my 401(k) to a self-directed IRA, will I be able to take out a loan against these funds and pay it back to the plan?

Loans are not permitted from an IRA to a disqualified person. Under IRC 4975 you, as the beneficial owner of the IRA, are a disqualified person. If you are a first-time home buyer, you may take a distribution of up to $10,000 from an IRA without penalty to help purchase your new home.

I understand that I can roll over funds from other qualified plans to a self-directed IRA without it being a taxable event. Are you limited to the $3000-per-year contributions, or can I roll over the full $75,000 in my plan at one time?

You may roll over any amount to an IRA without tax implications. Be sure to complete the rollover within 60 days of receipt from the plan if you received the assets personally.

I have an institutional lender who will lend my IRA the cost of a house that needs repair. Can that lender also lend the repair and holding costs to the IRA in the same loan? I know I can't guarantee the loan, but can someone else? Can other non-IRA property be used as collateral?

The lender can lend your IRA whatever amount the lender feels is appropriate, which can include repair and any other costs associated with the asset. Other assets in the IRA may be used as collateral. Although the IRS Code is silent about third-party guarantees to debt-financed property in IRAs, if they are made by disqualified persons, they may be considered contributions to your IRA. When contributions exceed your maximum limits, such contributions would be subject to excess contribution penalties of 6 percent per year on the excess, as long as it remains in the IRA.

If I use my IRA to invest $20,000 cash in a property and I debt finance the additional $80,000, administratively who manages the property? If I were to manage it, would there be tax issues? Alternatively, if the IRA purchased a 20-percent interest in an LLC and I purchased the 80-percent remainder for the purpose of purchasing real estate investments, how does this change the substance of the transaction and what ramifications would this have?

The property must be managed by someone other than a disqualified person. You, as owner of the IRA are a disqualified person. The manager may be an entity in which you own less than a 50-percent interest, and/or from which you receive an income or profit interest of less than 10 percent.

If a 20-percent interest in an LLC is purchased by the IRA, and you own the other 80 percent, your LLC will be making the purchase of real property. Both the purchase of the LLC interest and the purchase of the real property should be closed simultaneously, as the purchase by the IRA or you at any other time would be prohibited. Because you own more than 50 percent of the LLC, you are barred from having any management control over the LLC. The elements of the *Swanson v. Commissioner* decision, specifically relating to prohibited transactions, may be effective for the application you intend. This means that the LLC is a newly formed LLC, and you reserve the right to manage the assets in your IRA, among other things. If your LLC has debt-financed property, it will be subject to UBIT also. Be sure that you recognize that managing the assets in your IRA is distinct from managing the property. This applies in all cases.

I know that if a qualified plan or IRA buys an investment from an independent third party, it is not a prohibited transaction, but isn't it true that if you do multiple transactions with the same third party, it is a prohibited transaction if that third party does not qualify under the broker-dealer exemption to the prohibited transaction rules?

You are likely referring to Prohibited Transaction Exemption 97-11, which involves broker-dealer issues. You are correct that if your IRA or qualified plan buys securities from a third party, does multiple securities transactions with that third party, and that third party does not qualify under the exemption, the transaction would be prohibited. Of course, the individual who is selling the securities would have more problems than just prohibited transactions. Selling securities without a license is extremely problematic.

If your IRA or Qualified Plan buys investments other than securities or those investments not subject to the Securities Act, such as real property or notes, then no prohibited transaction issue exists. For example, if your IRA or Qualified Plan buys notes or real estate on many different occasions from the same party, and those notes or real estate are not securities under the Securities Act, and the third party is not a disqualified person under IRC 4975, then the transaction is not prohibited.

Isn't a promissory note a security? In my *Black's Law Dictionary*, a security is defined as: "Evidence of debt or property. Evidences of obligations to pay money or of rights to participate in earning and distributions of a corporation, trust, or other property. Stocks, bonds, notes, convertible debentures, warrants, or other documents that represent a share in a company or a debt owed by a company."

If the note you speak of is a corporate debenture and is covered under the Securities Act, it is a security. The Securities Act has a clear definition of what is and is not a security.

Buying and selling notes that are not securities or that are not covered under the Securities Act does not constitute a prohibited transaction if the transactions are executed between willing buyers and willing sellers. Examples include personal notes, individual mortgages, car liens, etc. If such notes were all required to be securities, then anyone who bought or sold such instruments would have to be licensed to negotiate the same.

If someone issues corporate bonds or debt covered by the Securities Act, and then buys or sells them in IRAs or Qualified Plans in violation of those laws and in violation of IRC 4975, then the purchases and sales are prohibited transactions by definition.

Is an investment in a corporation (other than a Subchapter S corporation), limited liability company (LLC), or limited partnership by an IRA, where the owner of the IRA is a manager and owner of the LLC, permissible with no adverse tax ramifications?

If the entity mentioned above does not violate Internal Revenue Code Section 4975, and as shown in the Swanson decision, or TC 2000-20A, wherein the original issue of the LLC stock is to the IRA, or the manager of the LLC who is also the beneficial owner of the LLC receives no real benefit from the LLC, except that the manager works in the interest of the IRA that receives all of the benefit, there should be no adverse tax consequences. (Also see LLCs and your IRA in this book for additional guidance.)

If the beneficial interest owned by a disqualified person is less than 50 percent, and the profit or income interest is less than 10 percent by that owner, there is also no problem.

Be sure that you also review the potential of unrelated business tax being applied to the profits of the corporation.

I would like to have my Roth IRA purchase 100 percent of the stock of a C corporation owned by a nondisqualified person, who is also the president of the corporation. This person would like to remain as president. My brother and sister are the directors. The C corporation also has a contract to provide services to an S Corporation, of which I own 90 percent. As long as the only transactions between the IRA and the C corporation are payments of dividends, are there any UBIT issues with this arrangement?

Section 4975 of the Internal Revenue Code contains specific restrictions regarding transactions between an IRA and a disqualified person. The transactions you intend your IRA to engage in with a corporation you own, such as an S-Corp, may very well be problematic, as you may receive a current personal benefit from the S-Corp which violates the current benefit rule. If all the benefits from the S-Corp accrue only to the IRA and non-disqualified persons, there may not be any problem.

The payment of dividends would not automatically result in Unrelated Business Income Tax.

Real Estate Transactions Using Plan Funds in General: The Process

The purchase of real property and notes using IRA and qualified plan funds has resulted in a number of questions from beneficial owners of those accounts, as well as trustees of plans. To help you with the transaction process, such as shown in the above examples, the following are guidelines of what is involved.

Beginning a Real Estate Transaction

Most trustees accept some form of a purchase or "buy" direction letter to begin a real estate purchase transaction. Direction letters are not legally required. In fact, you can use any agreed-upon method to notify your trustee about your purchase. However, direction letters are an easy and thorough way to authorize the purchase. Some trustees accept faxed or scanned copies of direction letters, followed by originals. It is always a good idea to confirm by telephone or e-mail that the direction letter was received.

The following information should be included in most Real Estate Buy Direction Letters.

- The correct name and number of the account making the purchase, as more than one account might be involved. For example, you might be using a Keogh, an SEP IRA, and a Roth IRA to fund the purchase. In such cases, each plan receives a proportionate interest in the asset purchased.
- The property's address and location. This information is helpful in identifying the property and for documenting the purchase.

- The Assessor's Parcel Number (APN) when available. In some jurisdictions, APNs are not used, so any other assessor identification could be used instead.
- The legal description of the property, especially if there is no APN. A legal description provides the most important source of identification for any real estate parcel.
- The names and contact information for the attorney, escrow agent, or title company handling the transaction, if any.
- The total purchase price for the property. This is the amount you paid to the seller for the property, not including any escrow fees, closing costs, or other adjustments that are assessed in the course of closing on the property.
- The amount that the trustee has advanced on your behalf. Sometimes this is referred to as an earnest money deposit.
- The percentage of ownership attributable to the account in question. The ownership interest determined based upon the proportionate amount of the money coming from this particular account only. If you have funds from other accounts (your own and/or other account holders), a direction letter must be completed for each account involved in the transaction. For example: (1) if you are funding 100 percent from your account, whether it is an entirely cash (no leverage) or leveraged transaction (down payment), the percentage of ownership for the account will be 100 percent; (2) if you are splitting the purchase in half between this account and someone else's, the percentage of ownership will be 50 percent; and (3) if the ownership percentage for this account is 25 percent, then the other ownership interests equal 75 percent. If you personally and/or other disqualified person(s) are going to own a certain percentage, and the account owns the remaining percentage, the percentage of ownership by the account is the difference between your percentage and 100 percent. Note that in this case, both transactions must close at the same time.
- The names of the lender and property manager, when applicable, to clarify who will be receiving the debt payments and who is collecting the rents that will be forwarded to this account.

Authorizing Periodic Payments

If periodic payments, such as mortgage payments, property taxes, or homeowner's association dues, need to be made from the account, you can set up payments with the administrator or trustee using a periodic payment authorization letter. Typical periodic payment authorization letters include the following:

- The correct name and number of the account making the payments, as more than one account might be involved.
- The address and location of the property for which payments are being made.
- The percentage of ownership held by this account, which is used to determine the proportionate amount of money that will be paid from this account. If any portion of the payments will be made from other accounts (your own and/or other account holders), an authorization letter must be completed for each account involved.
- Indicate the type of payments to be made.

Handling Expenses Related to Repairs and Remodeling

You can pay expenses for remodeling or rehabilitating property owned by your plan from your retirement account. In the following example, the plan owner rehabilitates mobile homes. To be reimbursed from the plan, a complete accounting, along with receipts, was provided to the plan's administrator. It is important to understand that all payments for goods and services need to come from the plan itself. When the purchase of goods and services is not administratively feasible, sometimes reimbursement is the only available method to effect the transaction. Such is the case when repairs are needed on an emergency basis (such as plumbing issues, roof repair, or electrical problems), or when the asset would be damaged if payment is not made at the time of service.

Selling Real Estate

Selling real estate that is part of your plan assets is similar to a regular real estate transaction, except that the administrator is handling it on your behalf. However, you always direct the process and approve the various transaction steps. Assets in your plan can never be sold without your permission.

You can use a sell direction letter to begin the sales transaction. A typical sell direction letter will include the following information:

- The correct name and number of the account making the sale, especially if more than one account has interest in the property. You might be selling only a portion of the property, while retaining proportionate interest in the other accounts.

- The property's address and location. This information is helpful in identifying the property and for documenting the sale.
- The Assessor Parcel Number (APN) when available. In some jurisdictions, APNs are not used, so any other assessor identification may be used instead.
- The legal description of the property to be sold, especially if there is no APN. A legal description provides the best source of identification for real property.
- The buyer's name and contact information.
- The total sales price. If at any point the sales price changes, an addendum to the letter will be needed. Addenda are customary in escrow. You should always review and approve such documents.
- Information on whether the plan will be financing all or part of the purchase price for the property being sold. Typically, this would be accomplished through a Carry Back Note. Keep in mind that if the plan will be financing any part of the transaction, you must complete a Buy Direction Letter for Real Estate Notes (see discussion below).
- Any escrow charges and administrative fees to be paid by the plan. Often, the allocation of escrow charges and administrative fees is negotiated between the buyer and seller and may be paid entirely by one party or shared to varying extents between buyer and seller. These costs can be important in the transaction. The instructions in the Sell Direction Letter should be examined against the escrow instructions to ensure that your intentions are carried out properly.
- The name and contact information for the escrow agent, if any. This way, the actual work of the closing can be completed by your designated representatives, including your administrator, escrow company, and title insurance carrier.
- Any special instructions or details regarding the transaction.

Purchasing a Real Estate Note

A Buy Direction Letter for Real Estate Notes is for when you carry back a note for a real estate sale, purchase an existing note, or create a new note.

The following items should be included in a typical Real Estate Note Buy Direction Letter:

- For a completely new note, attach all of the documentation, including the note. This can also be done through an escrow agent, a title company, an attorney, or a combination thereof.
- For a carryback note, the names of the borrowers and their contact information. The address provided should be the address where mailings, payment coupons (if applicable), and notices are sent. Telephone numbers are helpful in contacting borrowers if there are any problems with payments.
- The borrower's social security number. This information is required for 1098 mortgage interest reporting. The IRS is very strict about having social security numbers for all borrowers. In certain cases, fines are levied for reporting information without social security numbers.
- The percentage of ownership of the note for the particular account only.
- If the note is being purchased at discount, the amount and percentage of any such discount.
- Information on any loan servicer being used for the transaction. Some trustees and administrators collect payments and provide all of the necessary record-keeping functions. Because some trustees may not be set up as mortgage brokers, they may not provide true mortgage services as defined by individual state law. However, the record-keeping services provided by a plan trustee or record keeper may be very similar. Your selection of servicing options is largely dependent on costs and personal choice.

The administrator uses the above information to ensure proper recording of the note. When notes are purchased, it is not unusual for the terms of the transaction to change between the original purchase offer and the final deal. The trustee can only fund transactions that you have approved. Your trustee is responsible for protecting your interests at all times and ensuring that what you have directed is what is performed. You must approve any changes in writing.

Questions Regarding Asset Protection and Creditors

My broker, who works for a California bank, told me that my IRA could not be garnished by any agency, federal, state, or private. Is this accurate? I now live in Georgia, although my broker still has my account in California. The brokerage company is owned by a Canadian company. All this rather complicates getting a straight answer. Could you help me with an answer?

Under Section 72t of the Internal Revenue code, specific procedures are established regarding levies from the IRS. Therefore, the IRS can and does levy IRAs throughout the United States. In addition, some states have similar laws. Other states provide for IRAs being protected fully from creditors, but not government agencies.

For your purpose, you should check the laws in Georgia governing IRAs to determine what protection exists for you. The brokerage company ownership or location has no bearing on this matter. What is important is where you reside and the laws related to your IRA in that state.

C H A P T E R 3

Mechanics: Opening Accounts

Creating a Retirement Account or Qualified Plan

Opening an IRA, SEP-IRA, or SIMPLE-IRA

An IRA is a depository account from which you buy or sell assets. An account is created by a written document. Only an individual can establish an IRA. IRAs may not be established by trusts, joint tenants, or tenants-in-common. All the assets in the account are placed or "vested" in the name of the trustee, custodian, or administrator for the benefit of your name and/or your account. The following information is required to open an IRA, SEP-IRA, or SIMPLE-IRA account:

- For a regular IRA account, your full name.
- For an SEP-IRA, the employer name as it appears on the Simplified Employee Pension—Individual Retirement Accounts Contribution Agreement. This agreement is separate from the IRA in which the employer deposits the contributions made on the employee's behalf. (Even if the SEP is for the owner only, the same rules apply.)

- Your address and social security number. An Employer Identification Number is not required on the standard IRS form 5305-SEP document because each participating individual must have an IRA.
- The type of account to be opened: IRA (regular or Roth) or SEP. You cannot have an SEP connected to a Roth IRA. (For information on the different types of IRAs, refer to Chapter 1, "How to Get Started.")

In addition to the required information, the following additional information might also be requested:

- Designation of a beneficiary for the account, in the event of the account-holder's death. Beneficiary designation is not required at the time you open the account, but it is encouraged. Note that in community property states, the beneficiary must be the account-holder's spouse, unless the spouse signs a consent waiving his or her rights. Many custodians have merged the beneficiary designation with the application form, which generally includes a spousal consent form in community property states. Beneficiary designation may be complicated and should be determined based on each individual's situation. It is always important to update beneficiary information as personal situations change.
- Information on your preferences regarding contributions and investments. You only need to complete this portion if you make a contribution or transfer or roll over assets to your new account.
- Execution of an account agreement with the provider. The agreement is not required by the Internal Revenue Service as a condition for opening an IRA, except that the provision for a backup withholding clause must be certified by you, and is generally included in the application or agreement.

Creating a Qualified Plan or 401(k)

Selecting a Trustee for a Qualified Plan

If you are an employer, or self-employed with no other employees, you may act as the trustee for your Qualified Plan, which usually grants employees the right to defer pay. Unlike IRAs and SEP IRAs, there is no mandate to have a bank or other institution fulfill the role of trustee, although they usually offer such services. You can select yourself, another individual or individuals, a corporation, or a combination as the trustee of your plan. Your choice of trustee depends on the type of plan, who the plan administrator is, what the scope of the plan is, and to what extent investment discretion is permitted.

Determining Whether the Plan Is Self-Directed

The investment section of the plan document provided by the plan sponsor outlines the types of investments that are permitted by the plan. The plan sponsor can be a bank, another financial institution, or an administrator. Typically, banks and brokerages limit the investments to products they sell. Most individually designed plans leave the investment section as flexible as possible. You should carefully read all the information in the plan documents to ensure that the plan meets your tax-deferred investment needs and provides sufficient flexibility in investment options.

The following is a typical clause for complete self-direction:

> If so indicated in the Adoption Agreement, each Participant may individually direct the Trustee (or Custodian, if applicable) regarding the investment of part or all of his or her Individual Account. To the extent so directed, the Employer, Plan Administrator, Trustee (or Custodian) and all other fiduciaries are relieved of their fiduciary responsibility under Section 404 of ERISA.

Setting Up a Plan

Setting up a qualified plan often involves filling out an adoption agreement, which will be associated with a plan document unless it is an individually designed plan. The adoption agreement contains all the necessary information about the detailed functioning of the plan, and it determines how the plan operates in terms of eligibility, vesting, contributions, allocations, and so on. However, you can always amend your plan in the future. The adoption agreement is part of the Qualified Retirement Plan, which is the legal plan and trust under which your plan operates.

To set up a qualified plan, you can adopt an IRS-approved prototype or a master plan offered by a sponsoring organization, or you can prepare and adopt your own written plan that satisfies the qualification requirements of the Internal Revenue Code.

The plan you establish must be in writing and be communicated to your employees. The plan's provisions must be stated in the plan—it is not sufficient to merely refer to a requirement of the Internal Revenue Code. The plan must be for the exclusive benefit of employees or their beneficiaries, and you must allow them to participate in the plan if they meet the following minimum participation requirements:

- They are 21 years old.
- They have been employed at the company for at least one year (two years if the plan provides that after two years of employment, employees have a nonforfeitable right to all their accrued benefit).

A plan cannot exclude an employee because he or she has reached a specified age.

Opening a Bank Account for a Qualified Plan

Unless your plan is funded completely with insurance, it must have a trust account for depositing contributions to the plan. The following items are needed to open a trust account:

- Your Qualified Retirement Basic Plan Document
- Your adoption agreement
- The IRS Opinion Letter indicating approval of the plan

For the trust account, you must use the same taxpayer ID as the one used in your adoption agreement. You, or another person or entity designated by you, are the trustee, custodian, and administrator as indicated in your adoption agreement.

If your business is a corporation, a bank will often require a Corporate Resolution in order to do business with them. Usually, banks and other financial institutions, such as brokerages, supply the resolution.

Some banks have a difficult time understanding what type of account to open. The procedures can vary from one institution to another, and even from one branch office to another in the same bank! You can explain that it is like opening a living trust. If the financial institution has a trust division, that division may be able to help the person helping you! Stock brokerage firms are often more receptive to opening such trust accounts.

Tip: *Be careful that you do NOT open a qualified plan account with the financial institution. Let them know that you are opening a trust account for a retirement plan that you have established separately. To open a trust account, the financial institution should ask for copies of the above items. Often, the adoption agreement is sufficient. If they want to make a copy of the Basic Plan Document, they may do so.*

The title of your trust account should read:

"(Your company name) Profit Sharing Plan, for Benefit of (your name)"

For example:

Lee Wilson, Inc. Profit Sharing Plan, FBO Lee Wilson

Or

Lee Wilson, Inc. PS Plan, FBO Lee Wilson.

If that is too complex for the bank system, try

Lee Wilson PSP Trustee

For tax purposes, it is important to have all vesting documents and titles use these terms. If you receive account statements or title and escrow information and they do not name the type of account in the title, for example Profit Sharing or PSP, make sure that the financial institution corrects them immediately.

Once you have established an account, you can begin making contributions and investments. As the plan administrator, you must keep records for all assets in your trust account. This includes every credit, debit, gain, and loss. If you have just one brokerage account handling all your investments, you can use the statements they provide you. If you have multiple brokers and diverse assets, such as real property, notes, partnerships, and other investments, you should consolidate your records using a spreadsheet or accounting software.

Multiple Plans

You may always have an IRA, regardless of any other plans you have. You may also have a Qualified Plan, SIMPLE-IRA, or an SEP-IRA, and you may have both a qualified plan and an SEP IRA. The SEP-IRA and Qualified Plan will be "tested" together to make sure that you don't exceed the total contribution limits. It generally doesn't make sense to have an SEP-IRA and a Qualified Plan at the same time. Depending on your situation, as of 2004, a Profit Sharing 401(k) Plan (one of the qualified plan types) is far superior to any SEP-IRA or SIMPLE-IRA. If you have common law employees, you may make different choices.

Funding Your Account

Generally: You can make annual contributions to your retirement account with cash according to the amounts and in the manner established by IRS Code. Cash is defined as money, checks, money orders, and wire transfers.

You can also transfer assets (money or property) tax free from one retirement account to another eligible retirement plan.

It has been a common misconception that if you contributed to a qualified plan, including those which permitted employee deferrals, you could not also contribute to an IRA. The only issue in such a situation is whether you will be able to deduct your IRA contributions. If you contribute to an IRA and are also covered by an ERISA plan, the amount you can deduct for your IRA contributions simply gets reduced, and eventually goes away, depending on your income. This includes the profit sharing plans with 401(k) features, of course.

Transferring Assets from Other Retirement Accounts: The following kinds of transfers are permissible:

- Rollovers
- Transfers from one trustee to another
- Transfers due to a divorce

Initiating and Completing Transfers and Rollovers: For IRAs and Coverdell ESAs, the company to which you are transferring the funds will provide the appropriate forms for your transfer or rollover. Before initiating the transfer, you should confirm that the new custodian will accept the types of assets you are transferring or rolling over. This is generally not a problem for self-directed plans, except in the following cases:

- IRAs cannot accept life insurance policies from qualified plans;
- Some IRA Trustees do not accept collectibles that were once legal tender, or bullion;
- Some assets may not be acceptable to self-directed IRA trustees because of internal policies;
- Some investment product providers will not transfer or roll over an investment that they offer, such as a certain type of annuity or a certain class of mutual fund, to a new plan. In addition, a new provider will also not accept a rollover from another plan with assets that the new provider does not offer;
- Prior custodians or trustees do not provide the history of payments or other documents on a timely basis.

Payers will often continue to make payments to the old trustee or servicer, and it can take time to correct such problems. Tax and assessor information is often incorrect for up to one or two years, and notices of default are not always received. Your current provider normally marshals the assets into your account, but the cooperation of the old provider is always important.

In many cases, signatures must be notarized or medallion-guaranteed, which is an insured signature guarantee similar to a notary, and obtaining the proper signatures can take time.

There are restrictions regarding minimum distribution requirements if you have taken a distribution or are in the year in which distributions must be taken. The specifics are usually part of the transfer or rollover form. The restriction language includes information on the nature or method of calculations and beneficiaries. If this data is not included and you are in a minimum distribution year, your transfer might be rejected.

If you are taking a distribution from your IRA with the intent of rolling the asset over within 60 days, you may be subject to backup withholding just like any other conventional distribution. Be sure that the asset is conveyed to you legally.

Rollovers: A rollover is a distribution of cash or other assets from a retirement plan that is eligible to be put into another retirement plan. You can roll over a distribution tax free, unless it is a return of an excess contribution or a required distribution. You can have the funds paid to you and then within

60 days deposit all or part of such funds into a new account, or you can transfer the funds directly to a different account.

If an eligible rollover distribution is paid to you, the payer is required to withhold 20 percent of the distribution as federal tax withholding, so you actually receive only 80 percent of the distribution. This requirement applies even if you plan to roll over the distribution to an IRA or another qualified plan. To avoid the 20-percent withholding, you can roll over the funds directly to an IRA or an eligible retirement plan. You can use any reasonable means to complete a direct rollover, including mailing a check, wiring the funds, or hand-carrying the check to the receiving plan.

Rollovers are not tax deductible, but you must report the rollover distribution on your tax return. You must make the rollover within 60 days after you receive the distribution (the IRS can extend the time limit for certain hardship circumstances that are beyond your control). To defer taxes on the entire amount, you must roll over 100 percent of the distribution.

If you withdraw assets from a plan, you can roll over part of the withdrawal tax free into another retirement fund and keep the rest of it. The amount you keep is generally taxable (except for the part that is a return of nondeductible contributions) and might be subject to the 10-percent tax on premature distributions.

You can roll over assets from one IRA to another only once in a 12-month period. The time period begins on the date you received the distribution, not the date you rolled it over into another retirement plan. This once-a-year limit does not apply to employer-sponsored plans.

IRA distributions are exempt from the 12-month waiting period if the Federal Deposit Insurance Corporation (FDIC) makes distributions as a receiver for a failed financial institution. However, you must roll over the same property you received from your old IRA into the new IRA. To qualify for the exception, the distribution must satisfy both of the following requirements:

- It must not be initiated by either the custodial institution or the depositor.
- It must be made because the custodial institution is insolvent, and the receiver is unable to find a buyer for the institution.

Time Involved for Transferring or Rolling Over from One Plan to Another: The most challenging part of opening a self-directed account is rolling over or transferring assets to the new account. A transfer can take anywhere from days to months, depending on the assets and the capabilities of the institutions involved.

Cash usually takes up to 10 business days. You should allow at least 30 days for transferring assets other than cash. If you are rolling over from a qualified plan and the assets are deeds of trust, real estate, or privately held instruments, the process may take months.

The plan document for a qualified plan usually states the time period required to complete a rollover or distribution, which can be up to 18 months from the date you terminated employment. From that point forward, reregistration and clerical issues can take additional time.

In the case of an annuity product in a qualified plan, insurance carriers operate under a completely different set of rules. Usually, they do not impose surrender charges on assets being rolled over to an IRA, but the time required to roll over may be lengthy.

In many cases, you can shorten the time of transfer by having assets distributed to you directly and then rolling them over in the 60-day time period mandated by law. This works particularly well with assets held as cash, stocks, bonds, or mutual funds. It is less effective with any other types of assets.

If you have a deal that you want to make quickly, use the part of your portfolio that is easiest to liquidate. Then transfer or roll over those assets to your self-directed plan, or have them distributed and then roll them over to your self-directed plan. Pretax IRAs may now be rolled over to your Individual 401(k) or other qualified plan, if a plan permits such rollovers.

Transferring from One IRA Trustee to Another

Transferring funds in your IRA from one trustee directly to another, either at your request or at the trustee's request, is not a rollover. Because there is no distribution to you, the transfer is tax free. Because it is not a rollover, it is not subject to the one-year waiting period that is required between rollovers from one IRA to another.

Transfers Because of Divorce

If an interest in an IRA or qualified plan is transferred from your spouse or former spouse to you by a divorce, separate maintenance decree, or a written document related to such a decree, such as a qualified domestic relations order (QDRO) in the case of qualified plans, the IRA, or plan, is treated as your IRA or plan starting from the date of the transfer. The transfer is tax free.

Converting a Traditional IRA to a Roth IRA

Converting a traditional IRA to a Roth IRA is treated as a rollover. You can transfer contributions made to a traditional IRA into a Roth IRA without having to include them in your gross income if all of the following apply:

- You transfer the contributions by the due date (not including extensions) for filing your tax return for the year in which you made the contributions to the traditional IRA.
- You transfer any earnings on the contributions.
- You do not claim a deduction for the contributions for the year in which you convert.
- You cannot roll over amounts from a traditional IRA into a Roth IRA if your modified AGI for the year is more than $100,000, or if you are married and filing a separate return for the year. In addition, you cannot roll over required distributions from a traditional IRA.

You may convert property from a traditional IRA to a Roth IRA. The value of the property needs to be established as of the date you perform the conversion. You will receive a 1099-R from the traditional IRA (established by yourself, an SEP-IRA or SIMPLE- IRA) for the value of the property converted. For real property, the fair market value, as established by a recent bona fide offer to purchase or an appraisal by a third party, is acceptable, although in certain instances assessor's valuation may also be permitted. For notes, fair market value is also acceptable. For private offerings, the value needs to be substantiated through a formal valuation, or a recent purchase or sale.

For such valuations, you need to ensure that your documentation is clear and acceptable for examination by a third party, such as an IRS examiner.

The advantage of being able to convert from a qualified plan or traditional IRA to a Roth IRA can be significant. For example, if you paid tax on a rollover from a traditional IRA to a Roth, and the tax was $3000 (made in a year when your tax liability was low). If the Roth now has a value of $10,000, you will never have to pay tax on the $10,000 and all profit you make for the rest of your life.

Let's say you have $13,000 in a traditional IRA, and are able to transfer or convert it to a Roth IRA. You pay income tax at 30 percent. Assuming that you have no deductions and you pay $3000 in taxes from the traditional IRA, you will have $10,000 left. When you compare this to making a $13,000 investment, not having paid any tax with personal funds at 10 percent, the following results:

Your Roth $10,000 accumulation in 10 years slightly exceeds the $13,000 investment made with taxable funds or $25,937 versus $25,573. At 25 years it really gets better, the Roth will be at $108,357 versus $70,557. This is almost $38,000 more! And that is the worst-case scenario.

Even better, pay the $3000 tax from funds outside your conversion or rollover funds. This results in even greater benefits. After 25 years, assuming the investment made 10 percent per year, your Roth IRA will be worth more than $140,000, or double the $70,000 value of the personal funds invested the same way. Even adjusting for $3000 invested at 10 percent over 25 years and subtracting that return, which amounts to almost $17,000, the end result would still be $123,000 in the Roth IRA versus $70,000 in the person account. That is still a $53,000 difference.

Contributions

Contributing to a Traditional IRA

You can contribute to a traditional IRA up to the year you turn 70-1/2. However, if you or your spouse made contributions to any of the following employer retirement plans during the contribution year, the amount of your IRA contribution that you can deduct might be reduced or disappear entirely, depending on the amount of your income and your filing status:

- Qualified retirement, profit-sharing, stock bonus, money purchase pension plan, or Keogh plan.
- 401(k) plan.
- Union plan.

- Qualified annuity plan.
- Plan sponsored by government employers.
- Tax-sheltered annuity plan for employees of public schools and certain tax-exempt organizations (403(b) plan).
- SEC. 501(c)(18) trust (a tax-exempt trust created before June 25, 1959 that is funded only by employee contributions).
- SIMPLE. For the maximum allowable contribution amounts, see Table 3.2 later in this chapter.

Contributing to a Roth IRA

You can contribute to a Roth IRA regardless of your age. Unlike a traditional IRA, you cannot deduct contributions to a Roth IRA, but, if you satisfy the requirements, earnings grow tax free and withdrawals are tax free.

You can contribute to a Roth IRA if you have taxable compensation and your modified adjusted gross income (AGI) is less than $110,000 if you are single or, if you are married and filing jointly, it is less than $160,000 (as of 1/1/2002).

To determine your modified AGI, do the following:

- Subtract any income resulting from a rollover or conversion from a traditional IRA to a Roth IRA.
- Add the following exclusions:
  - Foreign earned income exclusion
  - Foreign housing exclusion or deduction
  - Exclusion of series EE bond interest shown on Form 8815
  - Exclusion of adoption expenses

If your AGI is above a certain amount, your contribution limit is gradually reduced. If you contribute to both a Roth IRA and a traditional IRA, the contribution limit for the Roth IRA must be reduced by all contributions for the year to all traditional IRAs. See Table 3.2 later in this chapter for the contribution limits.

Excess Contributions

To make an excess contribution to either a regular or Roth IRA is generally not permitted, and will generally be caught by the custodian, trustee, or administrator of your IRA. An IRA trustee may not accept a contribution in excess of statutory limits. Say you are under 50 years old. You could not make a contribution of over $3000 to a Roth IRA because you are ineligible as a result of your income being in excess of statutory limits, unlike traditional IRAs, where you may make contributions regardless of income, as long as it is Schedule C, Modified Adjusted or W-2 wages. If you are ineligible for a Roth IRA, for example, it would be an excess contribution. It could be recharacterized as a traditional IRA, but if you are also not eligible for a traditional IRA (you had no compensation acceptable for contribution purposes), then the $3000 would be an excess contribution. The same holds true if you mistakenly opened more than one Roth IRA at different institutions exceeding the total limit of $3000. If you opened three, for $3000 each, and you are only eligible for one $3000 contribution, you have an excess contribution of $6000.

Even if you do make excess contributions to your IRA, no penalties will accrue if you withdraw the excess contribution, as well as any income earned thereon, prior to your tax deadline. If you leave the excess in the IRA until after your tax deadline, the amount contributed will accrue penalties at 6 percent per year, until withdrawn. The profits may remain in the IRA and are not subject to penalties. The amount of the excess contribution is reduced each year following that you have not withdrawn for the contribution amount for which you are eligible. So in year two, you may be eligible for another $3000 contribution, and thus the excess is down to $3000, and the penalty of 6 percent is calculated on this amount. Again, there is no penalty on the earnings. For example: You made an excess contribution to a Roth IRA for which you are not eligible of $3000 in 2004. You did not withdraw it by the tax deadline of April 15, 2005. You must complete a form 5329 for excess contributions made and pay a 6-percent penalty. If you are eligible in 2005 to make a contribution to a Roth IRA of $3000, you will be able to use the $3000 you have in the existing IRA to count as this year's contribution. If you continue not to be eligible in 2005 for a Roth IRA, but are eligible to make a contribution to a traditional IRA, you may use up to the $3,000 you had in your Roth IRA to deposit to your traditional IRA. The same holds true for excess contributions to SEP-IRAs, SIMPLE IRAs, and rollovers that contain excess contributions. You must file IRS form 5329 to report the excess contribution and pay the penalty. The penalty does not need to be paid from your IRA and it is not deductible.

If you are under age 59-1/2 and have had a Roth IRA for less than five years, or a traditional, SEP-IRA or SIMPLE IRA, your withdrawal of the excess contribution will also be subject to a 10 percent premature distribution penalty.

Making Contributions to a SEP-IRA

You can contribute and deduct up to 25 percent of an employee's compensation (up to a maximum contribution of $41,000 in 2004) each year to each participant's SEP-IRA. When determining the 25-percent limit, compensation is limited to $200,000, not including the employer's contribution to the SEP-IRA. These contributions are funded by the employer.

An employer does not have to make contributions every year. Contributions must be based on a written allocation formula and must not discriminate in favor of highly compensated employees. In a year that contributions are made, the employer must contribute to the SEP-IRAs of all qualifying employees who performed personal services during the contribution year, even employees who die or terminate employment before contributions are made.

Deduction Limit for a Self-Employed Person

An SEP is treated as a profit-sharing plan. If you are self-employed, compensation is your net earnings from self-employment. The amount you can deduct for contributions on your behalf and your compensation are dependent upon each other. Your deduction for contributions on your behalf is determined using Rate Table for the Self-Employed (Table 3.1) or the Rate Worksheet for Self-Employed. If your contribution rate is a whole number (for example, 12 percent rather than 12-1/2 percent), you can use the table; otherwise, use the worksheet.

These rates apply only to unincorporated employers who have only one employer based plan.

To find your deduction rate, find your contribution allocation percent rate in the left column. Then read across to the rate under the right column. This is the rate to be applied for you.

TABLE 3.1 Rate Table for the Self-Employed

Plan contribution percentage	Self-employed rate (shown as a decimal)
1	.009901
2	.019608
3	.029126
4	.038462
5	.047619
6	.056604
7	.065421
8	.074074
9	.082569
10	.090909
11	.099099
12	.107143
13	.115044
14	.122807
15	.130435
16	.137931
17	.145299
18	.152542
19	.159664
20	.166667
22	.180328
23	.186992
24	.193548
25	.200000

Rate Worksheet for the Self-Employed

1. What is your contribution rate as a decimal? For example, 10-1/2 percent is 0.105.
2. Add 1 to the decimal rate in step 1. For example, 0.105 plus 1 is 1.105.
3. Divide the rate in step 1 by the number in step 2. This is your contribution/deduction rate.

If You Have More Than One Plan

To determine your deduction limit when you have more than one retirement plan, treat all your qualified defined contribution plans as a single plan, and all your qualified defined benefit plans as a single plan. An SEP is treated as if it were a separate profit-sharing defined contribution plan.

If you also contributed to a qualified profit-sharing plan, you must reduce the 25-percent deduction limit for that profit-sharing plan by the allowable deduction for contributions to the SEP-IRAs of those participating in both the SEP and the profit-sharing plan.

If you contribute to one or more defined contribution plans (including an SEP) and one or more defined benefit plans, special deduction limits may apply. If you made contributions in excess of the deduction limit (nondeductible contributions), you can carry over and deduct the excess in later years. However, the carryover, when combined with the contribution for the later year, cannot exceed the deduction limit for that year.

Making Contributions to a SIMPLE IRA

The employer's contribution on behalf of the employee (elective deferrals) is stated as a percentage of the employee's compensation and cannot exceed the allowable limit for the given tax year. Compensation for an employee is the total amount of wages reported on Form W-2, including elective deferrals. For a self-employed individual, compensation is the net earnings from self-employment, before subtracting any contributions made to a SIMPLE IRA.

The employer generally is required to match each employee's contributions on a dollar-for-dollar basis, not to exceed 3 percent of the employee's compensation. These contributions are deductible by the employer. If the employer elects a matching contribution that is less than 3 percent, it cannot be less than 1 percent. The employer must notify the employees of the lower match rate within a reasonable period of time before the employee's 60-day election period for the calendar year. A percentage of less than 3 percent cannot be elected for more than two years during a five-year period.

Instead of matching employee contributions, the employer can make nonelective contributions of 2 percent of compensation on behalf of each eligible employee. To use this contribution method, the employer must notify the employees within a reasonable period of time before the employee's 60-day election period for the calendar year.

The employer must contribute the elective deferrals to the SIMPLE retirement accounts within 30 days after the end of the month for which the payments to the employee were deferred. The employer's matching contributions or nonelective contributions must be made by the due date (including extensions) for filing the employer's income tax return for the year.

Qualified Plan Contributions

In 2003, Bill's income was $50,000 from his brokerage business. Because he received W-2 he had the company contribute 25 percent of his W-2 income or $12,500 to his Profit Sharing Account. The plan has a 401(k) feature, and he can therefore defer 100 percent of his compensation to a maximum of $13,000 to his 401(k) account, for a total of $25,500.

Bill knows that he can make IRA contributions to his Individual 401(k) plan, which can also be self-directed. He is also interested in the tax-free feature of Roth IRAs. Because it is in his interest to never have to pay tax again on investments in his Roth IRA, he realizes that having cash or assets at a low basis makes sense, especially if the assets have a high return. Bill also is aware that he can convert the assets in his traditional IRA to a Roth IRA because he is under the $100,000 income limit for a Roth conversion.

His traditional IRA has $40,000 in face value of notes that he will want to convert to the Roth IRA. He completes the Roth conversion paperwork, and sends it to his IRA custodian. He has a qualified valuation firm prepare a fair market valuation of the notes. The $40,000 face value notes are determined to have a fair market value of $18,000. On conversion, Bill will receive a 1099-R for 2004 reflecting the $18,000 and he will pay tax on that amount, together with tax on earned income for 2004.

Bill also purchased some notes at a discount in his qualified plan and wants to convert a portion of those to a Roth IRA. Because his plan has an in-service withdrawal provision, Bill can roll these notes over to a traditional IRA and then convert those notes into the same Roth IRA.

Contributions Deadline

You can make deductible contributions for a tax year up to the date for your return (plus extensions) is due for that year.

Self-Employed Individual

You can make contributions on behalf of yourself only if you have net earnings (compensation) from self-employment in the trade or business for which the plan was set up. Your net earnings must be from your personal service, not from your investments. If you have a net loss from self-employment, you cannot make contributions for yourself for the year, even if you can contribute for common-law employees based on their compensation.

When contributions are considered made:

- You generally apply your plan contributions to the year in which you make them. But you can apply them to the previous year if all the following requirements are met:
  - You make them by the due date of your tax return for the previous year (plus extensions).
  - The plan was established by the end of the previous year.
  - The plan treats the contributions as though it had received them on the last day of the previous year.
- You do either of the following:
  - You specify in writing to the plan administrator or trustee that the contributions apply to the previous year.
  - You deduct the contributions on your tax return for the previous year.

Limits on Employer Contributions and Benefits

Your plan must provide that contributions or benefits cannot exceed certain limits. The limits differ depending on whether your plan is a Defined Contribution Plan or a Defined Benefit Plan.

Defined Contribution Plan

For 2004, a Defined Contribution Plan's annual contributions and other additions (excluding earnings) to the account of a participant cannot exceed the lesser of the following amounts:

- 100 percent of the compensation actually paid to the participant; or $41,000.

- The maximum compensation that can be taken into account for this limit is $200,000.

Defined Benefit Plan

For 2004, the annual benefit for a participant under a Defined Benefit Plan cannot exceed the lesser of the following amounts:

100 percent of the participant's average compensation for his or her highest three consecutive calendar years; or $160,000.

Limits on Voluntary Employee Contributions to a Defined Benefit Plan: In addition to employer contributions, participants may make nondeductible voluntary contributions to their plans. Even though the contributions are not deductible, the earnings on them are tax-free until distributed in later years. The limits of these contributions are 10 percent each year and are subject to rules and limits.

Profit-Sharing Plan

Contributions are usually based on business profits, but according to the IRS rules, you can also contribute to your plan based on compensation. For sole proprietorships, there are exceptions for contributions made by the employer for their own account as an employee if the business did not have a profit. If you make contributions based on compensation, the Entrust plan for owners only—the Individual (k)—is set up so that you can make non-cash contributions, such as stock or Treasury bonds.

The maximum deductible contribution that can be made to a profit-sharing plan cannot exceed the following amounts:

25 percent of eligible compensation; or $41,000.

Eligible compensation is all the compensation that an employer pays to eligible plan participants during the employer's tax year. The annual compensation limit for 2002 contribution is $200,000.

Contributions are tax-deductible and earnings accumulate on a tax-deferred basis. The employer takes the deduction for this contribution. The employer's contribution to each employee's account is not considered taxable income to the employees for the contribution year. Funding is not required in any year.

A profit-sharing plan must set out a definite formula allocating both the contributions and distributions for each participant. In addition, distribution formulas must itemize the distribution terms, such as age, number of years in the plan, etc.

Profit-Sharing Plan Contribution/Deduction Limit

The employer deduction limit for profit-sharing plans has been increased from 15 percent to 25 percent. This allows substantially increased annual contributions for employers that use or allow multiple contribution options, such as profit sharing, matching, and after-tax contributions.

Contributions and Deductions

A plan is generally funded by employer contributions. However, employees participating in the plan may be permitted to make contributions.

If you are self-employed, you can make contributions for yourself only if you have net earnings (compensation) from self-employment in the trade or business for which the plan was established. If you have a net loss from self-employment, you cannot make contributions for yourself for the year, even if you can contribute for common-law employees based on their compensation. Your net earnings must be from your personal services, not from your investments, which does not include your deduction for one-half of self-employment tax, and the deduction for contributions on behalf of yourself to the plan.

As an employer, you can usually deduct contributions, including those made for your own retirement. Contributions and earnings are not taxed until distribution.

To deduct contributions for a tax year, your plan must be set up (adopted) by the last day of that tax year (December 31 for calendar-year employers). You can make deductible contributions for a tax year up to the due date of your return (plus extensions) for that year.

To determine your deduction limits if you contribute to more than one plan, treat all your qualified defined contribution plans as a single plan, and all your qualified defined benefit plans as a single plan. If you are contributing to a profit-sharing plan, you must reduce the 25-percent deduction limit by your deduction for contributions to the SEP-IRA.

The contribution deduction is similar to that of an SEP-IRA (see the previous section, "Deduction Rate for a Self-Employed Person" and the previous Table 3.1.

TABLE 3.2 Summary of Maximum Allowable Contributions

MAXIMUM CONTRIBUTIONS TO RETIREMENT PLANS								
	2002	2003	2004	2005	2006	2007	2008	2009
IRAs (REGULAR and ROTH)								
Up to age 50	$3,000	$3,000	$3,000	$4,000	$4,000	$4,000	$5,000	$5,000
Age 50+	$3,500	$3,500	$3,500	$4,500	$5,000	$5,000	$6,000	$6,000
401(k), 403(B), 457, and SAR-SEP PLANS								
Up to age 50	$11,000	$12,000	$13,000	$14,000	$15,000	$15,000*	$15,000*	$15,000*
Age 50+	$12,000	$14,000	$16,000	$18,000	$20,000	$20,000*	$20,000*	$20,000*
SIMPLE IRAs or SIMPLE 401(k)s								
Up to age 50	$7,000	$8,000	$9,000	$10,000*	$10,000*	$10,000*	$10,000*	$10,000*
Age 50+	$7,500	$9,000	$10,500	$12,000	$12,500	$12,500*	$12,500*	$12,500*
SEP-IRAs								
Self-employed individual or employer				Whichever is less: $41,000 or 25% of compensation.				
QUALIFIED PLANS: PROFIT-SHARING PLANS and KEOGHs								
Self-employed individual or employer				Whichever is less: $40,000 or 25% of compensation. Deduction limit is 20%.				

*Indexed to inflation in $500 increments

Carrying Over Excess Contributions

If you contribute more to your plans than you can deduct for the year (nondeductible contributions), you can carry over and deduct the excess in later years. However, the carryover deduction, when combined with the deduction for the later year, cannot exceed the deduction limit for that year. Nondeductible contributions may be subject to a 10-percent excise tax.

401(k) and Individual (k) Plans

There is generally a 55-percent-of-pay cap on the combined sum that employers and employees can contribute annually to 401(k) plans on a tax-favored basis, as much as $200,000 in pay.

An employee may defer up to 100 percent of compensation to a maximum of $13,000 in 2004, and indexed thereafter. This deferral does not count as part of the computation of the employer's contribution of 25 percent to a maximum of $41,000. For example, an employee who is 50 years old and has W-2 compensation of $50,000, makes a $14,000 deferral to his or her 401(k). As the employer that person may also make a $12,500 contribution to his or her profit sharing, for a total of $26,500.

For sole proprietorships, the percentage-of-pay limits apply to compensation after plan contributions are subtracted (and also after deducting one-half of self-employment tax), which makes the 25 percent figure actually 20 percent of earnings before those contributions. Also, the combined employer and employee contributions are subject to a flat-dollar cap—$40,000 per person in 2002.

The one-person 401(k) offers the biggest potential benefit for one-person businesses earning between $50,000 and $160,000.

You, as the business owner, must also consider that if you are also a corporate employee already participating in another 401(k) plan, an individual's deferrals in both plans together can't exceed the $14,000 per person cap in 2004, and higher thereafter.

401(k) contributions are considered separately for percentage calculations in profit-sharing plans, permitting the employee contribution not to be counted against the employer contribution 25 percent limitation. The employee deferral amount is, however, included as part of the $40,000 maximum contribution amount. This is a distinct benefit for owner-only plans in which income does not reach the dollar limitations ($160,000) and one wishes to make the highest contribution possible. In addition, beginning in 2006, 401(k) contributions will be eligible to be made on a posttax basis and be placed into a tax-free account, similar to a Roth IRA.

Money Purchase Pension Plans

Money Purchase Pension Plans permit employer contributions up to a maximum of 25 percent of the employee's compensation. Once the employer establishes the contribution level, the amount in subsequent contributions must be maintained and may only be decreased by a submission to the IRS.

For example, if your plan requires that contributions be 10 percent of compensation, the employer must contribute this amount to the plan regardless of whether the employer had profits (or whether you, as a self-employed person, had earned income). For all self-employed individuals, compensation is considered earned income derived from business profits.

In addition, you cannot make in-service withdrawals from a Money Purchase Pension Plan.

The maximum deductible contribution to a Money Purchase Pension Plan is the lesser of the following amounts:

- 100 percent of eligible compensation
- $41,000 indexed

This is the maximum that can be contributed for all Defined Contribution Plans.

Increased Contribution Limits

The annual contribution limits of qualified plans are described below.

401(k), 403(b), 457, and SAR-SEP Deferral Contributions

2004—$13,000
2005—$14,000
2006 and thereafter—$15,000 (indexed beginning in 2007)

Catch-Up Contributions: Participants age 50 or older that defer salary into 401(k), 403(b), 457, or SAR-SEP plans may make catch-up deferral contributions, as follows.

2004—$3,000
2005—$4,000
2006 and thereafter—$5,000 (indexed beginning in 2007)

Distributions

Generally

When you are eligible to take distributions from your retirement account, you can opt to receive either the entire sum or periodic distributions for the rest of your life. You can start taking distributions at age 59 1/2 (or earlier if you have a qualified plan that allows for retirement at age 55), even if you are still working. However, with the exception of a Roth IRA, you must start taking distributions in the year that you reach 70 1/2.

Distributions from a Traditional IRA

Your distributions from your traditional IRA might be fully or partly taxable, depending on whether your IRA includes nondeductible contributions. If you made only deductible contributions to your IRA, you have no basis in your IRA, which means that all distributions are taxed as part of your gross income. If you made nondeductible contributions to your IRA, you have a cost basis equal to the amount of those contributions. The nondeductible contributions are not taxed when they are distributed to you because they are a return of your investment in your IRA. If your IRA contains both deductible and nondeductible IRA contributions, your distributions consist of a nontaxable portion (your basis) and a taxable portion (deducted contributions, earnings, and gains). Until you run out of basis, each distribution is partly taxable and partly nontaxable.

If you have a loss on your IRA investment, you can include it on your income tax return after all the amounts in all your IRA accounts have been distributed to you and the total distributions are less than your unrecovered basis. You claim the loss as a miscellaneous itemized deduction, subject to the 2-percent limit.

Taking Early Distributions

If you withdraw assets (money or property) before age 59-1/2, you must pay a 10-percent penalty tax on the taxable distribution in addition to your regular income tax, unless the distribution falls within one of a specified list of exceptions. An early distribution will not be subject to any penalty tax if the distribution is made:

- To pay significant unreimbursed medical expenses
- To pay medical insurance premiums after losing your job
- For the purchase of a first home
- Due to a disability
- As the result of the death of the account holder
- As part of a divorce and separation proceeding

If you make a contribution to your retirement fund, take no deduction for it, and withdraw it and any earnings on it before the due date (including extensions) of your income tax return for that year, the 10-percent additional tax does not apply. However, any interest or other income earned on the contribution, which also must be withdrawn, is treated as income in the year the contribution was made. These earnings must be reported and may be subject to the 10-percent early-withdrawal tax.

Note that if you withdraw funds from a SIMPLE made within two years of date your participation began, you must pay a 25-percent tax.

Paying Unreimbursed Medical Expenses: You do not have to pay the 10-percent tax on amounts you withdraw that are not more than the amount you paid for unreimbursed medical expenses during the year of the withdrawal, minus 7.5 percent of your adjusted gross income for the year of the withdrawal.

Paying Medical Insurance: You may not have to pay the 10 percent tax on amounts you withdraw during the year that are not more than the amount you paid during the year for medical insurance for yourself, your spouse, and your dependents if all the following conditions apply:

- You lost your job.
- You received unemployment compensation paid under any federal or state law for 12 consecutive weeks.
- You make the withdrawals during either the year you received the unemployment compensation or the following year.
- You make the withdrawals no later than 60 days after you have been reemployed.

Purchasing a First Home (Not for Investment Purposes): You can withdraw $10,000 from your retirement fund for a first home without paying the 10-percent early-withdrawal tax. You must use the distribution to buy, build, or rebuild a first home that is the principal residence of yourself, your spouse, your child or grandchild, your spouse's child or grandchild, or for a parent or other ancestor of yours or your spouse's.

Disability: If you become disabled, any amounts you withdraw from your IRA because of your disability are not subject to the 10-percent additional tax. You must furnish proof that you cannot do any substantial gainful activity because of your physical or mental condition. A physician must determine that your condition is expected to result in death or to last a long and indefinite duration.

Death: If you die before age 59-1/2, the assets in your IRA can be distributed to your beneficiary or estate without paying the 10-percent tax. (For more information, see the section "Beneficiary Receipt of Assets" in this chapter.)

Divorce and Separation: The Internal Revenue code permits certain distributions relating to child support, alimony, or marital property resulting from divorce or legal separation actions. For qualified Plans, such as Individual 401(k)s, a Qualified Domestic Relations Order (QDRO) must be obtained from a court having jurisdiction over the divorce or separation proceedings in the case of a qualified plan. IRAs may be divided by court order. In both cases division may be made in accordance with a prenuptial agreement.

If you are required to transfer all of the assets in an IRA, you can just change the name on the IRA to your spouse or former spouse. If you need to transfer a portion of the funds, you can direct the trustee of the IRA to transfer the amount directly to the trustee of a new or an existing IRA set up in the name of your spouse or former spouse. If your spouse or former spouse is allowed to keep his or her portion of the IRA assets in your existing IRA, you can direct the trustee to transfer the assets you are permitted to keep directly to a new or existing IRA set up in your name. The name on the IRA containing your spouse's or former spouse's portion of the assets would then be changed to show his or her ownership.

If you receive a distribution from a qualified employer plan because of a divorce or similar proceedings, you may be able to roll over all or part of it into an IRA. To qualify, the distribution must be one that would have been an eligible rollover distribution if it had been made to an employee, and it must be made under a QDRO.

Lifetime Distributions before Age 59-1/2

You can receive distributions from your retirement plan as a series of substantially equal payments over your life (or your life expectancy), or over the lives of you and your beneficiary (or your joint life expectancies), without paying the 10-percent tax, even if you receive such distributions before age 59-1/2. To do this, you must use an IRS-approved distribution method, and you must take at least one distribution annually.

Two other IRS-approved distribution methods available are the amortization method and the annuity factor method. These methods are more complex and require professional assistance. The payments must continue for at least five years or until you reach age 59-1/2, whichever is longer. The five-year rule does not apply if the distribution method changes because of death or disability.

If the payments change before the end of the required period for any reason other than death or disability, you are subject to the 10 percent tax.

Questions Regarding Distributions from IRAs

I have small children who attend a private school. Tuition is costing me approximately $12,000 a year. Can I put this money into an IRA throughout the year and then take it out in August without penalty when their tuition is due?

Your contributions are limited to $3000 per year. You may withdraw that amount penalty free for certain education expenses such as tuition.

I'm 51 and retired. Can I roll my 401(k) to a self-directed IRA and split it so as to invest in real estate, for instance, and set up a 72t with part of it for usable money?

To do a 72t, or substantially equal periodic withdrawal, you need to have those assets in a different IRA than the one from which you wish to take only future distributions. You can set up one account to do the real estate investments, and then periodically transfer cash to the other for the 72t distributions. Please note that the 72t distributions will be calculated from the balance as of December 31 the previous year

If, however, you want to have the 72t calculation based on the total value of all investments, including both real estate and cash, you can keep all assets in one IRA, and then take the 72t distributions based on the total amount from that IRA.

Roth IRA Distributions

You are not required to take distributions from your Roth IRA at any age. Qualified distributions are not included in your gross income. A qualified distribution is any payment or distribution made after age 59-1/2 or, if before age 59-1/2, for the hardship exceptions described earlier.

A distribution is not a qualified distribution if it is made within five tax years from when you first contributed to your Roth IRA, or if you rolled over funds into the Roth IRA from a retirement fund other than a Roth IRA. A distribution that is not qualified is taxable.

Questions Regarding Roth IRA Distributions

Soon my Roth will be 5 years old. If I add to it this year, can the full amount be removed next year? Will the new money being contributed this year to a 5-year-old Roth IRA be eligible to be removed even if it has not been in the account for 5 years?

You may always take the basis out of your Roth at any time without tax consequences (a simple case would be those amounts originally contributed to the Roth). The only issue concerns earnings when you are under age 59-1/2, and have had contributions in the Roth for less than five years. Those earnings would be subject to a 10-percent penalty, as well.

Required Distributions

When you reach age 70-1/2, you are required to take distributions by April 1 of the following year (see Roth IRA exception above). You do not need to take the entire amount at once, but you must take a required minimum distribution (RMD) at least annually over your life expectancy. The RMD for any year after you reach 70-1/2 must be made by December 31 of that year.

Life expectancies are determined using the IRS life expectancy tables. If your spouse is your sole beneficiary and is more than 10 years younger than you, your life expectancy is based on your combined ages. If you have no beneficiary or if your beneficiary is not your spouse, the minimum distribution incidental benefit (MDIB) table is used to determine the distribution period. The MDIB rules establish a uniform distribution period based on a joint life expectancy of you and someone exactly 10 years younger than you.

If you do not withdraw funds as required, or if you withdraw an amount that is less than the RMD, you may have to pay a 50-percent excise tax on the amount not withdrawn. The IRS may waive the penalty if you can show that the excess was due to a reasonable error, and that appropriate steps have been or are being taken to remedy the shortfall.

If you choose to take distributions over your lifetime, you can either purchase an annuity or leave the balance in the plan and receive minimum distributions on an annual basis.

Distribution after Death

Your beneficiaries can be your spouse, estate, dependents, or anyone you choose to receive the benefits of your retirement fund after you die. The designated beneficiary is determined as of the end of the year following the year of the owner's death. If there is more than one beneficiary, the designated beneficiary is the one with the shortest life expectancy. The beneficiaries of your IRA must include the distributions to them in their gross incomes.

The designated beneficiary can receive payments over the beneficiary's life expectancy, regardless of whether the owner of the fund died before or after the RMD. The beneficiary's life expectancy is calculated using his or her age in the year following the owner's death and is reduced by one in each succeeding year.

If the owner does not have a designated beneficiary, the remaining payments must be made over the life expectancy of the owner, determined by the owner's age in the year of death and reduced by one each succeeding year.

If you inherit an IRA from your spouse, you can elect to treat it as your own after the RMD for the year of your spouse's death is distributed, as long as you are the sole beneficiary. Any distribution you take before you reach age 59-1/2 may be subject to the 10-percent tax.

If you inherit an IRA from someone other than your spouse, you cannot treat it as though you established it. You cannot roll the funds into another IRA, nor can you contribute or roll funds into the inherited IRA. The IRA cannot be rolled into or receive a rollover from another IRA. Deductions for amounts paid into the inherited IRA are not allowed, nor can nondeductible contributions be made to an inherited IRA.

A surviving spouse can roll over part or all of any eligible rollover distribution received from an employer's qualified plan into an IRA, but not into another qualified employer plan or annuity.

Qualified Plan Distributions

A plan must provide that each participant receives either the entire sum or regular lifetime periodic distributions by the required beginning date. Regular periodic distributions must meet the Required Minimum Distribution Rules as described earlier.

The minimum distribution rules apply individually to each qualified plan. You cannot satisfy the requirement for one plan by taking a distribution from another.

Distributions from a qualified plan are included in your gross income for the taxable year in which the distribution is made. You can roll over distributions, unless they are required distributions, or one in a series of equal periodic payments made over a single or joint life expectancy for a specified period of 10 or more years. Rolling over an eligible distribution into an IRA or another qualified plan is a way to defer the tax owed on a distribution.

If you receive a lump-sum distribution, you can use income averaging to lower the taxes. With income averaging, you must still pay tax on the distribution in the tax year in which the funds are distributed, but income averaging generally yields lower taxes because the amount of tax due is determined as if you had received the distribution in even amounts over a five-year period. If you use income averaging, you must file IRS Form 4972, Tax on Lump Sum Distributions.

If you receive a lump sum and choose to either income average or pay the capital gains, you cannot roll over any portion of the lump-sum distribution. Conversely, if you receive a lump-sum distribution and roll over a portion, you cannot use income averaging or capital gains tax options on the remaining amount.

The IRS periodically publishes annuity tables that permit recapturing taxes paid on contributions to be accounted for in annuity distributions. The annuity provider should provide you with the appropriate calculations if that is the distribution course chosen.

All retirement plan distributions of nonresidents (including former residents) are not subject to state taxation.

Questions about Qualified Plan Distributions

I received a rather large sum of money from a 401(k) account and company pension plan as part of a divorce settlement. What I'd like to do is take it out as cash to be used to either pay off my house or reinvest in real estate. By taking it out as part of the divorce settlement, there is no 10-percent penalty. However, the taxes on this are going to be humongous. Is there any way to protect this money from taxes?

If you receive the funds and spend them on paying off your home mortgage, the amount you receive as a result of the Qualified Domestic Relations Order is taxable.

If you choose to invest all or part of the amount in real estate, you may roll that amount over to a self-directed traditional IRA or to another qualified plan and have the IRA make the real estate investments. This avoids current tax. With a traditional IRA, you will eventually pay tax when you receive distributions, which must begin by your age 70-1/2.

You may, if you are eligible, convert all or part of those funds to a Roth IRA, by paying current tax and never pay tax again on the investment return you make on Real Estate or other investments.

Rollovers

If your distribution from an employer plan is more than $200 for the year, you must be given the option to have any part of an eligible rollover distribution paid directly to an IRA or to an eligible retirement plan. If you do a direct rollover, no tax is withheld. Involuntary cash-outs between $1000 and $5000 are automatically rolled into an IRA selected by the plan administrator if you do not specify how to distribute the assets.

If you receive property and cash in an eligible rollover distribution from your employer's plan, you can roll over either the property or the cash, or any combination of the two.

Contributing cash representing the fair market value of property received in a distribution from a qualified retirement plan to an IRA does not qualify as a rollover if you keep the property. You must either roll over the property or sell it and roll over the proceeds. You cannot substitute your own funds for property you receive from your employer's retirement plan.

If you sell the distributed property and roll over all the proceeds into an IRA, no gain or loss is recognized. The sale proceeds (including any increase in value) are treated as part of the distribution and are not included in your gross income. You cannot roll over a life insurance contract from a qualified plan into an IRA.

Distributions from 401(k) Plans

Generally, a distribution cannot be made until the employee retires, dies, becomes disabled, or separates from service. A distribution may be made if the plan ends and no other defined contribution plan is established or continued.

Distributions minus the prorated part of any cost basis are subject to income tax in the year they are distributed. Since most recipients have no cost basis, a distribution is generally fully taxable, unless it is rolled over into another retirement fund.

Inheritance

Inheriting an IRA with Basis

If you inherit an IRA with basis, that basis must remain with the IRA. Unless you are the spouse of the deceased and choose to treat the IRA as your own, you cannot combine the basis with any basis you have in your own IRAs or any basis in IRAs you inherited from other people. If you take a distribution from an inherited IRA as well as your own, and each has basis, you must complete Form 8606 for each IRA to determine the taxable and nontaxable portions of the distributions.

Deducting Federal Estate Tax

As a beneficiary, you may be able to deduct the estate tax paid on any part of a distribution that you must include as income from an inherited IRA. You can take the deduction for the tax year in which you report that income.

Any taxable part of a distribution that is not income with respect to a decedent is a payment you must include in income. However, you cannot take any estate tax deduction for this part.

Questions about Beneficiaries

I became a beneficiary of an IRA when my mother died a couple of years ago. I am 61 years old. It is my understanding that when I die, the funds in the IRA would have to be liquidated and taxes paid on the resulting amount. The fund is down now, as is everything else, but usually has had around $90,000 in it. Since I am still working, I take the required minimum distribution each year in order to avoid having to pay a large amount of tax. I will retire in June and will be in a lower tax bracket. I could begin to take larger amounts out and reinvest them, but prefer to continue taking the minimum and name beneficiaries. I now understand that certain institutions are allowing such decedent IRAs to be passed along to surviving spouses (as primary beneficiary) and our children (as secondary beneficiaries). I have also heard this can be risky. Where can I find correct information regarding this issue?

The assets in your plan would not have to be liquidated, and you may take larger amounts if you wish and also name beneficiaries. This is not risky and is permitted. The IRA must, however, remain in the name of your mother until it is depleted by the beneficiaries. You as a nonspouse beneficiary may not name additional beneficiaries. We suggest that one answer to the new rules be that you look at forming trusts to name as beneficiaries. Although this would be done best by properly trained attorneys, it may well be the best method to preserve an IRA for future generations.

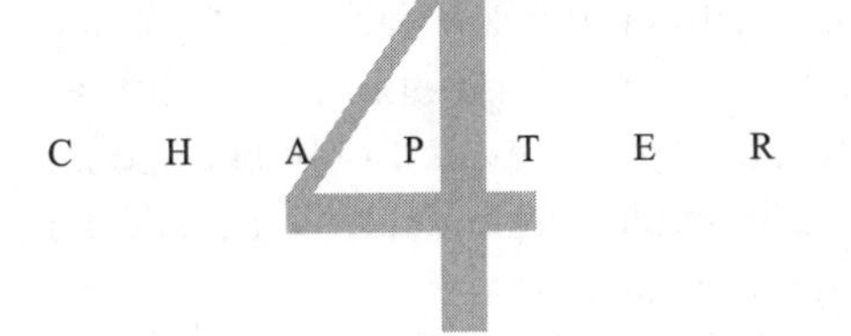

What to Do and Not Do to Get the Best Tax Results

If you are looking for a way to reduce tax on inheritance, one method that works in conjunction with beneficiary rules and distributions from IRAs and Qualified plans is gifting. Although you may not gift from an IRA or Qualified Plan, if your estate begins to be large, you may consider gifting real estate as part of your tax planning.

The Art of Gifting

If you have accumulated assets that you anticipate to be more than $3,500,000 by 2009, estate taxes could reduce the amount you will be able to pass to your beneficiaries. According to 2004 federal estate laws, estates larger than $1,000,000 are subject to tax rates as high as 49 percent. This figure does not include any applicable state taxes. An estate planning strategy that can help reduce the impact of estate taxes is gifting. Gifting of existing assets will assist in the reduction of estate taxes. The nature of the gift can take any form provided that the fair market value of the gift is established at the time the gift is given. The gift can be in kind, so real estate in any form is eligible. This includes undivided interests in real property.

The annual gift tax exclusion allows you give up to $11,000 (as of 2004), per calendar year, per recipient without gift tax liability. If you are married and your spouse consents to "splitting" the gift, the annual gift tax exclusion would increase to $22,000. This applies even if only one spouse actually performs the act of giving. The exclusion amount is indexed for inflation so it is likely to change in future years.

Making gifts during one's lifetime shifts any future appreciation of gifted property to the recipient.

By gifting real property, notes or portions thereof, assuming 2004 gift guidelines, it would take five years to gift a $100,000 property or the equivalent in notes. Taxable income may be then shifted from your potentially higher tax bracket to the gift recipient.

This applies in cases in which the gift recipient is 14 years of age or older. Because there are specific tax rules that apply to children, it is of utmost importance for you to obtain competent tax counsel regarding the income tax treatment of minors.

You would not be liable to pay any gift tax until the taxable gifts exceed the exclusion amount. If your total gifts exceed the total exclusion amount, gift tax would be payable.

Each year gift taxes are calculated by adding the total amount of taxable gifts made since December 1, 1976 to the total amount of taxable gifts made during the current year. Only cumulative taxable gifts in excess of $1,000,000 (as of 2003) will result in out-of-pocket gift tax payments by the donor. Under the Economic Growth and Tax Relief Reconciliation Act of 2001, the applicable estate tax exclusion amount will gradually increase until it reaches $3,500,000 in 2009.

If you have a partner, up to $11,000 of gifts that you make to your partner each year are tax-free under the annual gift tax exclusion (as of 2004). After that amount has been reached, you will begin to use up your unified credit. As of 2004, this credit exempts up to $1,500,000 for estate tax purposes or up to $1,000,000 for gift tax purposes.

Elementary Aspects of Tax Basis

Basis is used to determine gain upon the disposition of an asset. In simple terms, basis is an owner's investment in the asset. For purchased property, the starting basis is the original price paid (plus any acquisition costs). An asset's basis can be increased (e.g., by making improvements to real property) or decreased (e.g., after a casualty loss reduces the value of an asset). It can also change when factoring in how an asset was acquired and the circumstances surrounding the eventual disposition. Adjusted basis refers to changes in basis after an asset was acquired. Here is a closer look at basis and how it can affect capital gains:

Selling an Asset

Robin bought a condominium for $55,000. She discovered that the appraisal showed a current fair market value (FMV) of $75,000. Robin's basis is the original cost of $55,000. If she sold the condo at FMV, her taxable gain would be $20,000 ($75,000 selling price less her $55,000 basis).

"Gifting" an Asset

Robin decided to give the condo to her son, Don. Generally, the recipient assumes the basis of the donor, who, in this case, is Robin, at the time of the gift. The recipient also assumes a portion of any gift tax incurred by the transfer. However, if Robin were to sell the property, her gain or loss on the sale would depend upon whether the FMV of the condo at the time of the gift was greater than or less than its adjusted basis at that time.

If the FMV at the time of the gift is greater than Robin's basis of $55,000, then Robin's basis is used to determine the gain or loss. If the FMV at the time of the gift is less than Robin's basis, in this case we will assume an FMV of $45,000, the foundation for determining a gain or loss is different. In the case of a loss, Don's basis would be the lesser of Robin's original cost of $55,000 or the FMV at the time of the gift, which we assumed to be $45,000. In the case of a gain, if the condo is still valued at $75,000 when Robin sells it, the basis would continue to be Robin's original basis of $55,000.

Robin has a tough decision to make regarding gifting the property to her son. She needs to consider all of her alternatives. She is aware that there are possible gift tax consequences for any gift exceeding $11,000 per person per year (as of 2004). She thinks that perhaps marrying her fiancé, William, in 2004 rather than waiting until 2005 would be in her best interest if her primary goal is to avoid paying gift tax. If she marries William, deeds half of the condo to him, and in turn gifts it to her son, then she would be able to exclude $22,000 in gift tax instead of $11,000 if she chose to stay single or chose not to deed half of the condo to William. Within three years, she would be able to gift the property to Don and avoid paying gift tax.

Beneficiary Receipt of Assets

An additional option available to Robin is to make Don the beneficiary of the condo as part of her estate. The basis of property acquired by inheritance is adjusted to the FMV of the property at the time of the owner's death. This means that Don's basis would be the Fair Market Value of the condo at the time of Robin's death.

The main advantage of acquiring property through inheritance is that it allows the recipient to sell the property shortly after inheriting it with little or no capital gains tax. Assuming that an immediate sale of an inherited asset would be at the asset's FMV, there would be no recognized gain since the basis (FMV) would be the same. Even if the asset were held for some time after inheritance, an eventual sale would result in a smaller capital gains tax, due to the higher (stepped-up) basis established at inheritance.

Tax Issues for Self-Directed Plans

Before investing in real estate with your retirement funds, you should be aware of some of the tax issues involved.

Prohibited Transactions

Section 4975 defines a prohibited transaction as any direct or indirect transaction that involves the following:

- Selling, exchanging, or leasing any property between a plan and a disqualified person
- Lending of money or other extension of credit between a plan and a disqualified person
- Furnishing goods, services, or facilities between a plan and a disqualified person

- Transferring the assets of a plan to, or for the use or benefit of, a disqualified person
- Having a disqualified person who is a fiduciary using the income or assets of a plan in his or her own interests or account

In this context, a disqualified person can be one of the following:

- A fiduciary
- A person providing services to the plan
- An employer, any of whose employees are covered by the plan
- An employee organization, any of whose members are covered by the plan
- An owner, direct or indirect, of 50 percent or more of the business
- A 10 percent (or more) partner in a partnership having the plan

If you are a disqualified person, the following are also disqualified persons:

Members of your family (spouse, ancestors, direct descendants, and any spouse of a direct descendant)

Corporations, partnerships, trusts, or estates in which you own, directly or indirectly, at least half the total voting stock or the value of all stock of the corporation, capital interest, or profit interest of the partnership, or beneficial interest of the trust or estate.

Correcting Prohibited Transactions

If you are a disqualified person who participated in a prohibited transaction, you can minimize the tax by correcting it as soon as possible. Correcting it means undoing it as much as you can without putting the plan in a worse financial position than if you had acted under the highest fiduciary standards.

If you do not correct the transaction during the taxable period, you are subject to a 100 percent tax of the amount involved. The amount is based on the highest fair market value during the taxable period of any property given or received in the transaction.

You usually have an additional 90 days after the day the IRS mails a notice of deficiency for the 100-percent tax to correct the transaction. This correction period (the taxable period plus the 90 days) can be extended if the IRS grants a reasonable time needed to correct the transaction, or you can petition the Tax Court. If you correct the transaction within this period, the IRS will abate, credit, or refund the 100-percent tax.

Prohibited Transactions for Individual Retirement Arrangements

For IRAs Prohibited Transactions are defined as part of the Trust disclosed to each owner. A standard IRA provision on prohibited transactions is set forth below:

Prohibited Transactions: Notwithstanding anything contained herein to the contrary, the Custodian shall not lend any part of the corpus or income of the account to; pay any compensation for personal services rendered to the account to; make any part of its services available on a preferential basis to; acquire for the account any property, other than cash, from; or sell any property to, any Depositor, any member of a Depositor's family, or a corporation controlled by any Depositor through the ownership, directly or indirectly, of 50 percent or more of the total combined voting power of all classes of stock entitled to vote, or of 50 percent or more of the total value of shares of all classes of stock of such corporation.

You can purchase any asset that is legally permissible with your retirement plan funds. The Internal Revenue Code and Employee Retirement Income Security Act (ERISA) do not identify the types of investments you are allowed to make; they only state what you may not do. These restrictions are covered under Section 4975, Tax on Prohibited Transactions.

Generally, a prohibited transaction is any improper use of your IRA or annuity by you or any disqualified person. Disqualified persons include your fiduciary and members of your family (spouse, ancestor, lineal descendant, and any spouse of a lineal descendant).

Some examples of prohibited transactions with an IRA are:

- Borrowing money from it
- Selling your own property to it
- Receiving unreasonable compensation for managing it
- Using it as security for a loan
- Buying property for personal use (present or future)

If you or your beneficiary engage in a prohibited transaction in connection with your IRA at any time during the year, it will not be treated as an IRA as of the first day of the year. You (or your beneficiary) must also include the fair market value of all (or part, in certain cases) of the IRA assets in your gross income for that year.

The fair market value is the price at which the IRA assets would change hands between a willing buyer and a willing seller, when neither has any need to buy or sell, and both have reasonable knowledge of the relevant facts.

You must use the fair market value of the assets as of the first day of the year you engaged in the prohibited transaction. You may also have to pay a 10-percent tax if it is a premature distribution.

Borrowing on an Annuity Contract

If you borrow money against your IRA annuity contract, you must include the fair market value of the annuity contract in your gross income as of the first day of your tax year. You may also have to pay a 10-percent tax if it is a premature distribution.

Using Your IRA to Secure a Loan

If you use a part of your IRA account as security for a loan, for personal use, that part is treated as a distribution and is included in your gross income. You may also have to pay a 10-percent tax if it is a premature distribution.

Exemptions to Prohibited Transactions

The following transactions, which have previously been viewed as prohibited, have been granted exemption from prohibited transaction penalties by the Department of Labor if they meet the requirements for exemption:

- Payments by an IRA sponsor of cash, property, or other consideration to an individual (or family members) for whose benefit the IRA is established or maintained

- Receipt of services from a bank at reduced or no cost by an individual for whose benefit an IRA is established or maintained

All of the following requirements must be satisfied for the exemption for payments of cash, property, or other consideration:

- The payments must be given for establishing an IRA or for making additional contributions to it.
- The IRA must be established solely to benefit you, your spouse, and beneficiaries (yours and your spouse's).
- During the year, the total of the fair market value of the payments you receive cannot exceed $10 for IRA deposits of less than $5,000, $20 for IRA deposits of $5,000 or more.
- If the consideration you are provided is group term life insurance, the requirements do not apply provided that no more than $5,000 of the face value of the insurance is based on a dollar-for-dollar basis on the assets in your IRA.

Conditions on Use of Exemptions

All of the following conditions must be satisfied for the exemption for services you receive at reduced or no cost:

- The IRA taken into account for purposes of qualifying to receive the services must be established and maintained for the benefit of you, your spouse, or beneficiaries (yours and your spouse's).
- The services must be services the bank itself can legally offer.
- The services must be provided in the ordinary course of business by the bank (or a bank affiliate) to customers who qualify but do not maintain an IRA (or a Keogh Plan).
- For an IRA, the determination of who qualifies for these services must be based on an IRA (or a Keogh Plan) deposit balance equal to the lowest qualifying balance for any other type of account.
- The rate of return on an IRA investment that qualifies cannot be less than the return on an identical investment that could have been made at the same time at the same branch of the bank by a customer who is not eligible for (or does not receive) these services.

How to "Get Around" Prohibited Transactions to Deal with Real Estate in Your Plan: Distributions and Prohibited Transaction Exemptions from IRAs and Qualified Plans

The only rule about Prohibited Transactions and getting around them is that it isn't worth the risk. What follows are a number of perfectly legal strategies that will help you deal with assets in IRAs and Qualified Plans, and not violate prohibited transaction rules. Also, the indirect rule states that anything that may be done directly may not be done indirectly.

Distributions for Personal Use

Generally, distributions form IRAs are made for retirement purposes. At 59-1/2 you can start receiving distributions from all IRA types and at 70-1/2 you will have reached the age that distributions must be taken from every IRA type, except Roth IRAs, which have no required distribution age, as well as 401(k)s, and other qualified plans.

There are other reasons that you might consider receiving distributions form self-directed plans, at the age of 59-1/2 or earlier, whether from a Roth IRA or a traditional IRA. These reasons do not apply in most cases in a 401(k). Of course 401(k)s may permit you to take "in-service" withdrawals that may then be rolled over to traditional IRAs, which then would obviate issues with qualified plans and premature distributions. In some cases obtaining an exemption from the Department of Labor to purchase an asset from the IRA or plan is the best answer.

The reasons include:

- The home in the plan is one that you want to use as your personal residence.
- You want your own construction company to develop a tract of land.
- You want to sell the property to a family member.
- You want to rent out the property to a family member and receive current income.
- You want to control an LLC owned by your IRA without fear of running afoul of prohibited transaction rules.

An example of this distribution is: The home in the plan is one that you want to use as your personal residence.

Roth IRA

Ed is 59-1/2 and is eligible to take Roth IRA distributions. The distributions are tax free to Ed. The Roth IRA rules permit him to take tax-free distributions at that age, as long as the Roth has been in existence for five years. If Ed made conversions from traditional IRAs, each time he made a conversion, a five-year clock starts for the conversion amount only. Any assets Ed converted to a Roth IRA may be taken by Ed from his Roth IRA without any tax consequences, as such assets are considered his new non-taxable basis. Any additional cash contributions made by Ed in the future to his Roth IRA may also be removed from his Roth IRA without tax consequences, as he has also paid tax on such contributions, as is the net amount remaining from conversion the amount Ed contributed, at any time, as he has already paid tax. For converted assets, each time Ed converted, a five-year clock begins for that asset converted. Had Ed taken a distribution other than his basis (in other words income) at an age under 59-1/2 he would have to pay tax on the distribution amount, plus a 10-percent penalty. This example of distribution from a Roth IRA applies to all examples below.

IRA and Qualified Plans and 1031 Exchanges

When you receive a required distribution from a traditional IRA, generally including all IRA types other than Roth IRAs, and ESAs, you have options to deal with the property such as living in it. If you are going to take the property and pay tax on it, you could, after payment of the tax, exchange the property under 1031 rules. You could receive an undivided interest that comports with the lowest tax you are willing to pay, or not pay, as the case may be. The structure of this transaction is covered under "Co-ownership versus Partnership: Structuring Ownership of Income Real Property for Tax-Deferred Exchanges" in Part 3.

If you have a complete distribution of an asset, and the tax burden is relatively small, you can immediately look at exchanging it subsequent to title being conveyed to you.

For example: Jessica's IRA has a small condo on Maui. Knowing that she would have to pay tax on required minimum distributions, which was 10 years away, she made a judgment that as property values were on a rise, a tax now, when she would pay relatively little tax, was a good time to change her tax deferral strategy.

The Condo has an FMV of $125,000, which her IRA purchased for $70,000 in 1994. Jessica will include the FMV as part of her income from tax in 2003. She had sufficient deductions in the form of adjusted gross income and tax credits to cause her tax to be less than $5000. The lessees had been in the condo for five years and had renewed their two-year lease with her. The property continued to cash flow for her.

Jessica's basis in the property was $125,000, as that is the amount she paid tax on. The property could now be depreciated as one of her many rentals she had outside of her IRA. The positive cash flow was in cash and income was offset on a tax basis by expenses including depreciation.

She then elected to exchange the property for two others in a growing area along the Atlantic Coast. An appraisal later in 2003 placed the FMV at $185,000. She sold the property and realized a gain of $175,000. She then decided that the two properties worth $250,000 would be sufficient to make the deal attractive to her. She contributed cash to the exchange of $75,000 to complete the transaction.

In the end, she had two properties with an FMV of $250,000. She paid tax of $5000 and added $75,000 to the transaction, for a total of $80,000. This transaction is one that could not have been done in the IRA, as the $80,000 could not have been contributed. Her tax deferral capability has been preserved, and her portfolio enhanced, by taking a distribution in a timely manner.

Traditional IRA (Includes all IRA types, except Roth IRA); Using Home Exclusion Allowance

Mary is 59-1/2 and eligible to take distribution of the property. She obtains a Fair Market Value of the property which she wishes to make her home. She obtains an appropriate fair market value appraisal from a person who in the eyes of the IRS can make such appraisals, such as a broker, who may use comparative sales prices or other real estate or asset appraisers. She pays at her income tax rate on the full amount of the property, by the tax deadline plus extensions for the year in which she took distributions.

Had Mary done this one year prior, she would have had to pay a 10-percent penalty for a premature distribution, under normal circumstances. On sale of the property, if she lives in it as a primary residence she can also take advantage of a tax exclusion of up to $250,000 on the gain. This is further amplified in Part 3, Home Exclusion Allowance.

Using Your Own Construction Company to Develop a Tract of Land

Milt has been unable to find a buyer for his land and discovered that if he improved the property with homes, he could sell the properties and turn a nonearning asset into one that makes a profit. Milt's traditional IRA purchased the land 10 years ago and wants his construction company to develop the property. He also does not have sufficient capital in his traditional IRA, or other IRAs, to fund the building. In order for him to be able to turn this into an earning asset, he has two basic options:

1. Have the IRA obtain a nonrecourse loan to fund the build out, in which case he cannot use his or any person related to him to build out the land;
2. Apply for a Prohibited Transaction Exemption to purchase the property from his IRA.
3. Take the property as a distribution from his IRA and pay tax.

His game plan was to use his own company to build out the property, so option number one was not appealing. Option two was most appealing, as he had the cash to buy the property from his plan at Fair Market Value. Option three would be effective if he had no cash but could obtain a construction loan outside his IRA.

The process of obtaining a prohibited transaction exemption is straightforward. The Department of Labor is responsible for issuing such exemptions. They are generally following the format that includes:

- The transaction must be an arms-length transaction.
- It is a one-time-only transaction.
- The property must be valued at Fair Market Value.
- There is no commission paid.
- There are no disqualified persons involved in valuation or brokerage.
- The reason for purchase from the plan is for the benefit of the plan.

Renting Property to a Relative

Gary and Dee have a property as 50 percent each undivided interest holders in their individual 401(k) participant accounts. Their plan purchased a five-bedroom house in Bloomington, Illinois, 10 years ago. Their eldest son Dan is about to go to college at the University in Bloomington. Gary and Dee would like to have Dan live in that house. The house has students occupying it now, and it cash flows very nicely. When Dan attends University, he will have roommates that will continue the cash flow at a somewhat reduced rate. Gary and Dee had already used a Prohibited Transaction Exemption for other property, and also the justification to have the plan benefit from such a transaction would be questionable, as the property was cash flowing.

Dee and Gary looked at the possibilities of having their son live in someone else's apartment, but they did not see the benefit of paying someone else.

The taking of a distribution, in this case an in-service withdrawal from their Individual 401(k), involves the payment of tax at their ordinary income tax rate on the Fair Market Value (FMV) of the house. Dee knows an appraiser in Bloomington whom she has worked with before to provide a FMV that could be justified to the IRS. The value was determined to be $250,000. Over the previous ten years the home had appreciated by $200,000. They would be taxed at their income tax rate for the year in which they take the distribution. They would also have a basis of $250,000 in the distributed property.

The tax was $75,000. Because they decided to take the distribution early in the tax year, they would not have to pay the actual tax until April 15 of the following year, plus extensions. Gary and Dee figured that they would have a mortgage-backed line of credit on the house to pay the tax when due. The distributed amount would be includable in their income for the year, and they had quite a few other deductions that would lessen their overall tax bill.

Other alternatives could be: If they had known that they would like to use it for a relative, such as a son, they could have Rothized the transaction. Five years ago when their joint income was $95,000, Gary and Dee could have taken an in-service withdrawal from their 401(k). They then would roll their respective amounts into a traditional IRA and convert the asset (the home) to a Roth IRA. Their tax on a $150,000 FMV, using the same appraiser, would have been $45,000. They would have the property in the Roth IRA for the requisite five years. Income generation in the Roth is identical to any other IRA or plan, except that the gains are tax free. On distribution at $250,000 the property would be tax free, as was the gain from the original $50,000, as they were each over 59-1/2 years old. Effectively, Gary and Dee would have put a "stop-loss" on the tax they would have to pay in the future on any distributions, saving $35,000 in tax money. They could have also exchanged the house for other property and been the seller in a 1031 exchange.

Winding up with other property could easily diversify among other like-kind real estate. They could also exchange for unlike-kind property, if there was not a 1031 exchange. Any of the properties could then be treated as above. Dan could choose from several properties, Gary and Dee would not violate prohibited transaction rules, and they would still wind up with earning assets in their IRAs or 401(k)s.

If you decide to use a home in your IRA as a personal residence, you can always take a distribution of the house and pay the tax (Roth IRA property would not be taxed as long as you follow distribution rules). We cover this area under the Home Exclusion Allowance, Part 3 in this book.

Another possibility is that if you wish to live in the property for up to 60 days per year, you may have the property distributed to you for up to 60 days in every 12-month period. This distribution needs to formal, and property must be conveyed to you at fair market value. Remember the IRS nor your trustee or administrator know if you are going to roll the property over to your IRA. If you don't, the Fair Market Value of the property is taxable to you. During the time you have the property in your personal possession, you may not make any improvements to the property that would substantially add value to the property. The property rolled over must be the same that is distributed. Normal maintenance would not be considered a violation. Such maintenance expenses are covered in IRS Publication 527. Table 4.1 shows items that are considered improvements.

You may not use any property during the time it is in your IRA or qualified plan to maintain the property for any duration.

TABLE 4.1 Examples of Improvements

Caution: Work you do (or have done) on your home that does not add much to either the value or the life of the property, but rather keeps the property in good condition, is considered a repair, not an improvement.

Additions	Sprinkler system	Furnace	Flooring
Bedroom	Swimming pool	Duct work	Wall-to-wall carpeting
Bathroom	Miscellaneous	Central humidifier	Insulation
Deck	Storm windows,	Filtration system	Attic
Garage	doors	Plumbing	Walls, floor
Porch	New roof	Septic system	Pipes, duct work
Patio	Central vacuum	Water heater	
Lawn & Grounds	Wiring upgrades	Soft water system	
Landscaping	Satellite dish	Filtration system	
Driveway	Security system	Interior Improvements	
Walkway	Heating & Air	Built-in appliances	
Fence	Conditioning	Kitchen modernization	
Retaining wall	Heating system		
	Central air conditioning		

Example of What Not to Do

Not long ago, Virginia had a self-directed Individual Retirement Account that she built up to about $500,000. She made annual contributions for 20 years and also established an SEP IRA to help increase contribution limits. She directed the investment of her IRA carefully in real property that she sold for a profit. She also carried back notes so when the need arose, she, her IRA partner, and other interested parties took advantage of deals that would have been financially out of her reach if she had only personal funds to utilize.

She also directed her IRA to purchase a condominium for $180,000 in a college town, which she then rented to up to four students. This deal was a cash transaction, as Virginia didn't want to deal with debt-financed property in her IRA, especially since she possessed the funds to complete the transaction. We closed the deal for her IRA and Virginia made sure that the monthly rent payments were sent to us to credit her IRA. Sometimes we received one rental check and sometimes we received two. Either way, we always received the full rent payments on time. However, the rental agreements, though always completed in favor of the IRA, were rarely received on time.

One day, we received a check for the total rental amount and we noticed that the last name of the person who wrote the check was the same as Virginia's. The name was not a common name, so we asked Virginia what relationship, if any, she had with Lucy. The answer was not a positive one. Lucy was Virginia's daughter. Up to this point, the checks had always been written by other roommates, but summer had arrived and so the other roommates had gone home. Lucy, however, remained in the condo as she needed a place to stay. Since the rent still had to be paid to the IRA, Lucy made the payments. We informed Virginia that the law prohibits having her daughter in the condo, and that she needed to correct the problem right away. In other words, Lucy had to move. We didn't know how long Lucy had lived in the IRA's condo, but even one day was too many. The next month, to our surprise, we received another rent check from Lucy. So we made another call to Virginia to ask about the check once again. Virginia replied that Lucy needed a place to live and so was still residing in the condo. We told Virginia that we needed to meet with her to discuss what was permitted and what was not and to develop a plan to deal with and remediate the current issues. As one of us had another meeting near Virginia's home, she invited us to visit her there.

Virginia owns a vineyard. She sells the carefully tended grapes for top dollar and has been successful in her business. The visit was cordial. We provided her with information about the prohibited transaction codes from the IRS and left copies of the codes with her. She told us that she needed to have someone stay in the condo during the time that students were gone, and that her daughter Lucy had always served that purpose. She also told us that Lucy was there to make sure that the other roommates behaved in an appropriate manner and provided the funds to pay the rent. Lucy also made sure that one of the other roommates wrote the check for the rental payment. That comment appeared somewhat suspicious, but we ignored it as this was clearly a prohibited transaction in process. Virginia was informed about the $15,000 excise tax on prohibited transactions that may be applied if she did not correct the transaction. We also informed her that she would also face a potentially more severe penalty—disqualification of the IRA as of the beginning of the year. This would require a distribution of the entire amount in the IRA. Since this would be a premature distribution, as Virginia was under age 59-1/2, there would be an additional 10-percent premature distribution penalty. She would also have to pay tax on over $500,000 at her income tax rate. In addition, if she did not correct the prohibited transaction, she could face a 100-percent penalty on the amount distributed.

We left the idyllic setting, certain that she would correct her prohibited transaction. She could easily move Lucy to another condo and allow Lucy to look out for her IRA's best interest in a unit close by. It was certainly more difficult to rent the condo in the summer, but most owners factored in the loss of three months' rent by adjusting the rent over the other nine months. Surely, Lucy could be comfortable in another condo and still see to her mother's interest (with no compensation permitted, of course).

Four months after the first check had arrived from Lucy, we received rental payment through four checks. One was from Lucy. At this point we had no choice but to flag the account for detailed inspection of income and expense. We could no longer take liability for Virginia's actions, and we were obligated under the Internal Revenue Code to report the prohibited transaction. All of the assets in Virginia's IRA were distributed using a 1099-R reason code-prohibited transaction. The assets she held were assigned to her personally and the account was closed.

Two years later, we received a telephone call from Virginia. She had rolled the assets to another custodian, who accepted them. Through this conversation, we discovered that Virginia's daughter continued to live in the condo and also continued to make rental payments. Virginia had found a custodian who was either not as vigilant as we were or who simply didn't understand what a prohibited transaction was. Virginia stated that the IRS had sent her a notice of deficiency as a result of the 1099-R she received from us. She wanted us to help her. Because of our obligations under the code we could not do so. Virginia paid no attention to our advice or to her obligations as an IRA owner. She wanted to receive tax-deferred income while receiving two current benefits: a place for her daughter to live and further rental income. After the IRS assessed all the penalties, this cost Virginia not only her IRA, but also her beautiful income-producing vineyard. That was a big price to pay for so little gain.

Debt-Financed Property

You can have debt-financed property in any IRA or qualified plan (including a 401(k) option in a profit-sharing plan. However, if your net income on all your debt-financed property exceeds $1000 in a 12-month period, the portion of debt-financed property is subject to Unrelated Business Income Tax (UBIT).The IRA disclosure for UBIT is generally in the following format:

If the Depositor directs investment of the account in any investment that results in unrelated business taxable income, it shall be the responsibility of the Depositor to so advise the Custodian and to provide the Custodian with all information necessary to prepare and file any required returns or reports for the account. As the Custodian may deem necessary, and at the Depositor's expense, the Custodian may request a taxpayer identification number for the account, file any returns, reports, and applications for extension, and pay any taxes or estimated taxes owed with respect to the account. The Custodian may retain suitable accountants, attorneys, or other agents to assist it in performing such responsibilities.

UBIT is assessed when a retirement plan receives income from one of the following:

- A business owned or operated by the plan. Property that the plan improved through debt financing, such as real property in your account, or a margin account. Acquisition debt, such as a mortgage, is not subject to UBIT. Improvements in and of themselves are not subject to UBIT, only the debt used to finance them.
- A publicly traded partnership in which the plan owns an interest.

Certain exceptions to the normal UBIT rules apply to retirement plan investments. For example, a retirement fund that receives rent or lease income from real estate may be exempt from UBIT taxes. Rent or lease payments from personal property, such as a computer or MRI equipment, however, do not qualify for this exemption.

Rents that are not considered UBIT are:

- All rents from real property.
- All rents from personal property leased with real property if the rents attributable to the personal property are an incidental amount of the total rents received or accrued under the lease.

If rents attributable to personal property exceed 10 percent of the total rents from all the property leased, they are considered UBIT. For example, if personal property rents are $3000 per year, and the total rents from all property are $10,000 per year, the $3000 is UBIT and subject to tax.

Debt-financed property is any property held to produce income for which there is an acquisition indebtedness at any time during the tax year (or during the 12-month period before the date of the property's disposal if it was disposed of during the tax year). Such property includes rental real estate, tangible personal property, and corporate stock. Acquisition indebtedness is the unpaid amount of debt incurred when acquiring or improving the property, or before or after acquiring the property if the debt would not have been incurred except for the acquisition or improvement. If property (other than certain gifts, bequests, and devices) is acquired subject to a mortgage, the outstanding principal debt secured by that mortgage is treated as acquisition indebtedness. For example, if you paid $50,000 for real property valued at $150,000 and have a $100,000 mortgage, the $100,000 of outstanding principal debt is acquisition indebtedness.

In determining acquisition indebtedness, a lien similar to a mortgage is treated as a mortgage. A lien is similar to a mortgage if title to property is encumbered by the lien for a creditor's benefit. However, if state law provides that a lien for taxes or assessments attaches to property before the taxes or assessments become due and payable, the lien is not treated as a mortgage until after the taxes or assessments have become due and payable and you have had an opportunity to pay the lien in accordance with state law. Liens similar to mortgages include (but are not limited to):

- Deeds of trust
- Conditional sales contracts
- Chattel mortgages
- Security interests under the Uniform Commercial Code
- Pledges
- Agreements to hold title in escrow
- Liens for taxes or assessments

Extending, renewing, or refinancing an existing debt is considered a continuation of that debt if the outstanding principal does not increase. If the principal of the modified debt is more than the original outstanding principal, the excess is treated as a separate debt. The following are examples of acts resulting in the extension or renewal of a debt:

- Substituting liens to secure the debt
- Substituting obligees
- Renewing, extending, or accelerating the payment terms of the debt
- Adding, deleting, or substituting sureties or other primary or secondary obligors

For example, if you have an outstanding principal debt of $500,000 that is treated as acquisition indebtedness and you borrow another $100,000, which is not acquisition indebtedness, from the same lender, this results in a $600,000 note for the total obligation. A payment of $60,000 on the total obligation reduces the acquisition indebtedness by $50,000 and the excess debt by $10,000.

Acquisition indebtedness does not include an obligation, to the extent it is insured by the Federal Housing Administration, to finance the purchase, rehabilitation, or construction of housing for low or moderate income people.

If you sell debt-financed property, you must include a percentage of any gain or loss when computing the UBIT tax. The percentage is that of the highest acquisition indebtedness of the property during the 12-month period preceding the date of sale, in relation to the property's average adjusted basis.

The tax on this percentage of gain or loss is determined according to the usual rules for capital gains and losses. These amounts may be subject to the alternative minimum tax. If any part of the allowable capital loss is not taken into account in the current tax year, it may be carried back or carried over to another tax year without application of the debt/basis percentage for that year.

Average acquisition indebtedness is the average amount of outstanding principal debt during the part of the tax year that you hold the property. It is computed by determining how much principal debt is outstanding on the first day in each calendar month during the tax year that you hold the property, adding these amounts, and dividing the sum by the number of months during the year that you held the property. A partial month is treated as a full month.

The average adjusted basis of debt-financed property is the average of the adjusted basis of the property as of the first day and as of the last day that the organization holds the property during the tax year.

For example, on July 7, you buy an office building for $510,000 using $300,000 of borrowed funds, and you file your return on a calendar-year basis. During the year, the only adjustment to basis is $20,000 for depreciation. Starting July 28, you pay $20,000 each month on the mortgage principal plus interest. The debt/basis percentage for the year is calculated as shown in Table 4.2.

TABLE 4.2 Debt Basis Percentage Calculation

Month	Debt on 1st day of each month property is held
July	$300,000
August	$280,000
September	$260,000
October	$240,000
November	$220,000
December	$210,000
Total for each month	$1,500,000
Average acquisition indebtedness	$1,500,000 / 6 months = $250,000
Basis as of July 7	$510,000
Basis as of December 31	$490,000 (due to $20,000 depreciation)
Total basis	$1,000,000
Average adjusted basis	$1,000,000 / 2 = $500,000

Tax Forms for UBIT

The IRA trustee (or custodian or issuer) is responsible for filing Form 900-T and paying the tax, not the owner of the IRA. The tax is paid from your IRA funds. The problem is that the instructions for Form 990-T are not very clear. They state that the fiduciary of the IRA must file the form. The Department of Labor and IRS have stated that the IRA owner is a fiduciary under Internal Revenue Code 4975(e)(2), because IRA owners have the right to self-direct their investments. However, the IRS has stated that IRA trustees are also fiduciaries that must demonstrate fiduciary conduct. Yet the 990-T instructions also state that the trustee of more than one IRA can file a composite Form 990-T, but the law states that an individual (for example, an IRA owner) cannot act as trustee of an IRA. In fact, the IRS has ruled that if the IRA owner pays the UBIT tax, it is considered an IRA contribution. Form 990-T is not filed with your personal taxes. Instead, it is sent to the IRS.

Questions about Unrelated Business Income Tax Related to IRAs and Qualified Plans

What is debt-financed property in an IRA?

Debt-financed property is an IRS term for a mortgage or loan against an asset (among other definitions). For example, one type of debt-financed property is a loan secured by real estate in an IRA. The debt-financed portion is subject to unrelated business income tax. A tax may have to be paid depending on income and expense for the properties in question.

Specifics of unrelated business income tax are provided in the instructions for form 990-T. In addition, the IRA trustee (or custodian or issuer) is responsible for filing Form 900-T and paying the tax, not the IRA owner. The problem is that the Form 990-T instructions could be clearer. Page 2 of the 2000 990-T instructions states that the "fiduciary" of the IRA must file the form. The DOL & IRS have stated that the IRA owner is a fiduciary under IRC 4975(e)(2) because the IRA owner has the right to self-direct his investments. [Reg. 54.4975-6(a)(5); PLRs 8849001 and 8717079; DOL Advisory Opinion Letters 2000-10A and 90-20A] However, the IRS has stated that IRA trustees are also fiduciaries that must demonstrate fiduciary conduct. [Reg. 1.408-2(e)(2)] However on page 5, the 2000 990-T instructions "Composite Form 990-T" indicates that the trustee of more than one IRA may file a composite Form 990-T. An individual (e.g., IRA owner) cannot act as trustee of an IRA. [*Schoof v. Comm* (1998) No. 4265-96]

The IRA must pay UBIT. [PLR 9703026, ruling request #3] .... The IRS has ruled that if the IRA owner pays the UBIT, it is considered an IRA contribution. [PLR 88309061, ruling request #1]

[We] obtained a General Information Letter from IRS stating that the IRA owner is not responsible for preparing and filing Form 990-T. [IRS General Information Letter from Alan Pipkin, Manager Employee Plans Technical Group 5, March 26, 2001]. I also have spoken with the person [at

the] IRS responsible for Form 900-T, Joe Guilletti, a
is the IRA trustee who is responsible. Note: We are a
organizations incorrectly telling IRA owners that they

With respect to an IRA, Form 990-T does not get
sonal taxes," It gets filed to IRS at Ogden, UT. [200 ... uctions,
"Where to File", p. 3]

The custodian has no way of establishing the amount of UBIT for you. However, clients hire an outside accounting firm to first determine if UBIT exists and then prepare the 990-T for the IRA trustee. The fees for such accounting or legal services are deducted from the IRA balance.

When you direct your custodian to purchase leveraged real estate, whose credit is being evaluated? In other words, can you only buy leveraged real estate when the seller takes back paper, or can you or your IRA get a mortgage?

On a seller carryback, generally the seller's position is secured by the property sold to your IRA. Most often sellers don't evaluate the ability to repay, as they know they will get the real estate back.

An IRA can obtain a mortgage, provided that there is recourse only to the real property involved. The lender may not use your personal creditworthiness as part of the loan requirements, or make you guarantee the loan to the IRA. A guarantee or using your credit could be considered a contribution to and IRA, which is not in cash. Noncash contributions are not permitted to IRAs.

Hard-money lenders tend not to have a problem with this, but institutional lenders do. Institutional lenders also want to package loans and sell them, and loans made to IRAs and qualified plans are generally not readily marketable.

If you have a qualified plan that permits noncash contributions under certain conditions, the lender may lend you money based on your credit, but the loan payments must come from the plan and you may not personally guarantee payment. The value of the contribution would probably be the difference of what the lender would lend the funds at without the credit check. If it is acquisition debt, it would not be subject to Unrelated Business Income Tax. However, the contribution rules may still apply.

...s and Your IRA

Many individuals feel that they can obtain "control" of an IRA by having a company, such as an LLC, formed and having the IRA purchase original issue stock, subsequently directing the trustee of the IRA to name them as the managing director. In that way, the company owned by the IRA would be in a position to make all investment decisions, collect all income, and make all expense payments. At the time a distribution is taken, the trustee would make the required minimum distributions. The company would involve the trustee for any distributions made if a Roth IRA were involved, as distributions from Roth IRAs must also be reported.

After looking at this potential capability in light of the *Swanson v. Commissioner* case, we asked Maura Ann McBreen about certain aspects of such ownership and the issues that you might encounter in using the IRA owning a company which you "control." Her comments were:

IRA's Ownership in Operating and Nonoperating Companies

If the company is not an operating company, the company needs to make sure that the company does not engage in any prohibited transactions. In addition, IRA assets include a proportionate interest in each company asset; the company officers and directors are likely to be considered fiduciaries of the IRA; compensation and indemnification of officers and directors may give rise to prohibited transactions, and prohibited transactions may result if the company engages in business transactions with disqualified persons.

Under ERISA's plan asset regulation, "operating company" is defined as an entity that is:

"primarily engaged, directly or through a majority owned subsidiary or subsidiaries, in the production or sale of a product or service other than investment capital." (ERISA Reg. Section 2510.3-101(c)).

This definition lacks precision and accordingly creates a great deal of uncertainty as to what constitutes an operating company.

The preamble to the plan asset regulation provides, in pertinent part, as follows:

" This exclusion was intended to distinguish between companies that carry on an active trade or business, and which thus are not likely vehicles for the indirect provision of investment management services.... In general whether a particular company is, or is not, an operating company under the final regulation is a factual question to be resolved taking into account the particular characteristics of the entity under consideration....Although in most cases it is relatively easy to characterize an entity as either an operating company or an investment fund, some companies do carry on both kinds of activities. The Department of Labor has concluded...it would be impractical to provide detailed guidance concerning the types of activities necessary for characterization as an operating company. (51 FR 41262 (November 13, 1986)

An IRA or qualified plan cannot own 100 percent of an operating company if you want the IRA/plan assets to be limited to the equity interest in the entity. If the IRA or qualified plan owns all the outstanding equity interest in the (other than director's qualifying shares) entity (including an operating company) the IRA or Plan assets include those entity interests and all the underlying assets of the entity. ERISA Reg. Section 2510.3-101(h)(3). In other words, if the IRA or qualified plan owns all the outstanding stock of an operating company (other than director's qualifying shares), there is a "look through" to the underlying assets of the operating company, and such underlying assets (as well as shares of stock) are IRA or plan assets.

The non-IRA stockholder of the operating company would have veto power because of ERISA Reg. Section 2509.75-2 ("IB 75-2"). IB 75-2 is an Interpretive Ruling issued by the Department of Labor relating to prohibited transactions. IB 75-2 generally provide that if a transaction between a disqualified person and an IRA would be a prohibited transaction, then such transaction between a disqualified person and a corporation or partnership will be a prohibited transaction if the IRA may, by itself, require the corporation or partnership to engage in the transaction. For example, the sale of any property between the IRA owner and his IRA is a prohibited transaction. Code Section 4975 (c) (1) (A). The sale of any property between the IRA owner and a corporation would also be a prohibited transaction under IB 75-2, if the IRA could compel the corporation to sell the property to the IRA owner. If the non-IRA stockholder has veto power, the IRA cannot, by itself (and even if it owns 99 percent of the stock), compel the corporation to engage in a transaction.

Assuming that the IRA owns less than 100 percent of an operating company and that, the non-IRA stockholder has veto power, prohibited transaction issues can still arise. The stock of the operating company that is held by the IRA is an IRA asset, and a transaction involving such stock could be a prohibited transaction. In this regard, particular attention should be paid to the fact that Code Section 4975 prohibits indirect transactions that involve plan assets.

If the IRA or plan owns 100 percent of the original stock, then the stock and all the underlying assets of an LLC are assets of the IRA. As a result, the prohibited transaction rules attach to all such IRA assets—the stock and underlying assets of the LLC.

The IRA owner is a fiduciary of the IRA. Once the IRA acquired 100 percent of the original issue stock, consideration must first be given to whether appointing the IRA owner as the president or managing director is itself a prohibited transaction. In other words, the IRS has issued some private letter rulings to the effect that the IRA owner may have engaged in self-dealing if the investment by the IRA causes him to be named president or managing director.

Assuming that the naming of the IRA owner as president or managing director is not a prohibited transaction, then it is possible for the IRA owner as president or managing director to make all the decisions regarding the LLC without engaging in a prohibited transaction. However, each transaction would have to be carefully reviewed since all of the transactions would involve plan assets. Further, the absence of a current benefit to any Disqualified Person does not necessarily mean there is no prohibited transaction. Prohibited transactions are "per se" violations; it does not matter whether there is a benefit.

Because of the construction of LLCs and other such entities, including any other corporate format, we encourage that you only use this capability with sound and competent legal advice. The legal advice may be expensive, but it will be far less than prohibited transaction penalties and taxes.

24 Steps to Successful Tax-Deferred and Tax-Free Investing in Real Estate

1. You elect to obtain the best tax advantage from results of your real estate investment activity.
2. You compare the various tax-advantaged alternatives and decide which works best for you. Among these are:
   - Personal purchase and obtain various standard write-offs such as out of-pocket expenses associated with the investment and depreciation.
   - Use of Your and Other People's IRAs (OPI) or qualified plans to make the investment you wish.

- You review the possibility of Tax-Deferred Exchanges as a possible strategy for your real estate investments.
- You review the possibilities of using the Homeowners Exemption as an investment and tax-free strategy for income.
- You seek the assistance of a financial planner, accountant, and attorney to help guide you in the decision-making process.
- If you decide to use a retirement plan vehicle to fund your transaction, you continue with the steps below. If not, keep reading the following chapters in this book and then decide!

3. You decide to use your IRA or 401(k) and or OPI and other 401(k)s, or other qualified plan.
4. You decide what type of property that is permitted in the retirement plan.
5. You review the Prohibited Transaction Rules Carefully so that you know that you will self-deal or accidentally cause your IRA or Qualified plan to become disqualified.
6. You establish a budget concerning what you can spend. You can include personal funds under the right circumstances, as well as Other People's Money (OPM), and debt financed on a nonrecourse lender.
7. If you are going alone, make sure that you have sufficient cash in your account to meet all expenses and a contingency fund.
8. If you will be having partners, be sure that you are all in agreement regarding purchase and sale objectives. Define exit strategies for all concerned.
9. If you will be using a lender to debt finance your plan's purchase, nonrecourse lenders are not always easy to find. Find one first explaining to them that your plan is doing the borrowing, and that you will not be guaranteeing the debt. Remember, carryback loans are permitted, where the seller finances your acquisition. Any nondisqualified person may do so. If borrowing is not an alternative, or too expensive, rethink your plan, or find other partners.
10. Find a trustee or administrator close to you who sponsors and services self-directed IRAs and/or qualified plans.
11. Begin the opening account process. Opening the account takes about 20 minutes. Transferring or rolling over funds and other assets generally may take from two to four weeks. Plan accordingly. Make sure your partners and any financing is lined up solidly, and any retirement accounts are self-directed and in place.

12. You begin shopping for investment property that meets your and, if you have partners, their investment objectives.
13. Locate the property and write a purchase contract in your name for the benefit of your IRA or plan along with others participating with you.
14. Complete a Buy Direction Letter, which you send or fax to your trustee or local administrator, which establishes the parameters of the purchase.
15. Inform the title company, escrow company, and/or attorney you will be using to call your trustee or administrator. Provide them with the documentation needed to complete the purchase.
16. You will need to read and approve all documents involved in the purchase transaction. Don't skip any. In about 20 percent of purchases and sales, there is something wrong with documents, particularly settlement statements. Your trustee or administrator will sign all documents on behalf of your IRA or plan.
17. Your trustee or administrator will compare all documents to each other to ensure that your instructions and the purchase comport with each other. If changes are required you will need to ensure that your goals and objectives are met.
18. If property is rented, be sure that the assignment of any leases or rental agreements will be made at the time of closing.
19. If you are funding a note secured by real property, ensure that you have the payer's address and social security number for proper IRS reporting.
20. For debt financing of real estate, the lender will be paid from your IRA or plan account. Any invoices or payment books need to be sent to the trustee or administrator of your IRA. In the case of an Individual (k), where you are the trustee, you will be making payments from the trust's account.
21. All income from the investment will be credited to your trust account. All expenses, such as utilities, maintenance, etc., will be made from the same account.
22. You may hire a nondisqualified entity to service your properties. That entity can provide all income, expenses, and other services to your IRA or plan and send the net proceeds to your account.
23. If you decide to sell the property, or sell your interest in it, you will be completing a Sell Direction Letter when you have found a buyer. The

terms and conditions of the sale will be compared to the purchase contract you have completed.

24. The proceeds of the sale must come to your plan. You will then be able to make your next real estate transaction with the proceeds.

PART 2

REAL PROPERTY EXCHANGES

The Early Days

Since the early days of taxation and the development of the Internal Revenue Code of 1954, gains and losses on investment property have been subject to tax treatment. Of primary concern for most people is the potential tax on capital gains resulting from a sale of real property. Historically, if you realized a gain on real property but did not want to use the profit for personal purposes, the gain had to be recognized as a taxable event. One way to avoid paying capital gains tax was to trade or exchange properties. However, until 1979, the tax laws required that any properties being traded or exchanged had to be swapped simultaneously. This requirement made exchanging properties extremely difficult. In the 1979 *Starker* decision, the courts overruled the existing exchange rules and allowed delayed exchanges of real property to qualify for tax deferral. The *Starker* ruling made exchanges easier by granting investors time to find "replacement" property, generally through the services of a professional intermediary.

1991 and the Beginning of the Section 1031 Exchange

In 1991, the *Starker* decision was codified as Section 1031 of the Internal Revenue Code. Section 1031 both validated the concept of delayed exchange and simplified the exchange process. (The term 1031 is similar to the term 401(k). Both refer to sections of the tax laws that govern specific activities. Regulation 1031 refers to deferral of tax on property in an exchange, and 401(k) is a section of the Internal Revenue Code for qualified retirement plans allowing contributions through employee deferrals.)

The adoption of Section 1031 was an important development for real estate investors. Before the advent of delayed property exchanges, many real property investors preferred to hold their property for a long period of time in order to avoid paying taxes of up to 40 percent on their total capital gains when they sold their property. This made financial planning relative to real estate investments difficult in many cases. Effective financial planning generally needs to be able to adapt to evolving client and investment needs over time. Impetus for changes in investment objectives, goals, and needs can come from a variety of sources, including:

- International, national, and local economics
- Environmental issues
- Estate building
- Retirement
- Cash flow
- Personal circumstances

The exchange mechanism adopted by Section 1031 gives real estate investors a powerful tool for managing their real estate portfolios. By using Section 1031 exchanges, real estate investors can more easily adapt their real estate portfolio to their changing personal and financial objectives. Used properly, a 1031 tax-deferred exchange can help investors achieve their investment objectives without losing anticipated profit or potential equity increases to taxes in the short term.

In the period since 1991, 1031 exchanges have become a popular method for deferring taxes on a sale and subsequent purchase of investment property. The IRS specifies the exact requirements for the types of property that may be exchanged and provides definitions of terms specific to the exchange process. A thorough understanding of the relevant terms and basic requirements of Section 1031 is an important part of any determination as to whether the exchange process may be used in any particular circumstance.

How to Use This Part

This part will provide you with important information about deferring taxes through exchanging properties under specific, understandable rules. Each of the two chapters provides you with building blocks to enable you to work with professionals and make your tax-deferred real estate exchange a positive experience.

Chapter 5, "Like-Kind and Qualifying Property," provides a description of what kind of properties may be exchanged for others. This section also provides an overview of the process of using the tax-deferred exchange.

Chapter 6, "Exchange Transactions and How They Are Completed" gives you examples of actual transactions using the Exchange requirements established in Chapter 1. The mechanics of performing the tax-deferred exchanges are also included in this chapter. At the end of this part there are 14 steps to make a Real Estate 1031 exchange work for you.

CHAPTER 5

Like-Kind and Qualifying Property

A proper 1031 exchange requires that property be exchanged only for like-kind property. To qualify as a like-kind exchange, both the property being transferred away (the "relinquished property") and the property received (the "replacement property") must be considered to be:

- Like-kind property and
- Qualifying property.

The IRS specifies like-kind property as properties of the same nature or character, even if they differ in grade or quality. All real estate will generally be considered to qualify as like-kind, regardless of whether a property is improved or unimproved. For example, an exchange that swaps land improved with a single-family dwelling for a commercial building would be considered a like-kind exchange. The types of property that are not considered to be "like-kind" for exchange purposes are:

- Properties used for personal purposes, such as your home
- Real estate held by a dealer
- Accounts receivable, securities, or notes or other debt instruments
- Partnerships interests

- Foreign property, except as included in condemned property
- Goodwill

In addition, the Internal Revenue Code specifies that an exchange may be accomplished only if all of the properties involved in the exchange are located within the 50 United States. Real property outside the United States is not considered "like-kind" property.

Not only must the property being exchanged meet the like-kind requirements, it must also be considered qualifying property. With respect to the relinquished property, this means that the relinquished property must have been held for investment or use in a trade or business. Similarly, the replacement property must be intended solely for investment or use in a trade or business.

Identification of Replacement Property

In any 1031 exchange, you have 45 days after the sale of the relinquished property to locate the property or properties you wish to purchase for the exchange. The closing on the replacement property must occur within 180 days after the replacement property is identified.

There are three alternative rules that govern the identification process for replacement properties:

- Number of properties: You may purchase up to three properties of any fair market value.
- Value of properties: In the alternative, you may purchase any number of properties whose combined fair market value at the end of the identification period does not exceed 200 percent of the total fair market value of the relinquished property as of the date of closing.
- The 95-percent rule: If you identify more properties than prescribed by the regulations, the IRS will treat your exchange as if no properties had been identified, with two exceptions:
  - Any property you received before the end of the 45-day identification period will treated as identified.
  - Any single property you identified and received before the end of the identification period and having a fair market value of at least 95 per-

cent of the aggregate fair market value of all identified properties will be treated as identified.

Regulatory guidelines require that the replacement property(ies) must be properly identified by a legal description, such as an Assessor's Parcel Number, street address, or other description that distinguishes it from other potential property. This description needs to be in written form and delivered to a person who is not disqualified, such as a transfer agent for the property or qualified intermediary. Any change to or revocation of description must be provided in writing to the person(s) originally involved in the identification of the property.

Actual Exchange

In any valid 1031 exchange, there must be an actual "exchange," meaning that the proceeds from the sale of the relinquished property remain in escrow until they are used to purchase the replacement property. If you receive (or have the right to receive) any of the sale proceeds from the relinquished property, a subsequent purchase of a replacement property will not qualify for tax-deferred treatment.

Basis of Property

Determining the tax implications of sales and exchanges requires establishing the tax basis of the properties involved. Basis is used to determine gain upon the disposition of an asset. In simple terms, basis is an owner's investment in the asset. For purchased property, the starting basis is the original price paid (plus any acquisition costs). An asset's basis can be increased (e.g., by making improvements to real property) or decreased (e.g., after a casualty loss reduces the value of an asset). It can also change when factoring in how an asset was acquired and the circumstances surrounding the eventual disposition. Adjusted basis refers to changes in basis after an asset was acquired.

Tax basis for a particular year is calculated as follows:

1. Original purchase price
2. Plus capital improvements made

3. Minus depreciation expense or loss
4. Minus partial sales of property at fair market value
5. Minus fair market value of improvements removed
6. Equals property tax basis at the end of the tax year.

The key elements of the basis calculation are as follows:

1. Capital Improvements: These are defined in the Internal Revenue Code and must be distinguished from maintenance of property.
2. Depreciation Expense: This is determined by the IRS definitions of those expenses that are acceptable.
3. Partial sales of property: These are calculated at fair market value, as defined in the Code.
4. Improvements removed: The value is calculated after depreciation expense and at fair market value.

In an exchange, absent the need for an infusion of additional cash, the basis of the relinquished property will be the same as the basis of the replacement property. For example, if you have an adjusted basis of $100,000 in an investment property you sold and exchanged for other investment property, both of which properties have a fair market value of $200,000, the basis of the new property is the same as the old, or $100,000.

If you have to use additional cash to cover any difference between the sale price of the relinquished property and the purchase price of the replacement property, you still have no tax, or recognizable gain, as the additional cash simply increases your basis in the new property. For example: You have a property worth $100,000 and exchange it for property worth $150,000. If you use cash to make up the difference of $50,000, you will have no recognizable gain because of the cash infusion. If you decided to sell the investment property you originally owned for $100,000 and did not use an exchange to acquire a replacement property, you have a taxable event on the sale. If you later purchased a new investment property for $150,000, you have effectively lost the amount of any tax you paid on the gain the sale of the $100,000 property.

Exchange Expenses

Exchange expenses simply refer to the closing costs you pay in order to complete an exchange, including brokers' commissions, legal fees, title and escrow fees, and administration fees. The amount of any exchange expenses will be deducted from any amounts you receive in the exchange. If you realized a gain on the exchange, or received unlike-kind property in the exchange, the expense payments are subtracted from the fair market value of the property you received. The recognized gain is the net after deduction of the exchange expenses.

CHAPTER 6

Exchange Transactions and How They Are Completed

Example of an Exchange of Investment Property—Lisa's Exchange Transaction

Lisa has been an active investor since 1978 and, over time, she has determined that her personal capabilities and long-term objectives were oriented towards investment real estate and notes.

Lisa owns a rental property in California and decides to sell it after her long-time tenant opted not to exercise a purchase option on the property. After speaking with her financial planner and accountant, she decides that she also does not want to pay capital gains on the proceeds from the sale of the property. When she purchased the property five years earlier, the purchase price of the single-family starter home was $170,000 and the current value was $360,000. She decides to defer paying taxes on her gain by using a 1031 exchange. Lisa knows that under Section 1031 certain rules apply to her contemplated deferral of the gain. So, before she put the rental up for sale, Lisa did what every person contemplating a 1031 exchange does: She found out what the current exchange rules meant to her plan for deferral of taxes.

Provided that Lisa adheres to the rules under Section 1031, when Lisa exchanges her property, she will pay no capital gains or ordinary income tax. The taxes due on the exchanged property are deferred, meaning that at some point taxes will be paid by the owner of the property. However, in the interim, "[n]o gain or loss shall be recognized if property held for productive use in a trade or business or for investment purposes is exchanged solely for property of like-kind." (IRC Section 1031)

Step One: Lisa Must Satisfy the Like-Kind and Qualifying Property Requirements

In accordance with the rules governing 1031 exchanges, the property that Lisa looks for must be somewhere in the 50 United States and may be any of the following types of properties to qualify as a like-kind property:

- A rental home like what she sold in California for rental units elsewhere (as long as it cash flows)
- A retail strip center
- An apartment complex
- Bare land
- Improved property
- An office building

In addition to the types of properties listed above, the IRS also considers a leasehold estate with a remaining term of at least 30 years a "like-kind" property. As you can see, Lisa's options for exchanging her rental property are numerous, as she does not have to exchange her rental property for exactly the same type of property.

In order to ensure that she meets the qualifying property requirements, Lisa decides to look for a rental property that she will hold for investment purposes. Lisa is aware that any property she finds may not qualify as an investment property if she, or any member of her family, moves in for personal use soon after the exchange is made. Lisa's relinquished property already meets the qualifying property requirements because she held it as an investment property.

Step 2: Lisa Must Comply with the 45-Day Identification and 180-Day Acquisition Requirements

Lisa knows that within 45 days after the sale of her California property, she had to locate the property(ies) she wanted to purchase for the exchange. She also knew that the closing on the replacement property had to occur within 180 days after the replacement property was identified.

In an exchange, timing is everything, so Lisa had to keep in mind that if the property sold and closed quickly, she had only 45 days to identify replacement property. However, Lisa could extend the amount of time she had to locate the replacement property by establishing a longer escrow and later closing date for her California property. Before putting her California property on the market, Lisa had her real estate agent in California look at her property to determine if it was in salable condition. Lisa's agent determined that Lisa's current property needed some cosmetic maintenance, such as interior paint and replacement carpeting. Lisa hired a painter to paint the interior and a local carpet company to install new carpeting.

Lisa determined that the property she wanted as replacement property would be located in Florida, due to favorable market conditions there. Lisa took a trip to Florida to research the market. Before her trip to Florida, Lisa made sure she fully understood the "identification" rules that would apply to any replacement property she selected.

Lisa decided that her long-range plans were best fulfilled by acquiring at least three rental units with a minimum value equal to the sales price of her relinquished property. By using a 1031 exchange, Lisa was able to identify properties worth hundreds of thousand dollars, and then acquire them without any immediate tax consequence from the sale of her current property. Considering the anticipated sales price of $340,000 for her California property, Lisa decided to purchase three or more properties worth no more than a total of $700,000. After her trip to Florida and based on information from investors she knew in Florida, she signed a contract to put her California rental up for sale. Then, as required by the 1031 exchange rules, within 45 days after the "sale" of her California property, Lisa "identified" her replacement properties.

Step 3: Exchange

Before closing the sale of her relinquished property, Lisa arranged for the proceeds from the sale to be placed with a qualified intermediary. The intermediary will be responsible for handling the details of the 1031 exchange for the replacement property. This includes holding the proceeds of the sale of the California property in escrow, so that Lisa will not have actual or constructive possession of the sale proceeds from the relinquished property during the time period between sale of the relinquished property and acquisition of the Florida replacement property. Her 1031 qualified intermediary also made sure Lisa understood that the contract for sale in California needed to state that Lisa could assign the contract and that the contract is for the benefit of both Lisa and her assigns. This allows Lisa to assign the contract to the intermediary and is a further assurance that Lisa will not have actual or constructive possession of the sale proceeds.

Debt Financing in a 1031 Exchange—Lisa's Financing of Her Exchange

By "leveraging" the purchase of her replacement properties, Lisa is also able to purchase four to five times as much real estate than she would have otherwise.

If property appreciates by 10 percent, that appreciation is converted to a 50-percent profit with a 20-percent down payment. The amount available to invest is five times 20 percent, because of leverage. Five times 10 percent is 50 percent.

For example, in Lisa's case, the value of leverage from using an exchange versus a simple sale is shown by her tax rate of 40 percent on her gains from the sale:

$340,000 (anticipated sales proceeds) x 40 percent = $136,000

If she sold her California property with a gain of $340,000 after costs, she would pay taxes of $136,000 and have only $204,000 left to reinvest. On the other hand, if she uses an exchange, she pays no capital gains tax, leaving the entire $340,000 to reinvest (see Table 6.1).

Using the exchange process also increases the amount Lisa can afford to pay for her replacement properties. If Lisa simply sold her rental property and used the $204,000 she has to reinvest as a 20-percent down payment, she would be able to afford property totaling $1,020,000. By acquiring new property through a 1031 exchange, Lisa's 20-percent down payment would

TABLE 6.1 Lisa's Financing of Her Exchange

Sale		Exchange	
Proceeds	$340,000	Proceeds	$340,000
Tax Owed	–$136,000	Tax Owed	-0-
Cash to Reinvest	$204,000	Cash to Reinvest	$340,000

be the full $340,000 gained from the sale of her original property, which would allow her to purchase replacement properties totaling $1,700,000.

In other words, in a single transaction, Lisa could have an additional $680,000 with which to purchase property as a result of using an exchange rather than simply selling her property. In this case, Lisa has chosen to limit the value of her replacement properties to $700,000. As a result, with $340,000 in cash, she can easily obtain loans totaling $360,000 to reach her limit of $700,000. Lisa's decision on the maximum purchase value of her replacement properties was driven in part by her need to ensure that the replacement properties generate sufficient cash flow to make the underlying debt payment, at the very least.

Lisa has an excellent relationship with her lender, a community bank, and made sure to line up the credit before she went shopping. Lisa also knew that because the properties were nonowner occupied she would pay slightly more in interest to her lender. The lender knew the qualified intermediary, and also understood how 1031 exchanges work.

Lisa decided to look for three rental properties, all of which needed to have tenants who paid on time. The properties also had to have sufficient cash flow to pay both the debt as well as a reasonable profit. Lisa outlined these criteria to her real estate agent in Florida.

Lisa ended up acquiring four separate properties with purchase prices totaling $680,000. While the purchase of four houses exceeded the three-property rule, the purchase price was less than 200 percent of the fair market value of her relinquished property, which was $340,000, so Lisa's proposed replacement properties were properly identified.

The loan amount of $360,000 for the four properties had a loan to value ratio of 50 percent. The monthly rents on the combined properties amounted to $4800, which more than met the loan payments, property tax, and hazard insurance.

Using a 1031 Exchange to Obtain an Increase in the Amount of Depreciation

Depreciation refers to a method for adjusting the value of improvements to real estate over time, in order to either write off the property or recover costs. The IRS recognizes two systems for depreciating improvements to real property: the General Depreciation System and the Alternative Depreciation System. Both systems fall under the umbrella of the IRS "Modified Accelerated Cost Recovery System." The difference between the two systems is the length of time over which depreciation can be taken. The General Depreciation System allows depreciation over 27.5 years. The Alternative Depreciation System allows depreciation over 40 years.

Deductions for calculation of depreciation are posted against preadjusted taxable income. The effect of deductions for depreciation is a reduction in your tax basis in the property equal to the amount of depreciation.

Land is generally not a depreciable asset, however certain modifications and improvements to land, such as roads and culverts, may increase the value of land.

The following example shows how depreciation expense works in simple terms:

Your income is $50,000 before depreciation expense. Your tax basis in a rental unit is $500,000 and your depreciation on that unit is $25,000. Your taxable income, with all other factors remaining equal, is reduced by the amount of the depreciation on the rental unit, or $25,000. Your basis in the property is now also reduced by $25,000 to $475,000. If you were to sell the property for the amount of the previous year's tax basis ($500,000), your taxable gain on which you are taxed would be $25,000, or the amount of the depreciation expense.

From a tax-planning perspective, you can receive depreciation credit from the IRS and realize reductions in taxable income. Those reductions in taxable income translate into real dollars on which you do not pay taxes unless or until you sell the property.

Roger's Dilemma: Sell or Exchange

Roger has a property that he leases to two nondisqualified persons. (Nondisqualified persons are Roger's ascendants, descendants, siblings, spouses thereof, any one who may represent him in an exchange, which includes any person with whom he has any business, accounting, or legal personal or business connection.) He originally paid $60,000 for the property 15 years ago. The current market value is $275,000, which includes a $25,000 mortgage. Roger looked at the alternatives for selling the property versus exchanging. Part of his plan was to purchase a $950,000 fourplex, either directly or through a 1031 exchange. Roger is 45 years old and does not have any need for cash, but he is interested in keeping taxable events to a minimum.

On analyzing his options:

- Roger discovered that the tax on a sale was $75,000, whereas with the exchange there would be no tax.
- In addition, acquisition of the fourplex would cost Roger an additional $125,250 when he sold the property.
- Exchange of the property would mean that Roger only has to come up with an additional $50,000.
- Depreciation expense is about equal for a sale or an exchange.

The net result is that Roger opted to use a 1031 exchange. By using a 1031 exchange, the savings Roger would realize from not having to pay taxes on the sale of his existing property would be enough to allow Roger to make other more significant investments. The comparison of Roger's options is shown in Table 6.2.

Co-ownership, versus Partnership: Structuring Ownership of Income Real Property for Tax-Deferred Exchanges

Often individuals form partnerships with others in order to invest in real estate. This provides the group with more capital to make larger and more varied real estate purchases. However, if the group of investors wishes to use tax-deferred exchanges to transfer their individual interests in the jointly owned properties, only certain types of ownership structures may be used.

In 2002, the IRS issued Revenue Procedure 2002-22, 2002-14 Internal Revenue Bulletin 1 (the "Revenue Procedure"), which addressed the requirements that apply to a group of individuals who invest together in a

TABLE 6.2 Roger's Sale of Rental and Purchase of Fourplex

Sale and Purchase		Exchange	
Current depreciation	$0	Current Depreciation	$0
Current Equity	$250,000	Current Equity	$250,000
Existing Mortgage	$25,000	Existing Mortgage	$25,000
Net market value	$275,000	Net market value	$275,000
Sales Price	$275,000		
Original Basis	$60,000	Basis	$60,000
Taxable Gain	$215,000	Mortgage	–$25,000
Tax at 35%	$75,250	New Mortgage	$650,000
Mortgage	$25,000	Cash Paid by Roger at Closing	$50,000
Cash received by seller	$250,000		
Less capital Gains Tax	$75,250	Capital Gains Tax	0
Net cash to Roger	$174,750		
Purchase			
Price	$950,000	Price	$950,000
Mortgage	$650,000	Mortgage	$650,000
Cash Needed	$300,000		
Equity Rental Sold	$250,000		
Cash from above Sale	$174,750	Cash Roger Pays	$50,000
Additional Cash from Roger	$125,250	Equity Fourplex	$300,000
New Basis	$950,000	New Basis	$925,000
		Land	$231,250
Depreciation Basis		Building	$693,750
Relationship of Improvements to Land	$712,500		
Rate of Depreciation		Rate of Depreciation	
at Straight Line 27.5 years	$25,909	at Straight Line 27.5 years	$25,227
Cash Paid to Purchase		Cash Paid to Purchase	
Property	$125,250	Property	$50,000
Equity in Purchase	$300,000	Equity in Purchase	$300,000

real property transaction and wish to preserve ability to transfer their interests individually through 1031 exchanges. The most important requirement is that any such group of investors must apply for and obtain a Private Letter Ruling ("PLR") from the IRS affirming that the proposed co-ownership arrangement will give each individual investor an undivided ownership interest. Without a PLR, the IRS may treat the entire ownership arrangement as one in which each of the owners holds only an intangible property right, such as a partnership interest or stock interest, in an entity separate from its owners. This would make the disposition of each undivided interest ineligible for 1031 treatment.

Once a particular co-ownership arrangement has obtained the necessary PLR, they must then comply with the remaining requirements of the Revenue Procedure, which are as follows:

1. Formation. Each investor in the group must own an undivided interest and the group must hold the property as tenants-in-common under state law. The owners may not have previously held interests in the property through another legal entity, such as a partnership. Existing co-ownership arrangements formed as partnerships, limited liability companies (LLCs), or limited liability partnerships (LLPs), for example, will not be able to take advantage of the Revenue Procedure.
2. Management and control. The fees paid to sponsors or property or asset managers cannot be based on the income or profitability of the property. A sponsor is the person who structures the undivided interest arrangement for purposes of offering undivided interests for sale.

   Interest holders or owners must have the absolute right to vote on issues of disposition, leasing or re-leasing, and debt encumbrance of the property (in each case by unanimous consent). Other activities of the owners are limited to those customarily performed in connection with maintenance and repair of rental property.

   Third-party property managers must have their contracts renewed annually (by unanimous consent of the owners). Any such property manager must distribute revenue at least quarterly.

   No owner, sponsor, or manager may advance funds to cover payments due from another owner (such as an owner's share of operating or capital expenses) unless the debt is with recourse. Such debt must be repaid within 31 days.
3. Allocation. Allocation of income and expenses, as well as liabilities for comprehensive encumbrances, must be in direct relationship to each owner's percentage ownership interest.
4. Right to Cash Out. Each owner has the right to transfer, partition, and encumber his or her ownership interest, subject to any limits established

by a lien holder for the entire asset. Rights of first refusal from owners, as a condition to exercising their rights of transfer, are permitted provided the sale is made at fair market value as of the date of the offer.

The Revenue Procedure applies to all forms of co-ownership of rental real estate. While the Revenue Procedure is oriented towards sponsors, participants, and professional advisors of organized undivided interest programs, it is not limited to those entities or individuals. The Revenue Procedure should be understood and appreciated by anyone dealing with potential 1031 opportunities, so that ownership and operations of any real estate investment can be structured for maximum flexibility.

Bruce's Real Estate Exchange Ventures

Bruce has been a real estate investor for a number of years and often finds transactions that exceed the funds he has available. He has a number of business acquaintances who often invest alongside him in larger ventures. Some of these investors have found that they like to use exchanges to divest themselves of their interests as their personal requirements change. Accordingly, Bruce ensures that the purchases made by the group are structured so that the property is owned by the group as tenants-in-common, with each investor holding an undivided interest. Bruce acts as the sponsor for these transactions. In this way, each individual owner is able to use a 1031 exchange to transfer ownership of their undivided interest.

If Bruce and his friends were to form a partnership, LLC, or other such entity, the individual partners or shareholders would be unable to use a 1031 exchange with respect to their individual shares. The tax code prohibits exchanges by such ownership forms. Furthermore, the owners may not have held interests in the property through an ownership interest in any previous legal entity.

Generally, if the Revenue Procedure arrangements are followed, Bruce would have no issue with individuals exchanging out of a transaction that he sponsors. For added protection, Bruce could set forth the facts and circumstances of any of his transactions and apply for a Private Letter Ruling.

To summarize, tax-deferred exchanges provide another method to defer tax in real estate. The most significant difference between holding real property in a retirement account and exchanging property is that in a retirement account your IRA or Qualified plan owns the property, and you have no access to it. In a tax-deferred exchange you own the investment property and can sell it provided you have a QI in the middle when you acquire additional property. The rules for a tax-deferred exchange are significantly smaller in number than for retirement plans.

14 Steps in a Successful Tax-Deferred Exchange

1. You decide that it is in your interest to obtain the best tax advantages on the proceeds of an investment property you wish to sell.
2. You decide if there is any amount that you wish to keep as taxable income, or if you wish to add funds to a newly acquired property.
3. This is accomplished through a tax-deferred exchange. You put the real property up for sale.
4. You decide what type of property you wish to acquire that meets like kind exchange rules, and you begin looking for the replacement property.
5. You find a qualified intermediary for the exchange.
6. You enter into a contract with a buyer to sell the relinquished property. The contract is drafted so that you, the seller, have the right to assign the contract.
7. You notify the (QI) of the pending sale.
8. The QI prepares an exchange agreement between you and the QI with instructions to the escrow agent, title company, and/or attorney for completing the transaction as well as settlement statement requirements.
9. You transfer the relinquished property to the buyer, and the escrow agent disburses the net proceeds from the sale to the QI.
10. Within 45 days from closing on the relinquished property, you identify the replacement property(ies) from step 4 above, and notify the QI formally of the property(ies) you have identified.
11. You execute the purchase agreement(s) to purchase the replacement property(ies), which includes language allowing you to assign the agreement(s).
12. You assign the replacement property agreement(s) to the QI.

13. Within 180 days from the date you closed on the relinquished property, the QI completes the purchase of replacement property(ies) using net exchange proceeds, plus any additional funds needed to balance the transaction, with legal title transferred from the seller of the replacement property(ies) directly to you.
14. At end of the 180 days period, the QI sends you any funds due you, if any.

PART 3

HOME SALE EXCLUSION

In March of 2002, the Internal Revenue Service issued guidelines regarding the exclusion of gain on the sale of a principal residence. These guidelines included both final and temporary regulations. A 1997 law substituted an exclusion of up to $250,000 ($500,000 for a married couple filing jointly) for the old "replacement residence" rules. This law replaced old personal residence sale rules with new rules that provide an additional way to receive tax-free gain. The new rules also apply to a larger segment of the population. Previously, only a person over the age of 55 could exclude a maximum of $125,000 in gain and could do so only one time. The new exclusion may be claimed by any person who qualifies and may be claimed repeatedly, but in most circumstances only once every two years.

The new law also provided for partial exclusions and certain "safe harbors" for specific circumstances. An example of this would be an "Installment sale." An installment sale is defined as selling a home with a contract that provides for all or part of the proceeds to be paid in a later year. Further examples of partial exclusion will be explored later in the partial exclusion section.

The new law is somewhat equivalent to a Roth distribution in that no tax applies until you meet thresholds established by the Code. The exclusions are tax-free opposed to being tax deferred, and therefore add to the already great benefits of 1031 exchanges, Roth and traditional IRAs, and qualified plans. No longer do you have to "roll over" or "buy up" in order to defer your gain to a later tax year.

How to Use This Part

There are three chapters that describe the exclusion allowance, demonstrate examples, and also establish criteria of home ownership coupled with distribution of real estate from an IRA. This last example reviews a process that will be common in the future—when and how to pay tax on Real Estate Home distributions. As with 1031 Exchanges, this is another option using another tax-deferral method to continue deferring or paying tax.

Chapter 7: "Regulations." As with other tax-free and tax-deferred capabilities, there are rules. This chapter outlines the rules and determining factors permitting you to not pay tax on gains from sale of your primary residence.

Chapter 8: "Examples of Using the Exclusion Allowance." This section provides examples of various options and methods used to take advantage of the allowance. Because of some intricacies of timing, it establishes when one or more people can take advantage of the exclusion to not pay tax on the gain of sale.

Chapter 9: "Using Home Exclusion Allowance for Paying IRA Distribution Taxes."

CHAPTER 7

Regulations

The regulations include:

- How to determine if a home is a principal residence
- When gain from the sale of vacant land that was used as part of the residence may be excluded
- When and how to allocate the gain between residential and business use of the property
- How the exclusion applies to joint owners who are not married
- How to fulfill the requirement that the taxpayer own and use the home as a principal residence for two of the five years prior to the sale.
- Exceptional circumstances when partial or whole exclusions apply

For those with multiple homes, the regulations indicate what principal residence means. The factors include:

- How often the home is occupied
- The seller's place of employment
- Where other family members live
- The address used for tax returns, driver's license, car and voter registration, bills, and correspondence
- The location of the taxpayer's banks, religious organizations, or recreational clubs

The home sale exclusion may include gain from the sale of vacant land that has been used as part of the residence as long as the land sale occurs within two years before or after the sale of the residence.

If you sell a dwelling that was used as a residence and for business purposes, you do not need to allocate gain between the different categories. You simply pay tax on the gain equal to the total depreciation that occurred after May 6, 1997. You may exclude any additional gain on the residence, up to the maximum amount.

If the business-use property was separate from the living space, you must allocate the gain and are only able to exclude the gain on the residential portion of the principal residence.

If you own your property with your spouse, there is a $500,000 maximum exclusion allowed. If you own the property jointly with someone other than your spouse, each of you is entitled to up to $250,000 in tax-free gain. This also includes parties of more than two as long as all are tenants in common. Each party is entitled to his or her portion of the exclusion, up to $250,000 each.

Do You Qualify?

In order to qualify for the exclusion of gain, the following conditions must be met:

- If you own the property solely:
  - You must have owned the property for at least two of the five years preceding the sale of the home.
  - You must have used the home as a principal residence for at least two of the five years before the sale of the current home.
  - You may not have used the new exclusion on the sale of another residence within the two-year period prior to the current sale.
- If you are married:
  - You must file a joint tax return.
  - You or your spouse must have ownership of the property, or you may own the property jointly.

  - You or your spouse must have owned the property for at least two of the five years preceding the sale of the home.
  - You and your spouse must have used the home as a principal residence for at least two of the five years preceding the sale of the home.
  - Neither you nor your spouse may have used the new exclusion on the sale of another residence within the two-year period ending on the date of the current sale.
- If you owned the house with someone other than your spouse:
  - Both (or all) of you must have used the home as a principal residence for two of the five years prior to the sale.
  - You must not have excluded gain on another home sold during the two years before the current sale.

Please note that in all circumstances, the principal residence ownership and use periods need not be concurrent. The two-year requirement may be satisfied by 24 full months or 730 days. Short absences, such as a vacation, still qualify as use. Longer absences, however, do not. In addition, while the two years do not have to be consecutive, in most cases you can only take advantage of this gain exclusion provision once during a two-year period.

Also important to note is that the exclusion applies only to your principal residence, which is the home where you spend most of your time. The residence can be a single-family home, condominium, fabricated house, or even stock in a coop. However, if you reside in a retirement home, and do not have title to the property, you have effectively no ability to claim ownership and may not substitute the sale of a vacation home for the exclusion.

There are some exceptions in which you may be able to take a full or partial exclusion even if you do not meet the ownership and use qualifications. These will be described in detail in the Partial Exclusions section (Chapter 8).

These exclusion rules allow you to take your home sale profits tax-free. They apply regardless of your age and regardless of how many homes you might sell in the future or have sold in the past. An exclusion is available to you even if you previously took a "once-in-a-lifetime" exclusion. As long as you meet the qualifications, this exclusion is available for you with no waiting period.

A Special Note for Married Couples

Married couples often face some complex situations when selling a home. Here are some examples of how to handle these situations:

If you are filing a joint return, but did not share a primary residence with your spouse, you can claim an exclusion of up to $250,000 on the sale of your primary residence. Your spouse can also claim an exclusion of up to $250,000 on the sale of the property that was his or her primary residence. In short, if only one spouse meets the requirements for ownership and use on each residence, you and your spouse can take separate exclusions of up to $250,000.

If you marry someone who has used an exclusion within the last two years, you are limited to a maximum exclusion of $250,000 on a future primary residence sale. After two years have passed since either of you claimed an exclusion, you can exclude $500,000 of gain on your joint return the next time you sell a house as long as both of you meet the ownership and use qualifications. If two years have not yet passed, check with your accountant to see if you are eligible for a partial exclusion.

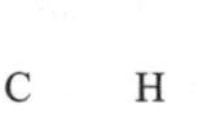

CHAPTER 8

Examples of Using the Exclusion Allowance

Roberto sold his primary residence for $350,000 in 2001. He purchased the property in 1998 for $125,000. Roberto's total gain was $225,000. Because Roberto met all eligibility requirements, his entire gain is excluded from tax. Roberto may use the gain for any purpose without further tax consequences. However, if Roberto decides to make any investments with these funds, gains or losses from those investments would not be excluded from future tax treatment.

If Roberto elects to buy another home with the $225,000 in tax-free proceeds from this sale and then proceeds to sell that home for $400,000 two years later, he has achieved a $175,000 tax-free gain on that property as well. Over a four-year period, Roberto has amassed a tax-free gain of $400,000.

Barbara and her husband Bill purchased a home in 1987 for $205,000 and sold it in 1992 for $365,000. To avoid tax, they decided to use their "once in a lifetime" exclusion on the gain of $160,000. They had met the qualifications for the exclusion, which at that time also included being over the age of 55. They decided to purchase another primary residence with the proceeds after using $10,000 for a vacation. The basis in the new home was $155,000. In 2003, they decided to move to a retirement community and sold their home for $800,000. The total gain was $645,000. Of that, $500,000 was tax free under the exclusion rules, and only $145,000 was taxable to them.

A married couple, Jo and Billy, paid $20,000 for a starter home. Ten years later, they sold the same home for $225,000. The met all the exclusion requirements. The combined exclusion allowance for a married couple is $500,000. Therefore, they assumed that they would be excluded from any tax on the proceeds as well as on their income tax return, which showed a combined income of $150,000. Of course, they were able to exclude the proceeds gain but not the income tax. They did not keep the rules in mind. The rules clearly state that no amount in excess of the total gain may be excluded. In Billy and Jo's case, this amount is $205,000.

Michael, a single man, bought his home in 1998 for $540,000. In June 2004, he sold his home for $1,300,000 after putting in more than $500,000 in improvements. Because he is single and the sole owner of the home, Michael can only exclude $250,000 of his total gain of $760,000. He has to pay tax on the remaining $510,000. This amount is subject to capital gain rules. However, this is preferable to paying income tax.

Irene owned her home and used it as her principal residence for eight years. In 1999, she married Bill. Bill moved into Irene's home and Irene transferred half of her ownership interest to Bill. In early 2000, they decided to move to another home. They sold the home and had a gain of $450,000. Noting the time of occupancy by Bill, it became apparent after the sale that they could not qualify for the full exclusion, as Bill did not use the home as his primary residence for the required two years. Had they known that, they might have reconsidered moving to a new home and instead have waited until both had been in the home the full two years. Because only Irene was eligible for the exclusion, they were only able to exclude $250,000. They had to pay tax on the remaining $200,000.

John owned a home. He married Kathy and she moved into John's home. They lived in the home together for five years. John never transferred ownership of half the interest in the home to Kathy. They decided to move to another state and sold the home. They qualified for the $500,000 exclusion even though John never transferred any ownership of their principal residence to Kathy. They fulfilled the requirement that either spouse may own the home for the two-year period. They also fulfilled the residency requirement of two years. Therefore, as long as they file a joint tax return, they are eligible for the entire exclusion amount of $500,000.

Nancy and Guido had been living happily together in a residence that had been owned solely by Nancy for 10 years. Knowing that the full $500,000 exclusion amount applies to married couples, Nancy and Guido decided to get married. First, they found their new dream house. Then they got married. They sold the old house and filed a joint income tax return. In this way, Nancy and Guido met the qualifications and were not taxed on the $450,000 gain they had on their old home.

Kim purchased a home for her principal residence in 1996. In 1998, after a full two years of living in the home, she decided to move in with Lee. In 2001, Kim felt that the real estate market was favorable in her area and so she decided to sell her old home. She had lived in the home for two of the last five years and had no one rent the property in the interim. She was entitled to the $250,000 exclusion allowance, which she happily accepted. Lee and Kim married in 2002. At that point, Lee had owned his home for seven years. Kim and Lee had been living in the home together for four years. They decided to sell the home. The underlying assumption was the two-year rule would benefit them with a $500,000 exclusion. However, they neglected to remember the rule that states that an exclusion may not be used more often than every two years. Kim had taken an exclusion in 2001 when she sold her property. Therefore, only Lee was eligible for the exclusion and they were only able to exclude $250,000 in gain, which was Lee's portion. If Kim and Lee had waited one more year to sell the home, they would have qualified for the full $500,000 exclusion.

These examples illustrate the value of planning. Proper planning can save you hundreds of thousands of tax dollars. Improper planning can cost you just as much.

Partial Exclusions

Partial exemptions from tax are not as clearly defined. The IRS has exemptions based on a specific computation. A computation worksheet for this purpose is included as part of the preparation of your taxes. Computing the portion allowable works as follows:

During the five-year period ending on the sale date, determine the number of days the spouse:

1. Used the home as his/her principal residence
2. Owned the home

(If one spouse owned the property longer than the other, both spouses are treated as owning the property for the longer period.) Next, you would enter the lesser of the result of 1 or 2. If the result of both and two is more than 730, enter 730 (as that is the maximum allowance). You would then divide this number by 730. Finally, multiply the final result by $250,000. Perform this computation for each spouse. The joint exclusion is the lesser of the actual gain on the sale or the total of the combined separate exclusions under the above formula. The following is an example of a partial exclusion using the formula:

Walter had owned his home since 1987. On August 1, 2000, he married Audrey. Walter transferred half of his ownership interest to Audrey at that time. On August 1, 2001, Walter and Audrey sold the home. At that time, Walter had lived in the home for 14 years and Audrey had lived in the home for one year. The gain on the sale of the home was $500,000.

Walter and Audrey were able to exclude $375,000 of gain. The remaining $125,000 gain was subject to tax. The calculation for the excluded amount was as follows:

Walter used the home as his primary residence well over 730 days and owned the home for well over 730 days; therefore, the computation would begin with 730. Divide 730 by 730 and the result is a factor of one. Multiply one by $250,000 and the final result is $250,000. Therefore, Walter qualifies for an exclusion of $250,000.

Audrey only lived in the home for one year, which is 365 days. This computation begins with 365. Divide 365 by 730 and arrive at a factor of 0.5. Multiply 0.5 by $250,000 and arrive at a final result of $125,000. Therefore, Audrey qualifies for an exclusion of $125,000. Together, Audrey and Walter qualified for an exclusion of $375,000. Now that the gains have been calculated, how are they reported to the IRS? If all of your gains can be excluded, you do not need to report the sale on your return.

If part of your gain is excluded, but the profit made on the home exceeds the amount of the allowable exclusion, you need to report the excess portion of the gain and pay taxes on it. Such taxable gain is reported on your 1040 return, Schedule D. If part of the home was used as a home office, then the sale of business property may also apply and is reported as such. The amount of the excess gain must be reported on either form 1040 or as part of the sale of business property.

If you have rented out the house at any time, you may take a depreciation allowance. However, you may not exclude the part of the gain equal to the depreciation amount that was deducted after May 6, 1997. Therefore, if you have taken a depreciation allowance of $5000 for the property on your tax returns since 1997 and realized a gain of $100,000, you may only exclude $95,000 from capital gains taxes.

Partial exclusions do not apply in all circumstances. In order to qualify, some conditions must be met. If you did not meet the ownership and use requirements, or if during the two-year period ending on the date of the sale or exchange you sold or exchanged another home at a gain and excluded all or part of that gain, you may be allowed to exclude a portion of the gain realized on the sale or exchange of your home if you sold your home due to a change in health, a change in employment, or due to unforeseen circumstances.

Change in Health

A sale or exchange due to a change in health only applies if the primary reason for the sale or exchange is to obtain, provide, or facilitate the diagnosis, cure, and mitigation and/or the treatment of disease, illness, or injury of a qualified individual. It can also apply if the primary reason for the sale is to obtain or provide medical or personal care for a qualified individual suffering from a disease, illness, or injury. A sale or exchange that is merely beneficial to the general health or well-being of the individual does not qualify as a sale or exchange due to health.

Qualified individuals include:

1. The taxpayer
2. The taxpayer's spouse
3. A co-owner of the residence
4. A person whose principal place of abode is the taxpayer's residence
5. An ascendant, descendant, or spouse thereof (this includes siblings)

It is important to note that the primary reason for the sale or exchange of the home can be due to health only if a physician recommends safe harbor for the individual. In other words, a physician must examine the person and attest to the fact that the sale or exchange is necessary in order to improve the health of the qualified person. The following two examples illustrate this concept:

Harriet and William bought a house in 2002 in the town of Mapleton, Minnesota. During that year, Harriet's doctor informed her that her chronic illness could be mitigated in a medical facility in Minneapolis. In 2003, Harriet and William sold their Mapleton home so that they could move to the medical care facility that would care for Harriet. Because this move was recommended by a physician and Harriet is a qualified individual, Harriet and William were able to claim a reduced maximum exclusion.

Joe's doctor informed him that he would have a longer and more fulfilling life if he participated in a regular physical fitness program, such as swimming. Joe enjoyed swimming in the ocean. Joe decided to move from Ames, Iowa, to Hana on the island of Maui in Hawaii because the ocean is warm year round in this area and he felt he could get the exercise he wanted. He bought and sold a house within one and one-half years. Joe had no major health problems. In this case, the sale of the Iowa home was simply for Joe's personal well being so a reduced maximum exclusion was not permitted.

Change in Employment

A change in employment can include working for a new employer, relocating while working for your current employer, or continuing to be self-employed but needing to relocate for the well being of your business.

The following conditions have to be met to make the exclusion effective:

- You must be living in the home as your primary residence at the time of the change of the place of your employment.
- The distance to your new place of employment must be 50 miles or more from the old workplace. If there is no old workplace, the residence must be 50 miles or more from the primary residence sold.

The following three examples illustrate this concept:

You accept a new job, which is 50 miles away from your current residence. You decide that the commute is very difficult, and you wish to move closer to your new office. You decide to sell your home. Because the distance to your new place of employment is 50 miles away, you are entitled to a reduced maximum exclusion. The rule in this circumstance states that if your place of employment is 50 miles or more away from your home, you may qualify for the reduced exclusion.

Monika purchased a home in 2002. She has a wonderful job with an employer who has offered her the opportunity to work in Shanghai. She is offered a three-month trial period in Shanghai to determine if she wanted to take the position. Monika decided to take the position. A year later, she decided to sell her home, as her position in Shanghai would last for four years. Monika's new place of employment in Shanghai is certainly more than 50 miles from her residence in the United States, so she qualified for a reduced maximum exclusion.

Audrey is employed in San Francisco. In June of 2000, she bought a house in Oakland, which is 15 miles from San Francisco. The following year she took a temporary assignment in San Jose, which is 54 miles from her old office, but only 35 miles from her house in Oakland. Audrey moved out of the house in Oakland but did not sell it. In July of 2004, she took a new assignment in Los Angeles, and decided that the time had come to sell her house.

Audrey is entitled to claim a reduced maximum exclusion. This is because her primary reason for the sale of her home was the fact that she took a new assignment in Los Angeles. She would not have qualified if she sold her home during the time she was working in San Jose because the distance from her home to San Jose was not more than 50 miles. However, Los Angeles is well over 50 miles from Oakland, so that change qualified her for the reduced exclusion.

Special rules apply for military personnel. If you were on qualified extended duty in the U.S. Armed Services or the Foreign Service, you may suspend the five-year test period for up to 10 years. In other words, you only need to occupy your primary residence for two of the preceding 10 years. You are on qualified extended duty when you are stationed somewhere that is at least 50 miles from the residence that was sold or you resided, under orders, in government housing for more than 90 days.

This change applies to home sales after May 6, 1997. You may use this provision for only one property at a time and on one sale every two years.

Unforeseen Circumstances

An unforeseen circumstance is an unanticipated event that could not reasonably be foreseen. Such an event would have to occur prior to the purchase of or the occupation of a new principal residence.

These include:

- The involuntary conversion of the residence
- Natural or man-made disasters, including acts of war or terrorism, which result in a casualty to the residence
- Death
- The cessation of employment which resulted in the individual becoming eligible for unemployment compensation
- A change in employment or self-employment status that results in the taxpayer's inability to pay housing costs and reasonable basic living expenses for the taxpayer's household. (This includes only basic living expenses such as food, clothing, medical expenses, taxes, transportation, court-ordered payments, and expenses reasonably necessary for the production of income. This does not include expenses that maintain an affluent or luxurious standard of living.)
- Divorce or legal separation under a decree of divorce or separate maintenance
- Multiple births resulting from the same pregnancy
- An event determined by the Commissioner to be an unforeseen circumstance to the extent provided in published guidance of general applicability or in a ruling directed to a specific taxpayer

The following four examples illustrate this concept:

In 2004, Barbara purchases a home in Hollister, California, for use as her primary residence. Later that year an earthquake damages that house. Barbara is able to sell the home, after making the necessary repairs, to a Nebraska couple. Barbara then decides to move back to her hometown in Oklahoma. The sale is within the safe harbor rules. In other words, Barbara qualifies to receive a reduced maximum exclusion, as the damage to her home was due to a natural disaster. Natural disasters are an unforeseen circumstance.

Peggy purchased a house in 2001 to use as a rental property. Later that year, the renter moved out and Peggy decided that she liked the home enough to use it as her primary residence. She claimed no depreciation expense for the home on her 2001 tax return. Peggy lost her job as a director of Human Resources for the IRS in 2004. She had to sell her home, as she could no longer meet her mortgage obligation. This sale complied with the safe harbor provisions and qualified as an unforeseen circumstance.

John and Marsha purchased a condominium in San Diego in the fall of 2002. In January of 2003, it was discovered that the condominiums had severe plumbing problems. The water lines for each condominium unit had to be replaced. The foundation also had to be dug up in order to repair the sewer connection and replace all pipes that led into the condominium complex. The contractor who originally built the condominiums was out of business and so not liable for repairs. The cost of the repairs then fell to the Homeowners Association. To cover the cost, the condominium Homeowners Association assessed each owner a portion of the bill. This would be a regular assessment for the following five years. John and Marsha discovered that the assessment, which totaled $1000 per month, was more than they could afford. They had to sell the property in order to preserve their equity. San Diego was a hot market for beachfront condominiums at the time and so they were able to sell at a profit. Because this was an unforeseen circumstance, John and Marsha were entitled to claim a reduced maximum exclusion.

Frank purchased a home as his principal residence. While inspecting the home, he heard a rush of wind. Through investigation, he discovered a very large Eucalyptus tree in the back yard. As the wind was blowing quite strongly at the time, Frank concluded that this was the source of the rush of wind. In the spring of 2003, he closed on the house. He moved into the home and enjoyed the dwelling and what he thought was the wind for a short period of time. Because he only inspected the home for a short period of time before purchasing it, he was unaware that the noise that he heard was that of a freeway. The freeway was about 200 yards up the hill from his house and was visibly obscured by other trees. He decided that this was not his dream home and promptly placed it on the market. It sold about one month later. He did not qualify for any special treatment and was not able to take a reduced maximum exclusion because the noise from the freeway was not an unforeseen circumstance.

C H A P T E R 9

Using Home Exclusion Allowance for Paying IRA Distribution Taxes

The Home Exclusion Allowance rules have benefited traditional IRA owners when they have taken normal distributions of a property. This is especially helpful to the IRA owners who do not possess the funds to pay tax.

The key to using the allowance is that the owner must move into a distributed house for a minimum of two years and use the house as his or her primary residence. The most important factors that determine effectiveness are the dollar amount of the distribution and market appreciation. In order for this process to work well, the gain on the property needs to be significant.

We will compare the effect of borrowing money to pay tax on the distribution from a traditional IRA with waiting to take the distribution when the market appreciated over the same period. This example is regarding a California property owned by Bruce's traditional IRA. Please note that if this were Bruce's 401(k) plan, the results would be identical.

Bruce lives in a major metropolitan area in California. He purchased a property originally intended for cash flow purposes and rented the property for 15 years. The original cost was $325,000. Over the years the property appreciated significantly and at age 70-1/2 he decided to take the property as a distribution. Here is why:

He could have taken distribution over the rest of his lifetime utilizing the required minimum distribution rules. These rules state that tax is based on his personal tax rate and not on capital gains. This means that he would have to take undivided interest and pay tax on the amount of distribution based on the fair market value. He would be required to do this at the end of each calendar year. The distributions could be any amount, as long as required minimum distributions were taken.

He wanted to reside in the home, and he had used it as a rental for the past 15 years. Partial distributions of the undivided interest would prohibit him from living in this property.

His IRA received significant income over the years. He had collected rent of up to $4250 per month at the end of the last year. His return on the rental was $360,000 over the 15 years that he owned the property. All of this income was tax deferred. Over time, he had continued to invest in real property with the rental and other proceeds from different Real Estate and Note investments in his IRA.

The real estate market where his IRA had property was hot at the time of his decision to take distribution. Taking undivided interest as distributions from his IRA would not be advantageous in a rising market.

Keeping the property in the IRA would be a continuous benefit. This was a situation in which Bruce could not lose. Bruce wanted to get cash out of the transaction. He could not do this if he received undivided interest.

Bruce's goals were simple. He wished to maximize the cash he would receive. He did not want to use personal cash to pay tax on the amount distributed. Bruce needed his cash for other purposes.

Bruce had several options:

- He could take a distribution and pay tax with cash on hand. This option did not appeal to Bruce because he did not have the cash to pay tax on a large distribution without liquidating other investments that were already very well placed.
- He could take a distribution and use borrowed funds secured by the real property being distributed. Bruce realized that debt was an alternative. He knew that the interest carried on the debt would be money he would

not recover, but he also understood that the appreciation of the property would compensate for that negative aspect.

- He could keep the home as a rental in the IRA and thus receive cash flow on a tax-deferred basis. If Bruce chose this option, he would have to change his plan. He wanted to use the property as a primary residence. However, if the value of this alternative would benefit him over a longer period of time, it may be in Bruce's best interest to take advantage of this option.

Bruce considered the following factors when choosing which option would suit his need the best:

1. The percentage of increase in property values over time
2. The value of the tax exclusion allowance
3. Capital gain taxes paid on any gain that exceeded the tax exclusion allowance
4. The interest rate of any loan he may have to take to pay taxes
5. The value of tax deferrals on income within a traditional IRA
6. Whether to live in the home or keep it as a rental

After careful consideration of all factors, Bruce determined that his most profitable option would be to take the home as a distribution, live in it for two years, and then sell it. To come to this conclusion, he carefully analyzed the market situation in the area and considered the value of comparable homes sold.

The cost of debt over two years was calculated at 8 percent, which was more than the market rate for owner occupied single-family dwellings. His Loan to value was 70 percent. Bruce easily prequalified for this loan amount. Bruce asked that the property be distributed to him. He paid the tax on the distribution amount at 35 percent, which totaled $437,500, with the loan proceeds. He netted a gain of $812,500 after ordinary income tax. He then financed the property and acquired the title. The deed of trust was recorded and Bruce and his family promptly moved into the home.

Over the next two years, the market rose significantly. Homes sold very quickly in this area, often for more than the original asking price. This absolutely delighted Bruce. He decided to put the house on the market after a little over two years after he had taken occupancy. This ensured that he satisfied the rule that he must own and occupy the home for at least 730 days within five years. By doing this, he qualified for the homeowner exemptions of $250,000 for himself and $250,000 for his wife, Jennifer. The asking price was $1,900,000. The house sold for far more within two hours without ever entering the Multiple Listing Service. The overbid was sufficient to cover his closing costs and commissions, leaving him with net proceeds of $1,875,000.

The loan payoff included $70,000 in interest expense. His loan was a two-year renewable loan, which resulted in no prepayment penalty. His gross gain on the profit over the basis he had received as a distribution of $1,250,000 two years prior was $625,000. The loan payoff of $507,500 left him with a profit of $117,000. This amount was not taxed, as he used his homeowner exclusion of up to $500,000. Had Bruce not chosen this option, he would have had to take additional taxable distributions from his plan simply to pay the tax on this home. Alternatively, he would have had to have sold the home at the time to pay the tax on the distribution.

Bruce also considered another alternative. This was to leave the property in the IRA for another two years and just take his required minimum distribution from a note. By doing this, he would have deferred the sale of the home, using the same criteria. The results in Table 9.1 show that his net gain would not have been as much as the anticipated gain he netted by living in the home. His gain would have been reduced by $80,500..

Because tax is not payable on the date of distribution, but is due with payment of tax for the year in which the distribution was made, Bruce had additional options. He could rent the home for one year and then sell it. By doing this, he would not qualify for the exclusion, but the rising market would result in approximately $312,500 in appreciation. This would raise the market value of the property to $1,561,500. Even after paying $62,500 in tax on that appreciation of $312,500, he would have an additional $250,000 to pay the tax due on the distribution. He would also be generating $40,000 in net income on the rental. His total profit would be $290,000. This would cover nearly two-thirds of the tax bill of $437,000 from the distribution of the home from the plan

Table 9.2 presents the alternative of using market appreciation as a tool to pay tax. The table compares both plans and shows the results of each alternative after a period of two years. If Bruce chose not to reside in the property, but instead rented it and then sold it after two years, he would leave the home in the IRA to continue to provide cash flow on a tax-

TABLE 9.1 Distribution with Loan (Cost of Debt at a 70-percent Loan toValue)

Annual Rate of Property	8% Interest Rate		
Value Increase	25%		
Time Held in Years	2		
Fair Market Value at Distribution	$1,250,000		
Tax Rate	35%		
Loan Amount	$437,500		
Net Asset Value of Gain after Tax	$812,500		
Sale After Two Years	$1,875,000		
Gross Gain	$625,000		
Loan Payoff	$507,500	$70,000 in Interest	
Net Cash to Seller	$1,367,500		
Gain After Payoff of Loan	$117,500 (Included in Exclusion Amount)		
Homeowner Exclusion	$500,000		
Exclusion Not Used	$382,500		
Amount Received	$1,367,500		
Retain Home in IRA and Sell After Two Years			
Take Distribution	$1,875,000		
Tax on Distribution	$656,250		
Net Gain	$1,218,750		
Rental Income Tax Deferred Over Two Years			
	Return	Amount	2-Year Gain
	4.20%	$52,500	$105,000
Tax When Distributed	$36,750		
Cash to IRA Owner	$68,250		
Gain + Cash	$1,287,000		
Alternatives	Borrow Money for Tax Payment		Wait and Distribute Later
Return: on Alternatives	$1,367,500	$1,287,000	
Gain: Borrow to Pay Tax rather than Waiting to Distribute Later	$80,500		

deferred basis. He would then sell it and receive the cash as a distribution. With all things remaining equal, the result favors taking the distribution at the beginning of two years and borrowing money to pay the tax. Bruce would have an additional profit of $57,000 by not letting the home remain in the IRA for the two-year period.

TABLE 9.2 Example without Home Exclusion Allowance

Distribution		With Loan	Cost of Debt with 70% Loan to Value
Annual Rate of Property			0.08
Value Increase	25%		
Time Held in Years	2		
Fair Market Value		$1,250,000	
Tax Rate	35%		
Loan Amount	$437,5000		$70,000
NAV / Amt Realized		$812,500	
Sale After Two Years			
		$1,875,000	
Gross Gain		$625,000	
Loan Payoff		$437,500	$70,000
Net Cash to Seller		$1,367,500	
Gain After Payoff After Basis		$117,500	
Homeowner Exclusion		$0	
Exclusion Not Used			
Capital Gains Tax		$23,500	
Amount Received		$1,344,000	
Retain Home in IRA and Sell After Two Years			
Take distribution			$1,875,000
Tax on distribution			$656,250
Net Gain			$1,218,750
Rental Income Tax Deferred Over Two Years			
	Return	Amount	2-Year Gain
	4.20%	$52,500	$105,000
Tax When Distributed (35%)			$36,750
Cash to IRA Owner			$68,250
Gain + Cash from Rental			$1,287,000
Alternatives			
	Borrow Money for Tax payment		Wait and Distribute Two Years Later
Return Alternatives	$1,344,000		$1,287,000
Excess Cash Obtained by Borrowing Money to Pay Tax versus Waiting to Distribute	$57,000		

Keep in mind that taxes are not due on the date of distribution, but actually due April 15 of the following year (and possibly later with proper extensions). Therefore, if the property was sold on January 1, it is possible that taxes would only be due for three months of interest. Using the tax rate of 8 percent on Bruce's loan amount of $437,500, the taxes due for the three-month period would only be $8000. That would offer Bruce further income in the amount of $62,000. This would raise his total amount received to $1,406,000.

Let's suppose that Bruce had personal funds to pay the tax on the distribution. How would this change his financial future?

If Bruce takes the distribution of the house, moves in, and is able to pay the tax due, his return would be significantly higher than it would be if he borrowed the funds from third parties to pay the tax due. In this case, when he sells the home in two years, he and his wife Jennifer would be eligible for the full $500,000 exclusion. This would cover the lions' share of the tax on the net gain. Although in this circumstance, he would be borrowing from himself to pay the tax, he would also be gaining back all of the tax he paid. His basis based on the fair market value of the home was $1,250,000. His total gain was $625,000. The exclusion for Bruce and Jennifer is $500,000 in total, so there was $125,000 in excess gain. Capital gain tax is found by multiplying the excess gain by 20 percent. This result is $25,000. Because Jennifer and Bruce lost the opportunity to invest $437,500, Table 9.3 shows an adjustment for lost income in the form of an opportunity cost. Opportunity cost is defined as income based on investment potential. This figure was based on the amount of $437,000 at 12 percent for two years. That final result is $105,000.

If Bruce chose not to live in the home, the tax exclusion would not be a factor. The results are still significant, however, because the funds to pay the distribution tax would not be borrowed. The tax exclusion would not be allowed, so the capital gains tax would be significantly higher. However, the net result still favors the payment of tax with personal funds.

As you can see from Table 9.4, Bruce's best option is to take the distribution, pay the distribution tax with personal funds, move his family into the home, and then sell it in two years. By doing this, he can take advantage of the full exclusion. Bruce would have a large profit and relatively little tax burden.

TABLE 9.3 Opportunity Cost Example

Distribution		With Loan	Cost of Debt Loan with 70% to Value	No Loan	Investment Return
Annual Rate of Property		0.08		12%	
Value Increase	25%				
Time Held in Years	2				
Fair Market Value		$1,250,000		$1,250,000	
Tax Rate	35%				
Loan Amount		$437,500		$437,500	$105,000
Net Amount Realized		$812,500		$812,500	
Sale After Two years		$1,875,000		$1,875,000	
Gross Gain		$625,000		$625,000	
Loan Payoff		$507,500	$70,000	$0	
Cash to Seller		$1,367,500		$1,875,000	
Gain After Payoff After Basis		$117,500		$625,000	
Homeowner Exclusion		$500,000		$500,000	
Exclusion Not Used		$382,500		–$125,000	
Capital Gains Tax				$25,000	
Amount Received		$1,367,500		$1,850,000	
Payback of Taxes Paid on Distribution		$0			
Effect of Opportunity Cost				–$105,000	
Net Including Opportunity Costs				$1,745,000	
Retain Home in IRA and Sell After Two years					
Take Distribution				$1,875,000	
Tax on Distribution				$656,250	
Net Gain				$1,218,750	
Rental Income Tax Deferred Over Two Years		4.20%	$52,500	$105,000	
Tax When Distributed				$36,750	
Cash to IRA Owner				$68,250	
Gain + Cash				$1,287,000	
ALTERNATIVES		Borrow Money for Tax Payment		Pay Tax	Wait and Distribute Later
Return Alternatives		$1,367,500		$1,720,000	$1,287,000
Pay Tax Increase Over Other Alternatives		$352,500			$433,000

TABLE 9.4 Best Option Example

Distribution		With Loan	Cost of Debt Rate 70% LTV	No Loan	Investment Return
Annual Rate of Property			0.08		12%
Value Increase	25%				
Time Held in Years	2				
FMV		$1,250,000		$1,250,000	
Tax Rate and Loan Amount	35%	$437,500		$437,500	$105,000
NAV/Amt Realized		$812,500		$812,500	
Sale After Two Years		$1,875,000		$1,875,000	
Gross Profit		$625,000		$625,000	
Loan Payoff		$507,500	$70,000	$0	
Net Cash to Seller		$1,367,500		$1,875,000	
Profit After Payoff After Basis		$117,500		$625,000	
Homeowner Exclusion					
Exclusion Not Used					
Capital Gains Tax		$23,500		$125,000	
Amount Received		$1,344,000		$1,750,000	
Opportunity Cost				–$105,000	
Net Including Opportunity Costs				$1,645,000	
Net After Capital Gain on Excess Over Deduction				$1,520,000	
Amount Received After Adjustments		$1,344,000		$1,520,000	
Retain Home in IRA and Sell After Two Years					
Take Distribution				$1,875,000	
Tax on Distribution				$656,250	
Net Profit				$1,218,750	
Rental Income Tax Deferred Over Two Years		4.20%	$52,500	$105,000	
Tax When Distributed				$36,750	
Cash to IRA Owner				$68,250	
Profit + Cash				$1,287,000	
Alternatives		Borrow Tax Payment	Pay Tax	Wait and Distribute Later	
Return Alternatives		$1,344,000	$1,520,000	$1,287,000	

APPENDIX A

Health Savings Accounts

Health Savings Accounts, (or HSAs) are tax-deferred accounts that provide a realtor with additional investment capital for real estate and note purchases. These accounts were established for those individual who have a high-deductible health plan (HDHP) to meet medical expenses. The funds that you contribute to the HSA must be in cash. Unlike IRAs and generally qualified plans, there is no earned income requirement to be able to make contributions. HSA investment may be in any legally permitted investment. The trustee or custodian of the HSA will determine what they permit as investments. Some self-directed plans permit investments in real estate and notes.

Benefits to a Real Estate Investor

HSAs have a number of benefits for the real estate investor:

- They may be combined with other investment capital to purchase undivided interests of an asset.
- Compensation is not required to be eligible to contribute to an HSA.
- You or an employer (could also be you) may make tax-deductible contributions.

- There is no required minimum distribution date; however, contributions cease at age 65.
- All distributions for health care purposes are not taxable.
- Distributions for medical expenses may be taken at any time.
- Distributions for any other purposes are subject to a 10-percent penalty plus income tax at your ordinary income tax rate for the year in which the distribution took place.
- Spouses may inherit HSAs and use the assets for their own health care or investment needs.
- An HSA may be established *in addition* to an IRA and *in addition* to a qualified plan, such as a 401(k) plan. (For example: You can have and contribute to a 401(k) plan, to IRS established limits, *and* a traditional or Roth IRA, and an HSA.) Potentially, a single person under age 50, earning $50,000 of W-2 income, could have an individual 401(k) with $26,500 in contributions, $3000 in a Roth IRA, and an HSA for $2600, for a total of $32,100 in tax-deferred and tax-free funds for investments, all in one year.

The rules for HSAs are straightforward and in many cases follow IRA rules. Some of the important details are summarized below.

Establishment of HSAs

The Medicare Prescription Drug, Improvement, and Modernization Act of 2003 was signed into law on December 08, 2003. This Act, among many other things, has created a new financial product, the Health Savings Account (HSA), which can be offered by various types of financial organizations.

An HSA is a tax-exempt trust or custodial account established exclusively for the purpose of paying qualified medical expenses of the account beneficiary who, for the months for which contributions are made to an HSA, is covered under a high-deductible health plan. A number of the rules that apply to an HSA are similar to rules that apply to an IRA. Thus, if the individual is an employee who later changes employers or leaves the work force, the HSA does not stay behind with the former employer, but stays with the individual.

An "eligible individual" can establish an HSA. An "eligible individual" means, with respect to any month, any individual who: (1) is covered under a high-deductible health plan (HDHP) on the first day of such month; (2) is not also covered by any other health plan that is not an HDHP (with certain exceptions for plans providing certain limited types of coverage); (3) is not entitled to benefits under Medicare (generally, has not yet reached age 65); and (4) may not be claimed as a dependent on another person's tax return. Employers may establish HSAs.

An HSA is generally exempt from tax. Earnings on amounts in an HSA are not includable in gross income while held in the HSA (i.e., inside buildup is not taxable). There are additional rules regarding the taxation of distributions to the account beneficiary. Contributions made by an eligible individual, or by a family member on behalf of an eligible individual, are deductible from income (or excluded from income if the HSA is funded by the employer), the earnings are not currently taxable, and distributions used to pay qualified medical expenses are tax free. In other words, instead of paying medical expenses with after-tax dollars, such individuals will be able to pay medical expenses with pretax dollars. Health Savings Accounts could be established by eligible individuals as of January 1, 2004.

Payment of Expenses

Qualified medical expenses include amounts paid with respect to the individual, the individual's spouse, and the individual's dependents, for medical care defined under Section 213(d) of the Internal Revenue Code, and such amounts are not compensated for by insurance or otherwise. Generally, qualified medical expenses shall not include payment for insurance. (There are some exceptions to this rule.)

Contributions

HSA contributions must be made in cash and may be made by an eligible individual, a family member on behalf of an eligible individual, or the employer of an eligible individual during any given year. Contributions may be made regardless of whether the eligible individual has compensation.

For an "eligible individual," a deduction is permitted for the taxable year equal to an amount that is the aggregate amount paid in cash during such taxable year to an HSA by either the Account Beneficiary or a family member.

HSA contributions are deductible whether or not the eligible individual itemizes deductions. An individual who may be claimed as a dependent on another person's tax return is not an eligible individual and may not deduct contributions to an HSA.

HSA rules are applied without regard to community property laws.

Employer contributions to an HSA are not subject to withholding from wages for income tax purposes or subject to FICA, FUTA, or the Railroad Retirement Tax Act. Contributions to an employee's HSA through a cafeteria plan (Section 125 plan) are treated as employer contributions. The employee cannot deduct employer HSA contributions on his or her federal income tax return as HSA contributions or as medical expense deductions.

Contribution Limits

For an eligible individual with self-only coverage, the 2004 maximum annual dollar limit is $2600. For an eligible individual with family coverage, the 2004 maximum annual dollar limit is $5150.

The maximum deduction permitted for a individual with self-coverage for a taxable year is the lesser of 100 percent of the deductible amount under the high-deductible health plan up to a maximum of $2600 for 2004. The maximum deduction for family coverage is the lesser of 100 percent of the deductible amount under the high-deductible health plan up to a maximum of $5150 for 2004.

HSA contributions must be made for a calendar year no later than the Account Beneficiary's tax filing deadline for that year, *not including extensions*. This date is normally the following April 15th.

Contributions for the taxable year can be made in one or more payments. Although the annual contribution limit is determined monthly, the maximum contribution may be made on the first day of the year.

For eligible individuals (and their spouses covered by the HDHP) the HSA contribution limit is increased each year. The monthly allowable catch-up contribution is computed in the same manner as the annual contribution limit.

The maximum annual catch-up amount is:

Year	Catch-up Amount
2004	$500
2005	$600
2006	$700
2007	$800
2008	$900
2009 and thereafter	$1000

Both spouses may make catch-up contributions, if eligible, without exceeding the family coverage limit.

If the aggregate amount of regular HSA contributions exceeds the applicable dollar limit, a 6-percent excise tax is imposed on the Account Beneficiary on the amount of the excess HSA contribution, until corrected.

To avoid the 6-percent excise tax, the taxpayer can withdraw the excess amount plus earnings attributable by the individual's tax filing due date plus extensions for the year *for* which the excess contribution was made. The earnings on the excess that are removed from the HSA are included in the Account Beneficiary's income in the year distributed and may be subject to the 10-percent additional income tax, unless another exception applies.

Distributions that are used exclusively to pay for qualified medical expenses are not includable in the taxpayer's income.

For calendar year 2004, qualified medical expenses incurred on or after the later of January 1, 2004 or the first day of the month the individual became eligible for an HSA may be reimbursed from the HSA, as long as the HSA is established on or before April 15, 2005.

Any amounts distributed from an HSA account that are not used to exclusively pay for qualified medical expenses are included in the gross income of the taxpayer and will be subject to an additional 10-percent tax. There are exceptions to the 10-percent penalty, such as disability, distributions to a beneficiary on the death of the HSA owner, and rollover to another HSA. If earnings removed due to excess contribution are not used for one of the exceptions, the 10-percent additional tax will apply.

Prohibited Transactions

If an individual engages in a prohibited transaction during a taxable year, the HSA account will be deemed distributed and the deemed distribution will be treated as not being used for qualified medical expenses. Therefore, the taxpayer will be subject to income taxes and to the 10-percent tax on HSA distributions that are not used for qualified medical expenses.

If the taxpayer pledges the HSA as security for a loan, the portion so pledged will be treated as a deemed distribution subject to taxes and the 10-percent additional income tax on HSA distributions that are not used for qualified medical expenses.

Until the IRS issues guidance to the contrary, HSAs should not be invested in collectibles defined under the IRS Code.

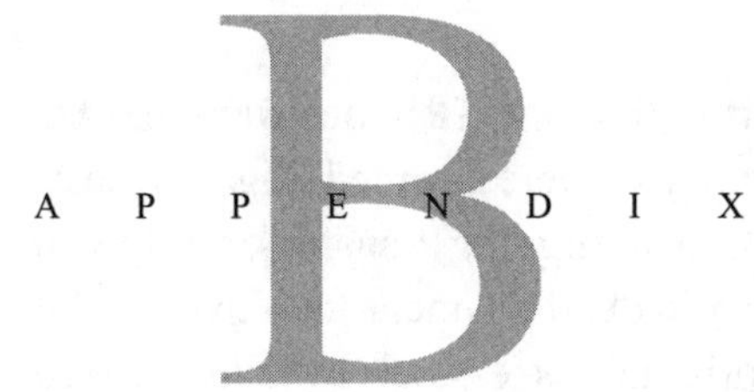

APPENDIX B

The Landmark Swanson Decision

James H. Swanson, et ux. v. Commissioner, 106 TC 76, Code Sec(s) 4975; 7430.

Tax Court & Board of Tax Appeals Reported Decisions

JAMES H. SWANSON AND JOSEPHINE A. SWANSON, Petitioners v. COMMISSIONER OF INTERNAL REVENUE, Respondent.

Case Information:

Code Sec(s):	4975; 7430 [pg. 76]
Docket:	Tax Ct. Dkt. No. 21203-92.
Date Issued:	2/14/1996.
Judge:	Opinion by Dean, *J.*
Tax Year(s):	Years 1986, 1988, 1989, 1990.
Disposition:	Decision for Taxpayers in part and for Commissioner in part.106 TC 76106 TC No. 3

HEADNOTE

1. Litigation costs—substantial justification for IRS position—IRAs; prohibited and sham transactions. Taxpayers were awarded litigation costs because IRS wasn't substantially justified in arguing transfer of 100% of DISC's original issue stock and DISC's dividend payment to taxpayer's 1st IRA, and transfer of 100% of FSC's original issue stock to taxpayer's 2d IRA, were Code Sec. 4975 prohibited transactions: DISC couldn't be disqualified person prior to its initial stock issuance; taxpayer- fiduciary didn't deal with IRA's assets in his own interest and only realized benefits from the payments as IRA participant; and IRS didn't promptly concede its position. But, costs were denied where IRS was substantially justified in arguing sale of taxpayers' home to trust was sham: taxpayers and daughter lived on property, paid expenses, and made repairs before it was sold to 3d party; and business purpose for trust's purchase was questionable.

Reference(s): ¶ 74,305.01(25); 49,755.01(35) Code Sec. 4975; 7430

2. Litigation costs—prevailing party—net worth calculation; exhaustion of administrative remedies; reasonable costs. Taxpayers properly calculated net worth by measuring their asset acquisition costs by amounts paid, against FMV, for litigation cost award purposes; didn't unreasonably protract proceedings; and exhausted administrative remedies per se, even though they didn't request Appeals Conference, because IRS hadn't issued 30 day letter before mailing deficiency notice. Court computed cost of living adjustment from Oct. 1, 1981, and adjusted award to reflect amount of attorney time and miscellaneous costs allocable to each issue.

Reference(s): ¶ 74,305.01(50); 74,305.01(10); 74,536.23151(10) Code Sec. 7430

Syllabus

Official Tax Court Syllabus

Ps filed a motion for reasonable litigation costs pursuant to Rule 231, Tax Court Rules of Practice and Procedure, and sec. 7430, I.R.C., claiming that R was not substantially justified in determining that: (1) Prohibited transactions had occurred under sec. 4975, I.R.C., with respect to a domestic international sales corporation, a foreign sales corporation, and two individual retirement accounts; and (2) the sale of Ps' Illinois residence to P's closely held corporation was a sham transaction.

[1] Held: R was not substantially justified with respect to the first issue, but was substantially justified with respect to the second issue.

[2] Held, further, net worth, for purposes of the Equal Access to Justice Act, 28 U.S.C. sec. 2412(d)(2)(B) (1994), as incorporated by sec. 7430(c)(4)(A)(iii), is determined based upon the cost of acquisition rather than the fair market value of assets, and was less than $2 million each with respect to Ps on the date their petition was filed.

[3] Held, further, Ps' failure to request an Appeals Office conference did not constitute a "[refusal] *** to participate in an Appeals office conference" within the meaning of sec. 301.7430-1(e)(2)(ii), Proced. & Admin. Regs., and, because no 30-day letter was issued to Ps prior to the mailing of their notice of deficiency, Ps are deemed to have per se exhausted their administrative remedies for purposes of sec. 7430(b)(1).

[4] Held, further, Ps have not unreasonably protracted the proceedings within the meaning of sec. 7430(b)(4).

[5] Held, further, the amount sought by Ps for litigation costs in this matter is not reasonable and must be adjusted to comport with the record.

Counsel

Neal J. Block and Maura Ann McBreen, for petitioners.

Gregory J. Stull, for respondent.

DAWSON, *Judge*:

OPINION

This case was assigned to Special Trial Judge John F. Dean pursuant to the provisions of section 7443A(b)(4) and Rules 180, 181, and 183.[1] The Court agrees [pg. 77] with and adopts the Special Trial Judge's opinion, which is set forth below.

OPINION OF THE SPECIAL TRIAL JUDGE

DEAN, *Special Trial Judge*: This matter is before the Court pursuant to petitioners' motion for award of reasonable litigation costs under section 7430 and Rule 231.

References to petitioner are to James H. Swanson.

The matter before us involves petitioners' combined use of a domestic international sales corporation, a foreign sales corporation, and two separate individual retirement accounts as a means of deferring the recognition of income. Respondent zealously strove to characterize this arrangement, as well as an unrelated sale by petitioners of their Illinois residence, as tax avoidance schemes. A protracted period of entrenchment ensued, during which the parties firmly established their respective positions, neither side wavering from its conviction that it was in the right. Ultimately, however, these issues were resolved by respondent's notice of no objection to petitioners' motion for partial summary judgment as well as the entry of an agreed decision document, which was later set aside and filed as a stipulation of settlement. As a consequence, petitioners now seek redress for what they claim were unreasonable positions taken by respondent.

A. *Factual Background*

Petitioners resided in Florida at the time the petition was filed. At all times relevant to the following discussion, petitioner was the sole shareholder of H & S Swansons' Tool Company (hereinafter, Swansons' Tool), which has operated as a Florida corporation since 1983.[2] Swansons' Tool elected to be taxed as a subchapter S corporation effective in 1987.

Swansons' Tool is in the business of building and painting component parts for various equipment manufacturers. As a part of these activities, Swansons' Tool manufactures and exports property for use outside the United States. [pg. 78]

1. *The DISC and IRA #1*

Following the advice of experienced counsel, petitioner arranged in the early part of January 1985 for the organization of Swansons' Worldwide, Inc., a domestic international sales corporation (hereinafter the DISC or Worldwide). During this period, petitioner also arranged for the formation of an individual retirement account (hereinafter IRA #1).

The articles of incorporation for Worldwide were filed on January 9, 1985, and under the terms thereof petitioner was named the corporation's initial director. Shortly thereafter, Worldwide filed a Form 4876A, Election to be Treated as an Interest Charge DISC.

A Form 5305, Individual Retirement Trust Account, was filed on January 28, 1985, establishing Florida National Bank (hereinafter Florida National) as trustee of IRA #1, and petitioner as the grantor for whose benefit the IRA was established. Under the terms of the IRA agreement, petitioner retained the power to direct IRA #1's investments.

On the same day that the Form 5305 was filed, petitioner directed Florida National to execute a subscription agreement for 2,500 shares of Worldwide original issue stock. The shares were subsequently issued to IRA #1, which became the sole shareholder of Worldwide.

For the taxable years 1985 to 1988, Swansons' Tool paid commissions to Worldwide with respect to the sale by Swansons' Tool of export property, as defined by section 993(c). In those same years, petitioner, who had been named president of Worldwide, directed, with Florida National's consent, that Worldwide pay dividends to IRA #1[3] Commissions paid to Worldwide received preferential treatment,[4] and the dividends paid to IRA #1 were tax deferred pursuant to section 408. Thus, the net effect of these transactions was to defer [pg. 79] recognition of dividend income that otherwise would have flowed through to any shareholders of the DISC.

In 1988, IRA #1 was transferred from Florida National Bank to First Florida Bank, N.A. (hereinafter First Florida), as custodian. Swansons' Tool stopped paying commissions to Worldwide after December 31, 1988, as petitioners no longer considered such payments to be advantageous from a tax planning perspective.

2. *The FSC and IRA #2*

In January 1989, petitioner directed First Florida to transfer $5,000 from IRA #1 to a new individual retirement custodial account (hereinafter IRA #2). Under the terms of the IRA agreement, First Florida was named custodian of IRA #2, and petitioner was named as the grantor for whose benefit the IRA was established. Under the terms of the IRA agreement, petitioner reserved the right to serve as the "Investment Manager" of IRA #2.

Contemporaneous with the formation of IRA #2, petitioner incorporated H & S Swansons' Trading Company (hereinafter Swansons' Trading or the FSC). Petitioner directed First Florida to execute a subscription agreement for 2,500 newly issued shares of Swansons' Trading stock. The shares were subsequently issued to IRA #2, which became the corporation's sole shareholder. Swansons' Trading filed a Form 8279, Election To Be Treated as an FSC or as a Small FSC, on March 31, 1989, and paid a dividend to IRA #2 in the amount of $28,000 during the taxable year 1990.

3. *The Algonquin Property*

In anticipation of Swansons' Tool's transferring its operations to Florida, petitioners moved during 1981 from their Algonquin, Illinois, residence (hereinafter, the Algonquin property or the property) to a condominium in St. Petersburg, Florida. The Algonquin property was not advertised for sale until sometime during 1983.

Conscious of a change in the Internal Revenue Code which would eliminate preferential treatment of capital gain recognized on the sale of their home, petitioners sought to sell the [pg. 80] Algonquin property prior to December 31, 1986.[5] As time was clearly a factor, petitioners arranged to sell the property to a trust of which Swansons' Tool was the beneficiary. Accordingly, on December 19, 1986, petitioners conveyed the Algonquin property to "Trust No. 234, Barry D. Elman, trustee," (hereinafter Trust No. 234) under a Deed in Trust, which was received and filed by the Recorder for the city of McHenry, Illinois. As a consequence of this transaction, petitioners reported a long-term capital gain of $141,120.78 on Schedule D, Capital Gains and Losses, of their 1986 Federal income tax return, reflecting a $225,000 sale price and an $83,879 basis.

Petitioners continued paying the electric bills, heating, exterior maintenance, and house sitting expenses of the Algonquin property through May or June of 1987. In March of 1988, Swansons' Tool reimbursed petitioners for maintenance and repair expenses incurred during the time period December 1986 through May 1987, as well as the expense of moving petitioners' personal belongings in September 1987. Swansons' Tool capitalized these expenditures as part of its basis in the Algonquin property. Subsequent to the signing of a "Real Estate Sales Contract" during March of 1988, the Algonquin property was sold by Swansons' Tool to an unrelated third party on June 23, 1988.

Petitioners' daughter, Jill, resided at the Algonquin residence from May of 1987 through June of 1988. Although the record is not clear as to the extent of usage, it appears that petitioners also periodically stayed at the residence subsequent to its sale on December 19, 1986.

4. *The Notice of Deficiency*

Despite petitioners' agreement to extend the period of limitations in their case until June 30, 1992, petitioners did not receive a 30-day letter prior to the notice of deficiency. Petitioners agreed to the extension in the hope of resolving the case at the administrative level.

In the notice of deficiency, dated June 29, 1992, respondent set forth one primary and three alternative positions for determining deficiencies in petitioners' Federal income taxes [pg. 81] and additions to tax for negligence with respect to petitioners' 1986, 1988, 1989, and 1990 taxable years. Of relevance to the present matter were respondent's determinations that: (1) "Prohibited transactions" had occurred which resulted in the termination of IRA's #1 and #2; and (2) the sale of the Algonquin property to a trust in 1986 was a "sham" transaction which could not be recognized for tax purposes.

a. *"Prohibited Transactions"*

Because the notice of deficiency failed to adequately explain respondent's bases for determining deficiencies and additions to tax with respect to the years at issue, petitioners requested and received the revenue agent's report in their case. As demonstrated by the revenue agent's report, respondent identified, as alternative positions, two "prohibited transactions" which resulted in the loss of IRA #1's status as a trust under section 408. First, respondent concluded that:

Mr. Swanson is a disqualified person within the meaning of section 4975(e)(2)(A) of the Code as a fiduciary because he has the express authority to control the investments of *** [IRA #1].

Mr. Swanson is also an Officer and Director of Swansons' Worldwide. Therefore, direct or indirect transactions described by section 4975(c)(1) between Swansons' Worldwide and *** [IRA #1] constitute prohibited transactions.

Mr. Swanson, as an Officer and Director of Worldwide directed the payment of dividends from Worldwide to *** [IRA #1] *** *The payment of dividends is a prohibited transaction within the meaning of section 4975(c)(1)(E) of the Code as an act of self-dealing where a disqualified person who is a fiduciary deals with the assets of the plan in his own interest.* The dividend paid to *** [IRA #1] December 30, 1988 will cause the IRA to cease to be an IRA effective January 1, 1988 by reason of section 408(e)(1). Therefore, by operation of section 408(d)(1), the fair market value of the IRA is deemed distributed January 1, 1988. [Emphasis added.]

As further demonstrated by the revenue agent's report, respondent's second basis for disqualifying IRA #1 under section 408 was that:

In his capacity as fiduciary of *** [IRA #1], Mr. Swanson directed the bank custodian, Florida National Bank, to purchase all of the stock of Swansons' Worldwide. At the time of the purchase, Mr. Swanson was the sole director of Swansons' Worldwide.

The sale of stock by Swansons' Worldwide to Mr. Swanson's Individual Retirement Account constitutes a [pg. 82] prohibited transaction within the meaning of section 4975(c)(1)(A) of the Code. The sale occurred February 15, 1985. By operation of section 408(e)(2)(A) of the Code, the Individual Retirement Account ceases to be an Individual Retirement Account effective January 1, 1985.

Effective January 1, 1985 the Individual Retirement Account is not exempt from tax under section 408(e)(1) of the Code. The fair market value of the account, including the 2500 shares of Swansons' Worldwide, is deemed to have been distributed to Mr. Swanson in accordance with section 408(e)(2)(B) of the Code. Therefore, Mr. Swanson effectively became the sole shareholder of Swansons' Worldwide, Inc. with the loss of the IRA's tax exemption. [Emphasis added.]

Although the record is not entirely clear on the matter, it appears that respondent imputed to IRA #2 the prohibited transactions found with respect to IRA #1 and used similar reasoning to disqualify IRA #2 as a valid trust under section 408(a).

b. *"Sham Transaction"*

With respect to the Algonquin property, respondent concluded in the notice of deficiency that:

the purported sale of your personal residence located in Algonquin, Illinois by you in 1986 to Trust #234, Barry D. Elman, Trustee, of which your corporation, H & S Swansons' Tool Company, Inc. is the beneficiary, can not be recognized for tax purposes. *The purported sale in 1986 was no more than a sham transaction which was entered into for tax avoidance purposes. It is determined that the purported sale served no other purpose than to enable you to obtain the tax benefit of a long term capital gain deduction of 60 percent that would not have been available had the sale occurred in tax years subsequent to 1986.* *** [Emphasis added.[6]]

5. *The Petition, Answer, Motion for Summary Judgment, and Settlement Agreement*

In their petition, filed September 21, 1992, petitioners stated with respect to respondent's determination of "prohibited transactions" that: (1) At all pertinent times IRA #1 was the sole shareholder of Worldwide; (2) since the 2,500 shares of Worldwide issued to IRA #1 were original issue, no sale or exchange of the stock occurred; (3) from and after the dates of his appointment as director and president of Worldwide, Mr. Swanson engaged in no activities on behalf of Worldwide [pg. 83] which benefited him other than as a beneficiary of IRA #1; (4) IRA #1 was not maintained, sponsored, or contributed to by Worldwide during the years at issue; (5) at no time did Worldwide have any active employees; and (6) Mr. Swanson engaged in no activities on behalf of Swansons' Trading which benefited him other than as a beneficiary of IRA #2.

With respect to the Algonquin residence, petitioners stated, in pertinent part, that: (1) On December 19, 1986, petitioners conveyed the Algonquin property by a Deed in Trust to a trust of which Swansons' Tool was the beneficiary; (2) the transfer documents conveyed full legal and beneficial ownership from petitioners to this trust; (3) at no time did petitioners act in any manner that was inconsistent with their transfer of all their right, title, and interest in the Algonquin property; and (4) subsequent to the sale, petitioners had no rights as tenants of the property other than as tenants at will.

Respondent filed an answer on November 13, 1992, denying, or denying for lack of knowledge, each of the allegations listed above.

Petitioners filed a motion for partial summary judgment on March 22, 1993. In their motion, petitioners restated their position, as set forth in their petition, that no prohibited transactions had occurred with respect to IRA's #1 and #2.

On July 12, 1993, respondent filed a notice of no objection to petitioners' motion for partial summary judgment, thereby ending the controversy on the DISC and FSC issues.

Respondent conceded the Algonquin property issue in a settlement agreement entered into on January 24, 1994. The parties agreed at that time to a total deficiency of $11,372.40, which reflected an amount conceded by petitioners in their petition as capital gain inadvertently omitted from their 1988 Federal income tax. A stipulated decision (hereinafter the decision) was submitted by the parties and entered on February 9, 1994.

6. *Motion for Award of Reasonable Litigation Costs*

On March 14, 1994, this Court received petitioner Josephine Swanson's motion for award of reasonable litigation costs (hereinafter also referred to as the motion). Finding that it was not petitioner Josephine Swanson's intent that the decision entered on February 9, 1994, be conclusive [pg. 84] as to the issue of attorney's fees, the Court ordered on April 29, 1994, that the decision be vacated and set aside. The Court further ordered that the decision of February 9, 1994, be filed as a stipulation of settlement, that petitioner Josephine Swanson's motion for award of reasonable litigation costs be filed, and that respondent file a response to petitioner Josephine Swanson's motion in accordance with Rule 232(c).

Respondent's objection to petitioner Josephine Swanson's motion for award of reasonable litigation costs was filed on June 29, 1994. Petitioners sought leave to file a response to respondent's objection by a motion filed August 3, 1994, which was granted.

Petitioners filed an amendment to the motion for award of reasonable litigation costs (hereinafter amendment to motion) on August 1, 1994, pursuant to which petitioner James Swanson joined petitioner Josephine Swanson as a party to the motion.

Petitioners filed their response to respondent's objection to petitioners' motion for award of reasonable litigation costs on September 15, 1994.

Following a conference call with the parties on March 20, 1995, the parties were ordered to file a stipulation of facts with respect to items of net worth reported by petitioners on attachment II of their amendment to motion. They were further ordered to file a stipulation of facts regarding the issue of attorney's fees paid or incurred by petitioners. If the parties could not stipulate facts with respect to either issue, they were ordered to file a status report with the Court on or before May 1, 1995.

On May 1, 1995, the parties participated in a conference call, during which they agreed to stipulate certain items of net worth reported on attachment II of petitioners' amendment to motion. The parties also agreed to stipulate that petitioners paid or incurred fees in this matter. The parties disagreed, however, as to the proper method for determining the acquisition cost of specific items on attachment II of petitioners' amendment to motion. With respect to these items, the parties were ordered to file, on or before June 1, 1995, simultaneous memoranda of law, and, on or before July 3, 1995, answering memoranda of law. [pg. 85]

B. *Discussion*

As an initial matter, we reject respondent's argument that it was improper for us to have vacated the decision of February 9, 1994, thereby allowing petitioners to file their motion for award of reasonable litigation costs. This Court may, in its sound discretion, set aside a decision that has not yet become final. See, e.g., *Cassuto v. Commissioner*, 93 T.C. 256, 260 (1989), affd. in part, revd. in part, and remanded on another issue 936 F.2d 736 [68 AFTR 2d 91-5096] (2d. Cir. 1991). Having so held, we turn to the merits of petitioners' motion.

Section 7430 provides that, in any court proceeding brought by or against the United States, the "prevailing party" may be awarded reasonable litigation costs. Sec. 7430(a). To qualify as a "prevailing party" for purposes of Section 7430, petitioners must establish that: (1) The position of the United States in the proceeding was not substantially justified; (2) they substantially prevailed with respect to the amount in controversy, or with respect to the most significant issue presented; and (3) they met the net worth requirements of 28 U.S.C. Sec. 2412(d)(2)(B) (1994), on the date the petition was filed. Sec. 7430(c)(4)(A). Petitioners must also establish that they exhausted the administrative remedies available to them within the Internal

Revenue Service and that they did not unreasonably protract the proceedings. Sec. 7430(b)(1), (4). Petitioners bear the burden of proof with respect to each of the preceding requirements. Rule 232(e).

Although it is conceded that petitioners substantially prevailed in this case, respondent does not agree that her litigation position was not substantially justified.[7] Furthermore, respondent asserts that petitioners: (1) Have not satisfied the net worth requirements, (2) failed to exhaust the administrative remedies available to them within the Internal Revenue Service, (3) unreasonably protracted the proceedings, and (4) [pg. 86] have not shown that the costs they have claimed are reasonable. We will address each contested point in turn.

1. *Whether Respondent's Litigation Position Was Substantially Justified*

In 1986, Congress amended section 7430 to conform that provision more closely to the Equal Access to Justice Act (EAJA). Tax Reform Act of 1986, Pub. L. 99-514, sec. 1551, 100 Stat. 2085, 2752. Where the prior statute required taxpayers to prove that the Government's position in a proceeding was "unreasonable," the statute as amended now requires a showing that the position of the United States was "not substantially justified." Sec. 7430(c)(4)(A)(i). This Court has concluded that the substantially justified standard is essentially a continuation of the prior law's reasonableness standard. *Sher v. Commissioner*, 89 T.C. 79, 84 (1987), affd. 861 F.2d 131 [63 AFTR 2d 89-422] (5th Cir. 1988). Thus, a position that is "substantially justified" is one that is "justified to a degree that could satisfy a reasonable person" or that has a "reasonable basis both in law and fact." *Pierce v. Underwood*, 487 U.S. 552, 565 (1988) (internal quote marks omitted) (defining "substantially justified" in the context of the EAJA).

Petitioners have not sought an award of administrative costs in this matter. Accordingly, we need only examine the question of whether respondent's litigation position was substantially justified.[8]

Respondent argues that we may not consider positions she took prior to the filing of the answer in determining whether her litigation position was substantially justified. In support, respondent cites, among other cases,[9] *Huffman v. Commissioner*, 978 F.2d 1139 [70 AFTR 2d 92-6016] (9th Cir. 1992), affg. in part and revg. in part T.C. Memo. 1991-144 [¶91,144 PH Memo TC].

Respondent is correct in stating that Huffman approves of a bifurcated analysis under section 7430, pursuant to which the two stages of a case, the administrative proceeding and the court proceeding, are considered separately. This bifurcated analysis: [pg. 87] not only ensures that the prevailing taxpayer is reimbursed for prelitigation and litigation costs, but also supports Congress's intent that before an award of attorney's fees is made, the taxpayer must meet the burden of proving that the Government's position was not substantially justified. It affords another opportunity for the United States to reconsider an inappropriate position. [Id. at 1146.]

Respondent's arguments on this point appear moot, however, as we find no discernible difference between the administrative and litigation positions she took in this matter.[10] See *Lennox v. Commissioner*, 998 F.2d 244, 247-249 [72 AFTR 2d 93- 5710] (5th Cir. 1993) (holding that the Government's position must be analyzed in the context of the circumstances that caused it to take that position), revg. in part and remanding T.C. Memo. 1992-382 [1992 RIA TC Memo ¶92,382].

a. *The DISC Issue*

Petitioners contend that respondent was not substantially justified in maintaining throughout the proceedings that prohibited transactions had occurred with respect to IRA #1, and by implication, IRA #2. We agree.

As stated previously, respondent based her determination of prohibited transactions on section 4975(c)(1)(A) and (E). Section 4975(c)(1)(A) defines a prohibited transaction as including any "sale or exchange, or leasing, of any property between a plan[11] and a disqualified person."[12] Section [pg. 88] 4975(c)(1)(E) further defines a prohibited transaction as including any "act by a disqualified person who is a fiduciary[13] whereby he deals with the income or assets of a plan in his own interest or for his own account."

We find that it was unreasonable for respondent to maintain that a prohibited transaction occurred when Worldwide's stock was acquired by IRA #1. The stock acquired in that transaction was newly issued — prior to that point in time, Worldwide had no shares or shareholders. A corporation without shares or shareholders does not fit within the definition of a disqualified person under section 4975(e)(2)(G).[14] It was only *after* Worldwide issued its stock to IRA #1 that petitioner held a beneficial interest in Worldwide's stock, thereby causing Worldwide to become a disqualified person under section 4975(e)(2)(G).[15] Accordingly, the issuance of stock to [pg. 89] IRA #1 did not, within the plain meaning of section 4975(c)(1)(A), qualify as a "sale or exchange, or leasing, of any property between a plan and a disqualified person."[16] Therefore, respondent's litigation position with respect to this issue was unreasonable as a matter of both law and fact.

We also find that respondent was not substantially justified in maintaining that the payments of dividends by Worldwide to IRA #1 qualified as prohibited transactions under section 4975(c)(1)(E). There is no support in that section for respondent's contention that such payments constituted acts of self-dealing, whereby petitioner, a "fiduciary," was dealing with the assets of IRA #1 in his own interest. Section 4975(c)(1)(E) addresses itself only to acts of disqualified persons who, as fiduciaries, deal directly or indirectly with the *income or assets of a plan* for their own benefit or account. Here, there was no such direct or indirect dealing with the income or assets of a plan, as the dividends paid by Worldwide did not become *income of IRA #1* until unqualifiedly made subject to the demand of IRA #1. Sec. 1.301-1(b), Income Tax Regs. Furthermore, respondent has never suggested that petitioner, acting as a "fiduciary" or otherwise, ever dealt with the corpus of IRA #1 for his own benefit.

Based on the record, the only direct or indirect benefit that petitioner realized from the payments of dividends by Worldwide related solely to his status as a participant of IRA #1. In this regard, petitioner benefited only insofar as IRA #1 [pg. 90] accumulated assets for future distribution. Section 4975(d)(9) states that section 4975(c) shall not apply to:

receipt by a disqualified person of any benefit to which he may be entitled as a participant or beneficiary in the plan, so long as the benefit is computed and paid on a basis which is consistent with the terms of the plan as applied to all other participants and beneficiaries.

Thus, we find that under the plain meaning[17] of section 4975(c)(1)(E), respondent was not substantially justified in maintaining that the payments of dividends to IRA #1 constituted prohibited transactions. Respondent's litigation position with respect to this issue was unreasonable as a matter of both law and fact.[18]

Respondent would have us believe that the delay in settling the DISC issue was due to a statement in petitioners' motion for partial summary judgment that IRA #1 was exempt from tax at all times. In her memorandum in objection to petitioners' motion for litigation costs, respondent contends that this was a "new and overriding issue" that required her to determine whether "any other" prohibited transactions had occurred during the period covered by the notice of deficiency. We disagree.

We need look no further than respondent's own memorandum to divine that the true reason for her delay in conceding the DISC issue was her desire to discover new facts with which to resuscitate her meritless litigation position. The following statements from respondent's memorandum are illuminating in this regard:

due to the complexity of the prohibited transaction rules and the many ways in which disqualified person status can be achieved through specific relationships described in I.R.C. section 4975(e)(2), it was imperative that [pg. 91] respondent explore other *possible violations* before conceding that the facts (as represented by petitioner's counsel) demonstrated no violation.

***

Petitioner husband established the IRA and created a DISC inside of his IRA to shelter from current income inclusion dividend payments made by an international trading company in which he was the sole shareholder. *But for the existence of the IRA*, such dividends would be currently taxable to him. *If he had created the DISC outside of the IRA*, and then sold some or all of the stock in the DISC to the IRA, the sale of stock in the DISC to his IRA would clearly violate the prohibited transactions rules under I.R.C. section 4975. Similarly, the payment of any dividends from his wholly owned corporation to his IRA that effectively allows him to avoid current income inclusion because he assigned his interest in the DISC to his IRA arguably represents an indirect benefit to him personally.

For example, both petitioner husband and petitioner wife indirectly received a significant current tax benefit derived from the payment of DISC dividends into his IRA, rather than to the husband as a direct shareholder.

But for the creation and maintenance of the IRA, petitioner husband (and, by virtue of her election to file a joint return, the petitioner wife) would have current income inclusion for payments from the trading corporation to the DISC. Accordingly, the transactions between his wholly-owned trading corporation to such entity are arguably indirect prohibited transactions between disqualified persons and the IRA. Also, since one slight variation in the structure or operation of the petitioner's transactions could have resulted in noncompliance with the prohibited transactions rules, it was clearly reasonable for respondent not to concede her position on answer and to analyze thoroughly all positions presented by petitioner's counsel during the litigation stage of the case. [Emphasis added.]

We read the preceding statements as an acknowledgment by respondent that her litigation position, as developed in the administrative proceedings and adopted in her answer, was without a foundation in fact or law. This case is distinguishable from those in which respondent promptly conceded an unreasonable position taken in her answer, thereby avoiding an award of litigation costs. Nothing occurred between the filing of respondent's answer and her notice of no objection to alter the fact that she had misapplied the prohibited transaction rules of section 4975 to petitioners' case. Accordingly, we find that respondent's litigation position with respect to IRA #1 was not substantially justified. Petitioners are therefore entitled to an award of litigation costs under section 7430.

As respondent's determination of deficiencies with respect to IRA #2 was inexorably linked to the fate of IRA #1, the [pg. 92] award of litigation costs is also intended to cover respondent's litigation position with respect to IRA #2.[19]

b. *The House Issue*

Petitioners contend that respondent was not substantially justified in determining that the sale of the Algonquin property to Trust No. 234 was a sham transaction. Respondent, on the other hand, argues that such a determination was reasonable, particularly in light of the postsale use by petitioners and their daughter.

A "sham" transaction is one which, though it may be proper in form, lacks economic substance beyond the creation of tax benefits. *Karr v. Commissioner*, 924 F.2d 1018, 1022-1023 [67 AFTR 2d 91- 653] (11th Cir.

1991), affg. *Smith v. Commissioner*, 91 T.C. 733 (1988). In the context of a sale transaction, as here, the inquiry is whether the parties have in fact done what the form of their agreement purports to do. *Grodt & McKay Realty, Inc. v. Commissioner*, 77 T.C. 1221, 1237 (1981).

The term "sale" is given its ordinary meaning for Federal income tax purposes and is generally defined as a transfer of property for money or a promise to pay money. *Commissioner v. Brown*, 380 U.S. 563, 570-571 [15 AFTR 2d 790] (1965). In deciding whether a particular transaction constitutes a sale, the question of whether the benefits and burdens of ownership have passed from seller to buyer must be answered. This is a question of fact which is to be ascertained from the intention of the parties, as evidenced by the written agreements read in light of the attendant facts and circumstances. *Haggard v. Commissioner*, 24 T.C. 1124, 1129 (1955), affd. 241 F.2d 288 [50 AFTR 1035] (9th Cir. 1956).

Various factors to consider in making a determination as to whether a sale has occurred were summarized in *Grodt & McKay Realty, Inc. v. Commissioner*, supra at 1237-1238, as follows:

(1) Whether legal title passes; (2) how the parties treat the transaction; (3) whether equity was acquired in the property; (4) whether the contract creates a present obligation on the seller to execute and deliver a deed and a present obligation on the purchaser to make payments; (5) whether the right of possession is vested in the purchaser; (6) which party pays the property taxes; (7) which party bears the risk of loss or damage to the [pg. 93] property; and (8) which party receives the profits from the operation and sale of the property. *** [Citations omitted.]

An additional factor to be weighed is the presence or absence of arm's-length dealing. *Falsetti v. Commissioner*, 85 T.C. 332, 348 (1985) (citing *Estate of Franklin v. Commissioner*, 64 T.C. 752 (1975), affd. 544 F.2d 1045 [38 AFTR 2d 76-6164] (9th Cir. 1976)).

We recognize that a number of the factors listed above favor petitioners' contention that the sale of the Algonquin property was not a "sham" transaction. Nevertheless, the fact remains that petitioners continued paying the heating, electricity, security, and maintenance expenses incurred for the property until sometime in June 1987; i.e., over 5 months after their sale of the property to Trust No. 234. Petitioners also paid for a number of repairs to the property prior to its sale to a third party in 1988. Although petitioners were ultimately reimbursed for all or part of these expenses, it appears that such reimbursement did not occur until proximate to the time a contract of sale was signed between Trust No. 234 and the third party. Finally, we cannot discount the fact that petitioners and their daughter occupied the property at various times between the time of its sale to the trust and its ultimate sale to a third party. In the case of the daughter, this period of occupancy lasted just over 1 year and ended shortly before the property was sold to the third party in June of 1988. The foregoing takes on added significance in light of the fact that petitioner was on "both sides" of the initial sale — both as owner of the property and as the sole shareholder of Swansons' Tool. Combined with the questionable business purpose behind a manufacturing corporation's purchase of a personal residence, we do not find it unreasonable that respondent would challenge the sale as not being at arm's-length.

Based on the record as a whole, we cannot say that respondent's position with respect to the house issue was unreasonable, as a matter of either law or fact. We recognize that petitioners have cited a number of cases supporting the proposition that sales to close corporations by shareholders are not "sham" transactions per se. We further note that petitioners cited cases supporting the permissible occupancy of a residence subsequent to its sale. A careful reading of each, however, does not persuade us that, based on the facts [pg. 94] of this case, respondent's litigation position was not substantially justified. Accordingly, we find that petitioners have failed to meet their burden of proof on this issue.[20]

Our conclusion is not diminished by the fact that respondent ultimately conceded this matter in petitioners' favor prior to trial. The determination of whether respondent's position was substantially justified is based on all the facts and circumstances surrounding a proceeding; the fact that respondent ultimately concedes or loses a case is not determinative. See *Wasie v. Commissioner*, 86 T.C. 962, 968-969 (1986); *DeVenney v. Commissioner*, 85 T.C. 927, 930 (1985).

2. *Net Worth*

Respondent contends that petitioners have failed to demonstrate that they satisfied the net worth requirement of section 7430(c)(4)(A)(iii).

To qualify as a prevailing party eligible for an award of litigation costs, a taxpayer must establish that he or she has a net worth that did not exceed $2 million "at the time the civil action was filed."[21] In the case of a husband and wife seeking an award of litigation costs, the net worth test is applied to each separately. *Hong v. Commissioner*, 100 T.C. 88, 91 (1993).

Although the term "net worth" is not statutorily defined, the legislative history to the EAJA states: "In determining the value of assets, the cost of acquisition rather than fair market value should be used." H. Rept. 96-1418, at 15 (1980); see also *United States v. 88.88 Acres of Land*, 907 F.2d 106, 107 (9th Cir. 1990); *American Pacific Concrete Pipe Co., Inc. v.* [pg. 95] *NLRB*, 788 F.2d 586, 590 (9th Cir. 1986); *Continental Web Press, Inc. v. NLRB*, 767 F.2d 321, 322-323 (7th Cir. 1985).

To demonstrate that they each had a net worth of less than $2,000,000 on the date their petition was filed, petitioners submitted, on August 1, 1994, a "STATEMENT OF NET WORTH AT ACQUISITION COST AS OF SEPTEMBER 21, 1992."[22] Petitioners' separate net worths were reported on this statement as follows:

Asset	Acq. Cost	James	Josephine
Cash/Checking	$48,375	$24,188	$24,188
Money Fund	188,657	188,657	-
Repo Account	184,155	184,155	-
Mortgage	76,225	38,113	38,113
Mortgage	40,000	40,000	-
Contract	34,433	34,433	-
Note-1	26,815	26,815	-
Note-2	2,300	2,300	-
Note-3	80,000	80,000	-
Note-4	17,500	17,500	-

IRA-Kemper	9,000	9,000	-
IRA-Kemper	8,250	-	8,250
IRA-1st Fla.	2,500	2,500	-
IRA-1st Fla.	5,000	5,000	-
401(k) Plan	45,000	45,000	-
Condo	185,000	-	185,000
Industrial Bldg.	107,500	-	107,500
Industrial Bldg.	260,000	-	260,000
Industrial Vacant	65,000	65,000	-
Stock - HSSTC	59,200	59,200	-
Prestige	23,500	-	23,500
Breck	25,000	25,000	-
West Coast	25,000	25,000	-
Sunshine	20,910	20,910	-
FSCC	5,000	5,000	-
Sailboat	85,000	85,000	-
Motorboat	8,000	8,000	-
Auto	17,000	-	20,000 [sic]
Art, etc.	40,000	20,000	20,000
Totals	1,694,322 [sic]	1,010,771	683,551

With an exception for the four IRA's, the 401(k) plan, and the stock of the six listed corporations, the parties stipulated on May 16, 1995, to the accuracy of the preceding statement.[23] [pg. 96]

Pursuant to our Order of May 1, 1995, the parties submitted simultaneous and answering memoranda of law, addressing the proper method for determining the acquisition cost of those assets for which there had been no stipulation. As set forth in these memoranda, petitioners argue for an approach whereby the amount paid for an asset, adjusted for depreciation, establishes the acquisition cost of an asset for purposes of the net worth computation. Respondent, on the other hand, argues that the acquisition cost of an asset should constantly be adjusted to reflect realized (if not recognized) income. To quote respondent:

In summary, acquisition costs of an asset are generated not only from external contributions but also from realized gains, the internal reinvestment of which acquires an increase, improvement, or enhancement in such asset.

Having carefully considered the parties' respective arguments, we accept petitioners' computation of their net worth under Section 7430(c)(4)(A)(iii). We find no basis in this case for disregarding the separate legal status of entities in which petitioners hold beneficial or legal interests. See, e.g., *Moline Properties, Inc. v. Commissioner*, 319 U.S. 436, 438-439 [30 AFTR 1291] (1943); *Webb v. United States*, 15 F.3d 203, 207 [73 AFTR 2d 94-1019] (1st Cir. 1994); *Bertoli v. Commissioner*, 103 T.C. 501, 511-512 (1994); *Allen v. Commissioner*, T.C. Memo. 1988-166 [¶88,166 PH Memo TC].

Respondent argues that even if Congress originally intended acquisition cost as the proper measure of net worth, relatively recent trends in generally accepted accounting principles (GAAP) require that such a measure be abandoned. We have considered respondent's arguments on this point and find them off the mark. While there has been a change in the rules regarding the method by which individuals prepare their financial statements, there has been no change in the definition of acquisition cost under GAAP, and as that was the standard set forth in the legislative history, it is the measure of net worth we apply to this case.[24] [pg. 97]

After careful review of the record, we find that petitioners have adequately set forth a statement of their net worth pursuant to Rule 231(b)(5) and have met the burden of proving that their separate net worths did not exceed $2 million on the date they filed their petition.

We have considered all other arguments raised by respondent regarding the net worth requirement and, to the extent not discussed above, find them to be without merit. Before continuing, however, we find it necessary to comment on some of the arguments raised by respondent in her memoranda.

While there was colorable merit to some of the contentions raised by respondent in her memoranda regarding the question of net worth, others border on being frivolous and vexatious. As an illustration, respondent set forth the following proposition in arguing that additional amounts should be added to petitioner Josephine Swanson's calculation of net worth:

Florida provides for the equitable distribution of property between spouses upon divorce. Fla. Stat. ch. 61.075 (1994). ***

Respondent notes that the record provides no indication of marital disharmony between the petitioners and presumes that Florida's equitable distribution statute does not expressly apply to this case. However, this significant expectancy to receive an equitable distribution in the event of divorce may itself constitute an asset of a spouse entitled to recognition for purposes of the net worth computation.

Such transparent sophistry speaks for itself and comes perilously close to meriting an award of fees to petitioners under section 6673(a)(2).

3. *Exhaustion of Administrative Remedies*

Notwithstanding our conclusion that respondent was not substantially justified with respect to the DISC issue, petitioners are not entitled to an award of litigation costs if it is found that they failed to exhaust their administrative remedies.

No "30-day letter" was issued to petitioners prior to the issuance of the statutory notice of deficiency. Respondent contends, however, that petitioners failed to exhaust their administrative remedies by not seeking an Appeals Office [pg. 98] conference prior to the filing of their motion for summary judgment. In support, respondent maintains that:

After commencing litigation, *** [petitioners'] attorneys forged quickly ahead by filing a motion for partial summary judgment without attempting to confer with either Appeals or District Counsel to seek a possible settlement — a conference which likely would have eliminated the need for the parties to prepare a prosecution and defense of the motion and its extensive exhibits and attachments, perhaps resulting in reduced litigation activities, saving time for the parties and the Court.

In opposition, petitioners state that, pursuant to section 301.7430-1(e)(2), Proced. & Admin. Regs., they have per se exhausted their administrative remedies.

In pertinent part, section 301.7430-1(e), Proced. & Admin. Regs., sets forth the following exception to the general rule that a party must participate[25] in an Appeals Office conference in order to exhaust its administrative remedies:

(e) Exception to requirement that party pursue administrative remedies. If the conditions set forth in paragraphs (e)(1), (e)(2), (e)(3), or (e)(4) of this section are satisfied, a party's administrative remedies within the Internal Revenue Service *shall be deemed to have been exhausted* for purposes of section 7430.

***

(2) In the case of a petition in the Tax Court —

(i) *The party did not receive a notice of proposed deficiency (30-day letter) prior to the issuance of the statutory notice and the failure to receive such notice was not due to actions of the party* (such as failure to supply requested information or a current mailing address to the district director or service center having jurisdiction over the tax matter); and

(ii) The party *does not refuse to participate* in an-Appeals office conference *while the case is in docketed status*. [Emphasis added.]

Section 301.7430-1, Proced. & Admin. Regs., fails to define the phrase "does not refuse to participate."

Respondent's arguments suggest that section 301.7430-1(e)(2), Proced. & Admin. Regs., is to be interpreted as requiring an affirmative act by petitioners; i.e., a request for an Appeals Office conference. Petitioners, on the other hand, [pg. 99] contend that the proper interpretation is one that puts the burden on respondent, requiring that she act affirmatively. Petitioners reason that they cannot "refuse to participate" in an Appeals Office conference unless and until respondent makes an offer of such a conference.[26]

We conclude that petitioners' reading of Section 301.7430-1(e)(2), Proced. & Admin. Regs., is correct. Section 601.106(d)(3), Statement of Procedural Rules, states that with respect to cases docketed in the Tax Court:

(iii) If the deficiency notice in a case docketed in the Tax Court was not issued by the Appeals office and no recommendation for criminal prosecution is pending, the case *will* be referred by the district counsel to the Appeals office for settlement as soon as it is at issue in the Tax Court. The settlement procedure *shall* be governed by the following rules:

(a) The Appeals office will have exclusive settlement jurisdiction for a period of 4 months over certain cases docketed in the Tax Court. The 4-month period will commence at the time Appeals receives the case from Counsel, which will be after the case is at issue. *Appeals will arrange settlement conferences in such cases within 45 days of receipt of the case.* *** [Emphasis added.]

The notice of deficiency in this matter was issued by the District Director for Jacksonville, Florida. There is no suggestion that a recommendation for criminal prosecution was ever pending against petitioners. Accordingly, pursuant to the procedural rules, respondent's Appeals Office gained settlement jurisdiction over petitioners' case after it was docketed in this Court and maintained such jurisdiction for a period of 4 months. Contrary to the language of Section 601.106(d)(3)(iii)(a), Statement of Procedural Rules, however, Appeals in this case did not arrange a settlement conference within 45 days of receipt of petitioners' case. Petitioners could not, therefore, have refused to participate in an Appeals Office conference, as none was ever offered.

We note that when a 30-day letter has been issued, the procedural rules provide that, in general, the taxpayer is entitled, as a matter of right, to an Appeals Office conference. See sec. 601.106(b), Statement of Procedural Rules. No such right exists, however, once the taxpayer's case is docketed in the Tax Court. Furthermore, once the case is [pg. 100] docketed, there is no provision in the procedural rules for a taxpayer request for an Appeals Office conference.

Based on the foregoing, we find that petitioners have exhausted their administrative remedies within the meaning of section 7430 and the regulations thereunder.

4. *Whether Petitioners Unreasonably Protracted the Proceedings*

Based upon the record, we find that petitioners did not protract the proceedings.

5. *Whether the Fees Sought in This Matter Are Reasonable*

As discussed below, we find that the amount sought by petitioners in this matter for litigation costs is not reasonable and must be adjusted to comport with the record.

C. *Award of Litigation Costs*

As an initial matter, we note that the parties disagree as to whether the cost of living adjustment (COLA), which applies to an award of attorney's fees under section 7430, should be computed from October 1, 1981, or from January 1, 1986.[27] Respectively, these are the two dates on which COLA's were first provided under the EAJA and section 7430.

Our position on this issue was addressed in *Bayer v. Commissioner*, 98 T.C. 19 (1992), where we concluded that Congress, in providing for cost of living adjustments in section 7430, intended the computation to start on the same date the COLA's were started under the EAJA; i.e., October 1, 1981. Id. at 23. Citing *Lawrence v. Commissioner*, 27 T.C. 713 (1957), revd. on other grounds 258 F.2d 562 [2 AFTR 2d 5073] (9th Cir. 1958), we stated that we would continue to use 1981 as the correct year for making the COLA calculation, unless, of course, the Court of Appeals to which appeal lay had held otherwise. *Golsen v. Commissioner*, 54 T.C. 742, 756-757 (1970), affd. 445 F.2d 985 [27 AFTR 2d 71-1583] (10th Cir. 1971).

This case is appealable to the Court of Appeals for the 11th Circuit, which has not addressed the question of whether 1981 or 1986 is the correct date for purposes of computing [pg. 101] the COLA adjustment under section 7430. Accordingly, we will follow our holding in Bayer, and we find October 1, 1981, to be the applicable date from which to make the adjustment.

1. *Amount of Litigation Costs*

Petitioners seek an award of litigation fees and expenses in the total amount of $140,580.46. Petitioners have also asked that they be awarded any additional costs incurred since March 1, 1994, to recover such fees and expenses. However, as explained in the affidavit of petitioners' counsel filed as a supplement to motion for litigation costs:

with counsel's acquiescence, Petitioners have paid to date only $56,588 of the fees incurred on their behalf. As a result of Baker & McKenzie's advisory role with regard to the DISC Issue, *Petitioners agreed after Respondent fully conceded the case to pay only $40,000 of the unbilled fees incurred from December 1992 on their behalf.* The $40,000 amount was paid by the Swansons from their Joint checking account. H.& S. Swansons' Tool Co., Mr. Swanson's closely held corporation and the client of record for bookkeeping purposes, had previously paid $16,588 for services rendered on petitioners' behalf between September and November, 1992.

Petitioners agreed to allow Baker & McKenzie to recover any remaining unbilled fees *in excess of the $56,588 Petitioners have paid to date* to the extent that Petitioners prevail on *** [their Motion for Reasonable Litigation Costs.] [Emphasis added.]

Thus, beyond the $40,000 agreed to, there is no legal obligation of petitioners to pay fees incurred on their behalf in the judicial proceeding.[28] Furthermore, based on the agreement detailed in the affidavits of petitioners' counsel, they incurred no fees with respect to the preparation of their motion. Petitioners did not, therefore, incur fees in this matter in an amount greater than $40,000. See *Marre v. United States*, 38 F.3d 823, 828-829 [74 AFTR 2d 94-7050] (5th Cir. 1994); *United States v. 122.00 Acres of Land*, 856 F.2d 56 (8th Cir. 1988) (applying sec. 304(a)(2) of the Uniform Relocation Assistance and Real Property Acquisition Policies Act of 1970, 42 U.S.C. sec. 4654(a); fees were not actually "incurred" because the taxpayer had no legal obligation to pay his attorney's fees); [pg. 102] accord *SEC v. Comserv Corp.*, 908 F.2d 1407, 1414 (8th Cir. 1990) (construing the EAJA, which language the Court did not find to be significantly different from that in *United States v. 122.00 Acres of Land*, supra); see also *Frisch v. Commissioner*, 87 T.C. 838, 846 (1986) (lawyer representing himself pro se was not entitled to fees for his own services because such fees were not paid or incurred).

Because there is no mention in the affidavits of counsel regarding the liability of petitioners for costs other than fees incurred after December 1992, we find that petitioners are not similarly restricted with respect to an award of "reasonable court costs" under section 7430(c)(1)(A) or those items listed in section 7430(c)(1)(B)(i) and (ii).

We must apportion the award of fees sought by petitioners between the DISC issue, for which respondent was not substantially justified, and the Algonquin property issue, for which respondent was substantially justified. Based on the record, we find that for the period December 1992 until September 1993,[29] a total of 312.9 hours was spent by counsel in connection with the Court proceedings. Of this amount, 158.8 hours were devoted to the DISC issue, 139.8 hours to the Algonquin property issue, and 14.3 hours to general case management. Based upon the $75-per- hour statutory rate, as adjusted by the COLA computed from 1981, we find that petitioners are entitled to an award for 166.4 hours of fees paid to counsel.[30]

As for expenses other than fees, petitioners have asked for total miscellaneous litigation costs in the amount of $6,512.33. Based upon our evaluation of the total time spent on the DISC issue, and our need to exclude miscellaneous expenses incurred with respect to the Algonquin property issue, we find that petitioners are entitled to an award of miscellaneous expenses in the amount of $3,300. [pg. 103]

To reflect the foregoing,

An appropriate order will be issued and decision will be entered pursuant to Rule 155.

1

Unless otherwise indicated, all section references are to the Internal Revenue Code. All Rule references are to the Tax Court Rules of Practice and Procedure.

2

Initially organized as a corporation in the State of Illinois, Swansons' Tool was subsequently merged into a newly formed Florida corporation of the same name on Dec. 30, 1983.

3

The following dividends were paid by Worldwide to IRA #1 during the taxable years 1986 through 1988:

Paid Date	Fiscal Year	Amount
4/8/86	12/31/86	$244,576
2/10/87	12/31/87	126,155
12/29/87	12/31/87	100,519

12/30/88	12/31/88	122,352
Total		593,602

No distributions were made to petitioners from the trust during the years at issue.

4

Under sec. 991, except for the taxes imposed by ch. 5, a DISC is not subject to income tax.

5

The Tax Reform Act of 1986 (TRA), Pub. L. 99-514, sec. 301(a), 100 Stat. 2085, 2216, eliminated the deduction under sec. 1202 for 60 percent of net long-term capital gains. The repeal was effective for tax years beginning after Dec. 31, 1986.

6

Respondent used substantially similar language in setting forth one primary and two alternative positions on this issue.

7

Respondent argues that our consideration of whether she was substantially justified in this matter should be based, in part, on the outcome of a related case involving IRA #1. In docket No. 21109-92, respondent determined, and IRA #1 ultimately conceded, that IRA #1 had unrelated business income for the taxable year 1988. IRA #1's concession in docket No. 21109-92, however, appears to have been a direct result of respondent's filing her notice of no objection to petitioners' motion for summary judgment in this case. In any event, we give no weight to the outcome of docket No. 21109-92 because it resulted from an agreement between the parties to that docket rather than a judicial determination.

8

Respondent's litigation position for purposes of this matter is that taken on Nov. 13, 1992, the date the answer was filed. See *Han v. Commissioner*, T.C. Memo. 1993-386 [1993 RIA TC Memo ¶93,386].

9

To the extent respondent has cited for support cases which discuss sec. 7430 prior to its amendment in 1986 by TRA sec. 1551, 100 Stat. 2085, 2752, and in 1988 by the Technical and Miscellaneous Revenue Act of 1988, Pub. L. 100-647, sec. 6239, 102 Stat. 3342, 3743, we find them to be inapposite. See *Sansom v. United States*, 703 F. Supp. 1505 [62 AFTR 2d 88-5304] (N.D. Fla. 1988).

10

Respondent's administrative position for purposes of this matter is that taken on June 29, 1992, the date of the notice of deficiency. Sec. 7430(c)(2).

11

A "plan" is defined by sec. 4975(e)(1) to encompass an individual retirement account as described under sec. 408.

12

As applicable to the following discussion, sec. 4975(e)(2) defines a disqualified person as:

(A) a *fiduciary*;

***

(C) an *employer* any of whose employees are covered by the plan;

(D) an *employee organization*, any of whose members are covered by the plan;

***

(G) a *corporation*, partnership, or *trust* or estate of which (or in which) *50 percent or more of*—

(i) *the combined voting power of all classes of stock entitled to vote or the total value of shares of all classes of stock of such corporation,*

(ii) the capital interest or profits interest of such partnership, or

(iii) t*he beneficial interest of such trust or estate, is owned directly or indirectly, or held by persons described in subparagraph (A), (B), (C), (D), or (E);*

***

(H) *an officer, director (or an individual having powers or responsibilities similar to those of officers or directors), a 10 percent or more shareholder*, or a highly compensated employee (earning 10 percent or more of the yearly wages of an employer) *of a person described in subpargraph (C), (D), (E), or (G)* *** [Emphasis added.]

13

In pertinent part, a "fiduciary" is defined by sec. 4975(e)(3) as any person who:

(A) exercises any discretionary authority or discretionary control respecting management of such plan or exercises any authority or control respecting management or disposition of its assets, [or]

***

(C) has any discretionary authority or discretionary responsibility in the administration of such plan.

At all relevant times, petitioner maintained and exercised the right to direct IRA #1's investments. Petitioner, therefore, was clearly a "fiduciary" with respect to IRA #1 and thereby a "disqualified person" as defined under sec. 4975(e)(2)(A). Furthermore, as petitioner was the sole individual for whose benefit IRA #1 was established, IRA #1 itself was a disqualified person pursuant to sec. 4975(e)(2)(G)(iii).

14

Furthermore, we find that at the time of the stock issuance, Worldwide was not, within the meaning of sec. 4975(e)(2)(C), an "employer," any of whose employees were beneficiaries of IRA #1. Although sec. 4975 does not define the term "employer," we find guidance in sec. 3(5) of the Employee Retirement Income Security Act of 1974 (ERISA), Pub. L. 93-406, 88 Stat. 829, 834. In pertinent part, ERISA sec. 3(5) provides that, for plans such as an IRA, an "'employer' means any person acting directly as an employer, or indirectly in the interest of an employer, in relation to an employee benefit plan *** ." Because Worldwide did not maintain, sponsor, or directly contribute to IRA #1, we find that Worldwide was not acting as an "employer" in relation to an employee plan, and was not, therefore, a disqualified person under sec. 4975(e)(2)(C). As there is no evidence that Worldwide was an "employee organization", any of whose members were participants in IRA #1, we also find that Worldwide was not a disqualified person under sec. 4975(e)(2)(D).

15

Sec. 4975(e)(4) incorporates the constructive ownership rule of sec. 267(c)(1), which states that:

Stock owned, directly or indirectly, by or for a corporation, partnership, estate, or trust shall be considered as being owned proportionately by or for its shareholders, partners, or beneficiaries. ***

Petitioner, as the sole individual for whose benefit IRA #1 was established, was therefore beneficial owner of all the outstanding shares of Worldwide after they were issued. Because petitioner, as the sole beneficial shareholder of Worldwide, was also a "fiduciary" with respect to IRA #1, Worldwide thus met the definition of a disqualified person under sec. 4975(e)(2)(G).

Contrary to respondent's representations, petitioner was not a "disqualified person" as president and director of Worldwide until *after* the stock was issued to IRA #1. Sec. 4975(e)(2)(H). Furthermore, petitioner was not a disqualified person under sec. 4975(e)(2)(H) solely due to his "shareholding" in Worldwide as the constructive attribution rules provided under sec. 267 are applicable only to sec. 4975(e)(2)(E)(i) and (G)(i). Sec. 4975(e)(4).

16

Ordinarily, controlling effect will be given to the plain language of a statute unless to do so would produce absurd or futile results. *Rath v. Commissioner*, 101 T.C. 196, 200 (1993) (citing *United States v. American Trucking Associations*, 310 U.S. 534, 543-544 (1940)). As the Supreme Court has stated:

in the absence of a clearly expressed legislative intention to the contrary, the language of the statute itself must ordinarily be regarded as conclusive. Unless exceptional circumstances dictate otherwise, when we find the terms of a statute unambiguous, judicial inquiry is complete. [*Burlington No. R. v. Oklahoma Tax Commn.*, 481 U.S. 454, 461 (1987); citations and internal quotation marks omitted.]

Accordingly, when, as here, a statute is clear on its face, we require unequivocal evidence of a contrary purpose before construing it in a manner that overrides the plain meaning of the statutory words. *Rath v. Commissioner*, supra at 200-201 (citing *Halpern v. Commissioner*, 96 T.C. 895, 899 (1991); *Huntsberry v. Commissioner*, 83 T.C. 742, 747-748 (1984)).

17
See the discussion supra note 16 regarding application of a statute's plain meaning.

18
In a letter accompanying the revenue agent's report, respondent stated that:

We believe the statutory Notice of Deficiency adequately describes the adjustments asserted therein. Moreover, during the course of the examination your client became fully cognizant of the transactions under scrutiny. However, as a convenience to you, enclosed is a copy of the revenue agent's report. Naturally, it is not the Service's intent by this letter to in any way limit the general language of the statutory notice. The Commissioner will stand on any ground fairly raised by the statutory notice as a basis for her determination.

In finding that respondent was not substantially justified with respect to the DISC issue, we have considered all grounds upon which respondent could fairly raise a question of prohibited transactions under sec. 4975.

19
See discussion of IRA #2 supra p. 82.

20
For similar reasons, we find that it was not unreasonable as a matter of fact or law for respondent to contend in alternative positions that the proceeds from the sale of the Algonquin property should be adjusted between petitioners and Swansons' Tool. Having carefully considered petitioners' arguments, we find that they have not met their burden of proving that respondent was not substantially justified on this point.

21
This requirement is set forth by implication in sec. 7430(c)(4), which states in pertinent part that:

(A) In general. — The term "prevailing party" means any party in any proceeding to which subsection (a) applies

***

(iii) which meets the requirements of *** section 2412(d)(2)(B) of title 28, United States Code (as in effect on October 22, 1986) *** .

As applicable to this case, 28 U.S.C. sec. 2412(d)(2)(B) provides that a "party" means "an individual whose net worth did not exceed $2,000,000 at the time the civil action was filed."

22
This statement of net worth was submitted as "attachment II" to petitioners' amendment to motion for award of reasonable litigation costs. As noted by petitioners, the figures presented therein are unadjusted for depreciation.

23
We note that petitioners omitted the asset identified as "Florida Bonds" from their Aug. 1, 1994, statement of net worth in the amount of $60,000 to be allocated half to each petition-

er. Petitioners have explained, and we accept, that this was an accidental omission. The stipulation of facts contains other nonmaterial modifications and corrections.

24

As noted by the Courts of Appeals for the Ninth and Seventh Circuits, "the cost of acquisition" under GAAP is arrived at by subtracting accumulated depreciation from the original cost of an asset. *American Pacific Concrete Pipe Co., Inc. v. NLRB*, 788 F.2d 586, 590- 591 (9th Cir. 1986); *Continental Web Press, Inc. v. NLRB*, 767 F.2d 321, 322-323 (7th Cir. 1985). We do not here decide whether depreciation should be used in determining net worth for purposes of sec. 7430(c)(4)(A), as petitioners' separate net worths, whether computed using depreciation or not, do not exceed $2 million.

25

Sec. 301.7430-1(b)(2), Proced. & Admin. Regs., provides that:

a party or qualified representative of the party *** participates in an Appeals office conference if the party or qualified representative discloses to the Appeals office all relevant information regarding the party's tax matter to the extent such information and its relevance were known or should have been known to the party or qualified representative at the time of such conference.

26

As we have not found any prior cases addressing this issue, it appears that the correct interpretation of the meaning of the regulation is one of first impression.

27

Petitioners are seeking an award of fees based solely upon the statutorily provided rate of $75 an hour, as adjusted by the COLA. Sec. 7430(c)(1)(B)(iii). Petitioners have not argued that there are "special factors" which would justify a higher rate in this case. Id.

28

We find that to the extent of the $16,588 paid by Swansons' Tool, petitioners did not "pay or incur" fees within the meaning of sec. 7430. Although the nature of the agreement under which such payment was made is unclear, the ultimate effect was to diminish the deterrent effect of the expense involved in seeking review of, or defending against, unreasonable Government action. See, e.g., *SEC v. Comserv Corp.*, 908 F.2d 1407, 1413-1415 (8th Cir. 1990).

29

Pursuant to petitioners' agreement with counsel, December 1992 was the month from which they agreed to pay $40,000 of unbilled fees incurred on their behalf. According to the affidavits of counsel, September 1993 was the last month in which fees were incurred to defend the DISC issue. Thus, this is the only period for which petitioners may recover fees in this matter.

30

We reach this figure based upon 158.8 hours devoted to the DISC issue and 7.6 of general case management apportioned to the DISC issue ((158.8 / (158.8 + 139.8) x 14.3 = 7.6).

Federal Regulations Reg § 1.408-2. Individual Retirement Accounts.

(a) In general. An individual retirement account must be a trust or a custodial account (see paragraph (d) of this section). It must satisfy the requirements of paragraph (b) of this section in order to qualify as an individual retirement account. It may be established and maintained by an individual, by an employer for the benefit of his employees (see paragraph (c) of this section), or by an employee association for the benefit of its members (see paragraph (c) of this section).

(b) Requirements. An individual retirement account must be a trust created or organized in the United States (as defined in section 7701(a)(9)) for the exclusive benefit of an individual or his beneficiaries. Such trust must be maintained at all times as a domestic trust in the United States. The instrument creating the trust must be in writing and the following requirements must be satisfied.

(1) Amount of acceptable contributions. Except in the case of a contribution to a simplified employee pension described in section 408(k) and a rollover contribution described in section 408(d)(3), 402(a)(5), 402(a)(7), 403(a)(4), 403(b)(8), or 409(b)(3)(C), the trust instrument must provide that contributions may not be accepted by the trustee for the taxable year in excess of $1,500 on behalf of any individual for whom the trust is maintained. An individual retirement account maintained as a simplified employee pension may provide for the receipt of up to $7,500 for a calendar year.

(2) Trustee.

(i) The trustee must be a bank (as defined in section 408(n) and the regulations thereunder) or another person who demonstrates, in the manner described in paragraph (e) of this section, to the satisfaction of the Commissioner, that the manner in which the trust will be administered will be consistent with the requirements of section 408 and this section.

(ii) Section 11.408(a)(2)-1 of the Temporary Income Tax Regulations under the Employee Retirement Income Security Act of 1974 is superseded by this subparagraph (2).

(3) Life insurance contracts. No part of the trust funds may be invested in life insurance contracts. An individual retirement account may invest in annuity contracts which provide, in the case of death prior to the time distributions commence, for a payment equal to the sum of the premiums paid or, if greater, the cash value of the contract.

(4) Nonforfeitability. The interest of any individual on whose behalf the trust is maintained in the balance of his account must be nonforfeitable.

(5) Prohibition against commingling.

(i) The assets of the trust must not be commingled with other property except in a common trust fund or common investment fund.

(ii) For purposes of this subparagraph, the term "common investment fund" means a group trust created for the purpose of providing a satisfactory diversification or investments or a reduction of administrative expenses for the individual participating trusts, and which group trust satisfies the requirements of section 408(c) (except that it need not be established by an employer or an association of employees) and the requirements of section 401(a) in the case of a group trust in which one of the individual participating trusts is an employees' trust described in section 401(a) which is exempt from tax under section 501(a).

(iii) For purposes of this subparagraph, the term "individual participating trust" means an employees' trust described in section 401(a) which is exempt from tax under section 501(a) or a trust which satisfies the requirements of section 408(a) provided that in the case of such an employees' trust, such trust would be permitted to participate in such a group trust if all the other individual participating trusts were employees' trusts described in section 401(a) which are exempt from tax under section 501(a).

(6) Distribution of interest.

(i) The trust instrument must provide that the entire interest of the individual for whose benefit the trust is maintained must be distributed to him in accordance with paragraph (b)(6)(ii) or (iii) of this section.

(ii) Unless the provisions of paragraph (b)(6)(iii) of this section apply, the entire interest of the individual must be actually distributed to him not later than the close of his taxable year in which he attains age 70-1/2 .

(iii) In lieu of distributing the individual's entire interest as provided in paragraph (b)(6)(ii) of this section, the interest may be distributed commencing not later than the taxable year described in such paragraph (b)(6)(ii). In such case, the trust must expressly provide that the entire interest of the individual will be distributed to the individual and the individual's beneficiaries, in a manner which satisfies the requirements of paragraph (b)(6)(v) of this section, over any of the following periods (or any combination thereof)—

(A) The life of the individual,

(B) The lives of the individual and spouse,

(C) A period certain not extending beyond the life expectancy of the individual, or

(D) A period certain not extending beyond the joint life and last survivor expectancy of the individual and spouse.

(iv) The life expectancy of the individual or the joint life and last survivor expectancy of the individual and spouse cannot exceed the period computed by use of the expected return multiples in §1.72-9, or, in the case of payments under a contract issued by an insurance company, the period computed by use of the mortality tables of such company.

(v) If an individual's entire interest is to be distributed over a period described in paragraph (b)(6)(iii) of this section, beginning in the year the individual attains 70-1/2 the amount to be distributed each year must be not less than the lesser of the balance of the individual's entire interest or an amount equal to the quotient obtained by dividing the entire interest of the individual in the trust at the beginning of such year (including amounts not in the individual retirement account at the beginning of the year because they have been withdrawn for the purpose of making a rollover contribution to another individual retirement plan) by the life expectancy of the individual [or the joint life and last survivor expectancy of the individual and spouse (whichever is applicable)], determined in either case as of the date the individual attains age 70 in accordance with paragraph (b)(6)(iv) of this section, reduced by one for each taxable year commencing after the individual's attainment of age 70-1/2. An annuity or endowment contract issued by an insurance company which provides for nonincreasing payments over one of the periods described in paragraph (b)(6)(iii) of this section beginning not later than the close of the taxable year in which the individual attains age 70-1/2 satisfies this provision. However, no distribution need be made in any year, or a lesser amount may be distributed, if beginning with the year the individual attains age 70-1/2 the aggregate amounts distributed by the end of any year are at least equal to the aggregate of the minimum amounts required by this subdivision to have been distributed by the end of such year.

(vi) If an individual's entire interest is distributed in the form of an annuity contract, then the requirements of section 408(a)(6) are satisfied if the distribution of such contract takes place before the close of the taxable year described in subdivision (ii) of this subparagraph, and if the individual's interest will be paid over a period described in subdivision (iii) of this subparagraph and at a rate which satisfies the requirements of subdivision (v) of this subparagraph.

(vii) In determining whether paragraph (b)(6)(v) of this section is satisfied, all individual retirement plans maintained for an individual's benefit (except those under which he is a beneficiary described in section 408(a)(7)) at the close of the taxable year in which he reaches age 70-1/2 must be aggregated. Thus, the total payments which such individual receives in any taxable year must be at least equal to the amount he would have been required to receive had all the plans been one plan at the close of the taxable year in which he attained age 70-1/2.

(7) Distribution upon death.

(i) The trust instrument must provide that if the individual for whose benefit the trust is maintained dies before the entire interest in the trust has been distributed to him, or if distribution has been commenced as provided in paragraph (b)(6) of this section to the surviving spouse and such spouse dies before the entire interest has been distributed to such spouse, the entire interest (or the remaining part of such interest if distribution thereof has commenced) must, within 5 years after the individual's death (or the death of the surviving spouse) be distributed or applied to the purchase of an immediate annuity for this beneficiary or beneficiaries (or the beneficiary or beneficiaries of the surviving spouse) which will be payable for the life of such beneficiary or beneficiaries (or for a term certain not extending beyond the life expectancy of such beneficiary or beneficiaries) and which annuity contract will be immediately distributed to such beneficiary or beneficiaries. A contract described in the preceding sentence is not includible in gross income upon distribution. Section 1.408-4(e) provides rules applicable to the taxation of such contracts. The first sentence of this paragraph (b)(7) shall have no application if distributions over a term certain commenced before the death of the individual for whose benefit the trust was maintained and the term certain is for a period permitted under paragraph (b)(6)(iii)(C) or (D) of this section.

(ii) Each such beneficiary (or beneficiary of a surviving spouse) may elect to treat the entire interest in the trust (or the remaining part of such interest if distribution thereof has commenced) as an account subject to the distribution requirements of section 408(a)(6) and paragraph (b)(6) of this section instead of those of section 408(a)(7) and paragraph (b)(7) of this section. Such an election will be deemed to have been made if such beneficiary treats the account in accordance with the requirements of section 408(a)(6) and paragraph (b)(6) of this section. An election will be considered to have been made by such beneficiary if either of the following occurs: (A) any amounts in the account (including any amounts that have been rolled over, in accordance with the requirements of section 408(d)(3)(A)(i), into an individual retirement account, individual retirement annuity, or retirement bond for the benefit of such individual) have not been distributed within the appropriate time period required by section 408(a)(7) and paragraph (b)(7) of this section; or (B) any additional amounts are contributed to the account (or to the account, annuity, or bond to which the beneficiary has rolled such amounts over, as described in (1) above) which are subject, or deemed to be subject, to the distribution requirements of section 408(a)(6) and paragraph (b)(6) of this section.

(8) Definition of beneficiaries. The term "beneficiaries" on whose behalf an individual retirement account is established includes (except where the context indicates otherwise) the estate of the individual, dependents of the individual, and any person designated by the individual to share in the benefits of the account after the death of the individual.

(c) Accounts established by employers and certain association of employees.

(1) In general. A trust created or organized in the United States [as defined in section 7701(a)(9)] by an employer for the exclusive benefit of his employees or their beneficiaries, or by an association of employees for the exclusive benefit of its members or their beneficiaries, is treated as an individual retirement account if the requirements of paragraphs (c)(2) and (c)(3) of this section are satisfied under the written governing instrument creating the trust. A trust described in the preceding sentence is for the exclusive benefit of employees or members even though it may maintain an account for former employees or members and employees who are temporarily on leave.

(2) General requirements. The trust must satisfy the requirements of paragraphs (b)(1) through (7) of this section.

(3) Special requirement. There must be a separate accounting for the interest of each employee or member.

(4) Definitions.

(i) Separate accounting. For purposes of paragraph (c)(3) of this section, the term "separate accounting" means that separate records must be maintained with respect to the interest of each individual for whose benefit the trust is maintained. The assets of the trust may be held in a common trust fund, common investment fund, or common fund for the account of all individuals who have an interest in the trust.

(ii) Employee association. For purposes of this paragraph and section 408(c), the term "employee association" means any organization composed of two or more employees, including but not limited to, an employee association described in section 501(c)(4). Such association may include employees within the meaning of section 401(c)(1). There must be, however, some nexus between the employees (e.g., employees of same employer, employees in the same industry, etc.) in order to qualify as an employee association described in this subdivision (ii).

(d) Custodial accounts. For purposes of this section and section 408(a), a custodial account is treated as a trust described in section 408(a) if such account satisfies the requirements of section 408(a) except that it is not a trust and if the assets of such account are held by a bank (as defined in section 401(d)(1) and the regulations thereunder) or such other person who satisfies the requirements of paragraph (b)(2)(ii) of this section. For purposes of this chapter, in the case of a custodial account treated as a trust by reason of the preceding sentence, the custodian of such account will be treated as the trustee thereof.

(e) Nonbank trustee.

(1) In general. The trustee of a trust described in paragraph (b) of this section may be a person other than a bank if the person demonstrates to the satisfaction of the Commissioner that the manner in which the person will administer trusts will be consistent with the requirements of section 408. The person must demonstrate by written application that the requirements of paragraph (e)(2) to (e)(6) of this section will be met. The written application must be sent to the address prescribed by the Commissioner in revenue rulings, notices, and other guidance published in the Internal Revenue Bulletin [see §601.601(d)(2)(ii)(b) of this chapter. For procedural and administrative rules, see paragraph (e)(7) of this section].

(2) Fiduciary ability. The applicant must demonstrate in detail its ability to act within the accepted rules of fiduciary conduct. Such demonstration must include the following elements of proof:

(i) Continuity.

(A) The applicant must assure the uninterrupted performance of its fiduciary duties notwithstanding the death or change of its owners. Thus, for example, there must be sufficient diversity in the ownership of the applicant to ensure that the death or change of its owners will not interrupt the conduct of its business. Therefore, the applicant cannot be an individual.

(B) Sufficient diversity in the ownership of an incorporated applicant is demonstrated in the following circumstances:

(1) Individuals each of whom owns more than 20 percent of the voting stock in the applicant own, in the aggregate, no more than 50 percent of such stock;

(2) The applicant has issued securities registered under section 12(b) of the Securities Exchange Act of 1934 (15 U.S.C. 78l(b)) or required to be registered under section 12(g)(1) of that Act (15 U.S.C. 78l(g)(1)); or

(3) The applicant has a parent corporation within the meaning of section 1563(a)(1) that has issued securities registered under section 12(b) of the Securities Exchange Act of 1934 (15 U.S.C. 78l(b)) or required to be registered under Section 12(g)(1) of that Act (15 U.S.C. 78l(g)(1)).

(C) Sufficient diversity in the ownership of an applicant that is a partnership means that—

(1) Individuals each of whom owns more than 20 percent of the profits interest in the partnership own, in the aggregate, no more than 50 percent of such profits interest, and

(2) Individuals each of whom owns more than 20 percent of the capital interest in the partnership own, in the aggregate, no more than 50 percent of such capital interest.

(D) For purposes of this subdivision, the ownership of stock and of capital and profits interests shall be determined in accordance with the rules for constructive ownership of stock provided in section 1563(e) and (f)(2). For this purpose, the rules for constructive ownership of stock provided in section 1563(e) and (f)(2) shall apply to a capital or profits interest in a partnership as if it were a stock interest.

(ii) Established location. The applicant must have an established place of business in the United States where it is accessible during every business day.

(iii) Fiduciary experience. The applicant must have fiduciary experience or expertise sufficient to ensure that it will be able to perform its fiduciary duties. Evidence of fiduciary experience must include proof that a significant part of the business of the applicant consists of exercising fiduciary powers similar to those it will exercise if its application is approved. Evidence of fiduciary expertise must include proof that the applicant employs personnel experienced in the administration of fiduciary powers similar to those the applicant will exercise if its application is approved.

(iv) Fiduciary responsibility. The applicant must assure compliance with the rules of fiduciary conduct set out in paragraph (e)(5) of this section.

(v) Financial responsibility. The applicant must exhibit a high degree of solvency commensurate with the obligations imposed by this paragraph. Among the factors to be taken into account are the applicant's net worth, its liquidity, and its ability to pay its debts as they come due.

(3) Capacity to account. The applicant must demonstrate in detail its experience and competence with respect to accounting for the interests of a large number of individuals (including calculating and allocating income earned and paying out distributions to payees). Examples of accounting for the interests of a large number of individuals include accounting for the interests of a large number of shareholders in a regulated investment company and accounting for the interests of a large number of variable annuity contract holders.

(4) Fitness to handle funds.

(i) In general. The applicant must demonstrate in detail its experience and competence with respect to other activities normally associated with the handling of retirement funds.

(ii) Examples. Examples of activities normally associated with the handling of retirement funds include:

(A) To receive, issue receipts for, and safely keep securities;

(B) To collect income;

(C) To execute such ownership certificates, to keep such records, make such returns, and render such statements as are required for Federal tax purposes;

(D) To give proper notification regarding all collections;

(E) To collect matured or called principal and properly report all such collections;

(F) To exchange temporary for definitive securities;

(G) To give proper notification of calls, subscription rights, defaults in principal or interest, and the formation of protective committees;

(H) To buy, sell, receive, or deliver securities on specific directions.

(5) Rules of fiduciary conduct. The applicant must demonstrate that under applicable regulatory requirements, corporate or other governing instruments, or its established operating procedures:

(i) Administration of fiduciary powers.

(A)

(1) The owners or directors of the applicant will be responsible for the proper exercise of fiduciary powers by the applicant. Thus, all matters pertinent thereto, including the determination of policies, the investment and disposition of property held in a fiduciary capacity, and the direction and review of the actions of all employees utilized by the applicant in the exercise of its fiduciary powers, will be the responsibility of the owners or directors. In discharging this responsibility, the owners or directors may assign to designated employees, by action duly recorded, the administration of such of the applicant's fiduciary powers as may be proper to assign.

(2) A written record will be made of the acceptance and of the relinquishment or closing out of all fiduciary accounts, and of the assets held for each account.

(3) If the applicant has the authority or the responsibility to render any investment advice with regard to the assets held in or for each fiduciary account, the advisability of retaining or disposing of the assets will be determined at least once during each period of 12 months.

(B) All employees taking part in the performance of the applicant's fiduciary duties will be adequately bonded.

Nothing in this subdivision (i)(B) shall require any person to be bonded in contravention of section 412(d) of the Employee Retirement Income Security Act of 1974 (29 U.S.C. 1112(d)).

(C) The applicant will employ or retain legal counsel who will be readily available to pass upon fiduciary matters and to advise the applicant.

(D) In order to segregate the performance of its fiduciary duties from other business activities, the applicant will maintain a separate trust division under the immediate supervision of an individual designated for that purpose. The trust division may utilize the personnel and facilities of other divisions of the applicant, and other divisions of the applicant may utilize the personnel and facilities of the trust division, as long as the separate identity of the trust division is preserved.

(ii) Adequacy of net worth.

(A) Initial net worth requirement. In the case of applications received after January 5, 1995, no initial application will be accepted by the Commissioner unless the applicant has a net worth of not less than $250,000 (determined as of the end of the most recent taxable year). Thereafter, the applicant must satisfy the adequacy of net worth requirements of paragraph (e)(5)(ii)(B) and (C) of this section.

(B) No fiduciary account will be accepted by the applicant unless the applicant's net worth (determined as of the end of the most recent taxable year) exceeds the greater of—

(1) $100,000, or

(2) Four percent (or, in the case of a passive trustee described in paragraph (e)(6)(i)(A) of this section, two percent) of the value of all of the assets held by the applicant in fiduciary accounts (determined as of the most recent valuation date).

(C) The applicant will take whatever lawful steps are necessary (including the relinquishment of fiduciary accounts) to ensure that its net worth (determined as of the close of each taxable year) exceeds the greater of—

(1) $50,000, or

(2) Two percent (or, in the case of a passive trustee described in paragraph (e)(6)(i)(A) of this section, one percent) of the value of all of the assets held by the applicant in fiduciary accounts (determined as of the most recent valuation date).

(D) Assets held by members of SIPC.

(1) For purposes of satisfying the adequacy-of-net worth requirement of this paragraph, a special rule is provided for nonbank trustees that are members of the Securities Investor Protection Corporation (SIPC) created under the Securities Investor Protection Act of 1970 (SIPA)(15 U.S.C. §78aaa et seq, as amended). The amount that the net worth of a nonbank

trustee that is a member of SIPC must exceed is reduced by two percent for purposes of paragraph (e)(5)(ii)(B)(2), and one percent for purposes of paragraph (e)(5)(ii)(C)(2), of the value of assets (determined on an account-by-account basis) held for the benefit of customers (as defined in 15 U.S.C. §78fff-2(e)(4)) in fiduciary accounts by the nonbank trustee to the extent of the portion of each account that does not exceed the dollar limit on advances described in 15 U.S.C. §78fff-3(a), as amended, that would apply to the assets in that account in the event of a liquidation proceeding under the SIPA.

(2) The provisions of this special rule for assets held in fiduciary accounts by members of SIPC are illustrated in the following example.

Example. (a) Trustee X is a broker-dealer and is a member of the Securities Investment Protection Corporation. Trustee X also has been approved as a nonbank trustee for individual retirement accounts (IRAs) by the Commissioner but not as a passive nonbank trustee. Trustee X is the trustee for four IRAs. The total assets of each IRA (for which Trustee X is the trustee) as of the most recent valuation date before the last day of Trustee X's taxable year ending in 1995 are as follows: The total assets for IRA-1 is $3,000,000 (all of which is invested in securities); the value of the total assets for IRA-2 is $500,000 ($200,000 of which is cash and $300,000 of which is invested in securities), the value of the total assets for IRA-3 is $400,000 (all of which is invested in securities); and the value of the total assets of IRA-4 is $200,000 (all of which is cash). The value of all assets held in fiduciary accounts, as defined in §1.408-2(e)(6)(viii)(A), is $4,100,000.

(b) The dollar limit on advances described in 15 U.S.C. §78fff-3(a) that would apply to the assets in each account in the event of a liquidation proceeding under the Securities Investor Protection Act of 1970 in effect as of the last day of Trustee X's taxable year ending in 1995 is $500,000 per account (no more that $100,000 of which is permitted to be cash). Thus, the dollar limit that would apply to IRA-1 is $500,000; the dollar limit for IRA-2 is $400,000 ($100,000 of the cash and the $300,000 of the value of the securities); the dollar limit for IRA-3 is $400,000 (the full value of the account because the value of the account is less than $500,000 and no portion of the account is cash); and the dollar limit for IRA-4 is $100,000 (the entire account is cash and the dollar limit per account for cash is $100,000). The aggregate dollar limits of the four IRAs is $1,400,000.

(c) For 1996, the amount determined under §1.408-2(e)(5)(ii)(B) is determined as follows for Trustee X: (1) four percent of $4,100,000 equals $164,000; (2) two percent of $1,400,000 equals $28,000; and (3) $164,000 minus $28,000 equals $136,000. Thus, because $136,000 exceeds $100,000 the minimum net worth necessary for Trustee X to accept new accounts for 1996 is $136,000.

(d) For 1996, the amount determined under §1.408-2(e)(5)(ii)(C) for Trustee X is determined as follows: (1) two percent of $4,100,000 equals $82,000; (2) one percent of $1,400,000 equals $14,000; and (3) $82,000 minus $14,000 equals $68,000. Thus, because $68,000 exceeds $50,000, the minimum net worth necessary for Trustee X to avoid a mandatory relinquishment of accounts for 1996 is $68,000.

(E) The applicant will determine the value of the assets held by it in trust at least once in each calendar year and no more than 18 months after the preceding valuation. The assets will be valued at their fair market value, except that the assets of an employee pension benefit plan to which section 103(b)(3)(A) of the Employee Retirement Income Security Act of 1974 (29 U.S.C. 1023(b)(3)(A)) applies will be considered to have the value stated in the most recent annual report of the plan.

(iii) Audits.

(A) At least once during each period of 12 months, the applicant will cause detailed audits of the fiduciary books and records to be made by a qualified public accountant. At that time, the applicant will ascertain whether the fiduciary accounts have been administered in accordance with law, this paragraph, and sound fiduciary principles. The audits shall be conducted in accordance with generally accepted auditing standards, and shall involve whatever tests of the fiduciary books and records of the applicant are considered necessary by the qualified public accountant.

(B) In the case of an applicant which is regulated, supervised, and subject to periodic examination by a State or Federal agency, such applicant may adopt an adequate continuous audit system in lieu of the periodic audits required by paragraph (e)(5)(iii)(A) of this section.

(C) A report of the audits and examinations required under this subdivision, together with the action taken thereon, will be noted in the fiduciary records of the applicant.

(iv) Funds awaiting investment or distribution. Funds held in a fiduciary capacity by the applicant awaiting investment or distribution will not be held uninvested or undistributed any longer than is reasonable for the proper management of the account.

(v) Custody of investments.

(A) Except for investments pooled in a common interest fund in accordance with the provisions of paragraph (e)(5)(vi) of this section, the investments of each account will not be commingled with any other property.

(B) Assets of accounts requiring safekeeping will be deposited in an adequate vault. A permanent record will be kept of assets deposited in or withdrawn from the vault.

(vi) Common investment funds. The assets of an account may be pooled in a common investment fund (as defined in paragraph (e)(5)(viii)(C) of this section) if the applicant is authorized under applicable law to administer a common investment fund and if pooling the assets in a common investment fund is not in contravention of the plan documents or applicable law. The common investment fund must be administered as follows:

(A) Each common investment fund must be established and maintained in accordance with a written agreement, containing appropriate provisions as to the manner in which the fund is to be operated, including provisions relating to the investment powers and a general statement of the investment policy of the applicant with respect to the fund; the allocation of income, profits and losses; the terms and conditions governing the admission or withdrawal of participations in the funds; the auditing of accounts of the applicant with respect to the fund; the basis and method of valuing assets held by the fund, setting forth specific criteria for each type of asset; the minimum frequency for valuation of assets of the fund; the period following each such valuation date during which the valuation may be made (which period in usual circumstances may not exceed 10 business days); the basis upon which the fund may be terminated; and such other matters as may be necessary to define clearly the rights of participants in the fund. A copy of the agreement must be available at the principal office of the applicant for inspection during all business hours, and upon request a copy of the agreement must be furnished to the employer, the plan administrator, any participant or beneficiary of an account, or the individual for whose benefit the account is established or that individual's beneficiary.

(B) All participations in the common investment fund must be on the basis of a proportionate interest in all of the investments.

(C) Not less frequently than once during each period of 3 months the applicant must determine the value of the assets in the fund as of the date set for the valuation of assets. No participation may be admitted to or withdrawn from the fund except (1) on the basis of such valuation and (2) as of such valuation date. No participation may be admitted to or withdrawn from the fund unless a written request for or notice of intention of taking such action has been entered on or before the valuation date in the fiduciary records of the applicant. No request or notice may be canceled or countermanded after the valuation date.

(D)

(1) The applicant must at least once during each period of 12 months cause an adequate audit to be made of the common investment fund by a qualified public accountant.

(2) The applicant must at least once during each period of 12 months prepare a financial report of the fund which, based upon the above audit, must contain a list of investments in the fund showing the cost and current value of each investment; a statement for the period since the previous report showing purchases, with cost; sales, with profit or loss; any other investment changes; income and disbursements; and an appropriate notation as to any investments in default.

(3) The applicant must transmit and certify the accuracy of the financial report to the administrator of each plan participating in the common investment fund within 120 days after the end of the plan year.

(E) When participations are withdrawn from a common investment fund, distributions may be made in cash or ratably in kind, or partly in cash and partly in kind: Provided, That all distributions as of any one valuation date must be made on the same basis.

(F) If for any reason an investment is withdrawn in kind from a common investment fund for the benefit of all participants in the fund at the time of such withdrawal and such investment is not distributed ratably in kind, it must be segregated and administered or realized upon for the benefit ratably of all participants in the common investment fund at the time of withdrawal.

(vii) Books and records.

(A) The applicant must keep its fiduciary records separate and distinct from other records. All fiduciary records must be so kept and retained for as long as the contents thereof may become material in the administration of any internal revenue law. The fiduciary records must contain full information relative to each account.

(B) The applicant must keep an adequate record of all pending litigation to which it is a party in connection with the exercise of fiduciary powers.

(viii) Definitions. For purposes of this paragraph (e)(5) and paragraph (e)(2)(v), and paragraph (e)(7) of this section—

(A) The term "account" or "fiduciary account" means a trust described in section 401(a) (including a custodial account described in section 401(f)), a custodial account described in section 403(b)(7), or an individual retirement account described in section 408(a) (including a custodial account described in section 408(h)).

(B) The term "plan administrator" means an administrator as defined in §1.414(g)-1.

(C) The term "common investment fund" means a trust that satisfies the following requirements:

(1) The trust consists of all or part of the assets of several accounts that have been established with the applicant, and

(2) The trust is described in section 401(a) and is exempt from tax under section 501(a), or is a trust that is created for the purpose of provid-

ing a satisfactory diversification of investments or a reduction of administrative expenses for the participating accounts and that satisfies the requirements of section 408(c).

(D) The term "fiduciary records" means all matters which are written, transcribed, recorded, received or otherwise come into the possession of the applicant and are necessary to preserve information concerning the acts and events relevant to the fiduciary activities of the applicant.

(E) The term "qualified public accountant" means a qualified public accountant, as defined in section 103(a)(3)(D) of the Employee Retirement Income Security Act of 1974, 29 U.S.C. 1023(a)(3)(D), who is independent of the applicant.

(F) The term "net worth" means the amount of the applicant's assets less the amount of its liabilities, as determined in accordance with generally accepted accounting principles.

(6) Special rules.

(i) Passive trustee.

(A) An applicant that undertakes to act only as a passive trustee may be relieved of one or more of the requirements of this paragraph upon clear and convincing proof that such requirements are not germane, under all the facts and circumstances, to the manner in which the applicant will administer any trust. A trustee is a passive trustee only if under the written trust instrument the trustee has no discretion to direct the investment of the trust funds or any other aspect of the business administration of the trust, but is merely authorized to acquire and hold particular investments specified by the trust instrument. Thus, for example, in the case of an applicant that undertakes merely to acquire and hold the stock of regulated investment companies, the requirements of paragraph (e)(5)(i)(A)(3), (i)(D), and (vi) of this section shall not apply and no negative inference shall be drawn from the applicant's failure to demonstrate its experience of competence with respect to the activities described in paragraph (e)(4)(ii)(E) to (H) of this section.

(B) The notice of approval issued to an applicant that is approved by reason of this subdivision shall state that the applicant is authorized to act only as a passive trustee.

(ii) Federal or State regulation. Evidence that an applicant is subject to Federal or State regulation with respect to one or more relevant factors shall be given weight in proportion to the extent that such regulatory standards are consonant with the requirements of section 401. Such evidence may be submitted in addition to, or in lieu of, the specific proofs required by this paragraph.

(iii) Savings account.

(A) An applicant will be approved to act as trustee under this subdivision if the following requirements are satisfied:

(1) The applicant is a credit union, industrial loan company, or other financial institution designated by the Commissioner;

(2) The investment of the trust assets will be solely in deposits in the applicant;

(3) Deposits in the applicant are insured (up to the dollar limit prescribed by applicable law) by an agency or instrumentality of the United States, or by an organization established under a special statute the business of which is limited to insuring deposits in financial institutions and providing related services.

(B) Any applicant that satisfies the requirements of this subdivision is hereby approved, and (notwithstanding subparagraph (2) of this paragraph) is not required to submit a written application. This approval takes effect on the first day after December 22, 1976, on which the applicant satisfies the requirements of this subdivision, and continues in effect for so long as the applicant continues to satisfy those requirements.

(C) If deposits are insured, but not in the manner provided in paragraph (e)(6)(iii)(A)(3) of this section, the applicant must submit an application. The application, notwithstanding subparagraph (2) of this paragraph, will be limited to a complete description of the insurance of applicant's deposits. The applicant will be approved if the Commissioner approves of the applicant's insurance.

(iv) Notification of Commissioner. The applicant must notify the Commissioner in writing of any change that affects the continuing accuracy of any representation made in the application required by this paragraph, whether the change occurs before or after the applicant receives a notice of approval. The notification must be addressed to the address prescribed by the Commissioner in revenue rulings, notices, and other guidance published in the Internal Revenue Bulletin [see §601.601(d)(2)(ii)(b) of this chapter].

(v) Substitution of trustee. No applicant will be approved unless the applicant undertakes to act as trustee only under trust instruments which contain a provision to the effect that the grantor is to substitute another trustee upon notification by the Commissioner that such substitution is required because the applicant has failed to comply with the requirements of this paragraph or is not keeping such records, or making such returns, or rendering such statements as are required by forms or regulations.

(7) Procedure and administration.

(i) Notice of approval. If the applicant is approved, a written notice of approval will be issued to the applicant. The notice of approval will state the day on which it becomes effective, and (except as otherwise provided therein) will remain effective until revoked. This paragraph does not authorize the applicant to accept any fiduciary account before such notice of approval becomes effective.

(ii) Notice of disapproval. If the applicant is not approved, a written notice will be furnished to the applicant containing a statement of the reasons why the applicant has not been approved.

(iii) Copy to be furnished. The applicant must not accept a fiduciary account until after the plan administrator or the person for whose benefit the account is to be established is furnished with a copy of the written notice of approval issued to the applicant. This provision is effective six months after April 20, 1979 for new accounts accepted thereafter. For accounts accepted before that date, the administrator must be notified before the later of the effective date of this provision or six months after acceptance of the account.

(iv) Grounds for revocation. The notice of approval issued to an applicant will be revoked if the Commissioner determines that the applicant is unwilling or unable to administer fiduciary accounts in a manner consistent with the requirements of this paragraph. Generally, the notice will not be revoked unless the Commissioner determines that the applicant has knowingly, willfully, or repeatedly failed to administer fiduciary accounts in a manner consistent with the requirements of this paragraph, or has administered a fiduciary account in a grossly negligent manner.

(v) Procedures for revocation. The notice of approval issued to an applicant may be revoked in accordance with the following procedures:

(A) If the Commissioner proposes to revoke the notice of approval issued to an applicant, the Commissioner will advise the applicant in writing of the proposed revocation and of the reasons therefor.

(B) Within 60 days after the receipt of such written advice, the applicant may protest the proposed revocation by submitting a written statement of facts, law, and arguments opposing such revocation to the address prescribed by the Commissioner in revenue rulings, notices, and other guidance published in the Internal Revenue Bulletin [see §601.601(d)(2)(ii)(b) of this chapter]. In addition, the applicant may request a conference in the National Office.

(C) If the applicant consents to the proposed revocation, either before or after a National Office conference, or if the applicant fails to file a timely protest, the Commissioner will revoke the notice of approval that was issued to the applicant.

(D) If, after considering the applicant's protest and any information developed in conference, the Commissioner determines that the applicant is unwilling or unable to administer fiduciary accounts in a manner consistent with the requirements of this paragraph, the Commissioner will revoke the notice of approval that was issued to the applicant and will furnish the applicant with a written statement of findings on which the revocation is based.

(E) If at any time the Commissioner determines that immediate action is necessary to protect the interest of the Internal Revenue Service or of any fiduciary account, the notice of approval issued to the applicant will be suspended at once, pending a final decision to be based on the applicant's protest and any information developed in conference.

Index

NOTE: Boldface numbers indicate illustrations or tables.

About the Author

Hubert Bromma is the CEO of Entrust Administration, Inc., and Entrust Bank and Trust, and Principal of the Entrust Group. Entrust provides IRA and qualified plan record keeping, administration, and continuing education services to discriminating investors, accountants, financial planners, and realtors. Entrust and its affiliates have been providing such services to thousands of clients internationally since 1981. The company was founded originally by Bromma as Consulting Associates, Inc. The company has the largest network of third-party administrators providing self-directed investment services in the nation.

Bromma is a frequent speaker to real estate, real estate investor, retirement, financial planner, and accountant groups. He has written numerous articles for various publications for three decades. He has appeared on many television and radio programs internationally primarily discussing the diversification of assets in tax-free and tax-deferred environments. These include KABC, KNBC, KCBS, KJSL, KNBR, KRMS, FNN, ORF, WCIU-TV, WebFN, Bloomberg, and many others.

He has also an active real estate and note investor since 1978. His degrees are in economics and political science, and has also taught at Southern Methodist University Graduate School of Banking. His career started in 1967 and extended though being a banker, bank examiner, bank regulator, and merger and acquisition specialist. He also was a Member of the Blue Ribbon Committee on Management, City of San Francisco, as well as a Special Consultant to the Municipal Court of San Francisco, Instructor for Operation Hope in Los Angeles, and Guest lecturer at LA City College.